THE FACE OF FORGIVENESS

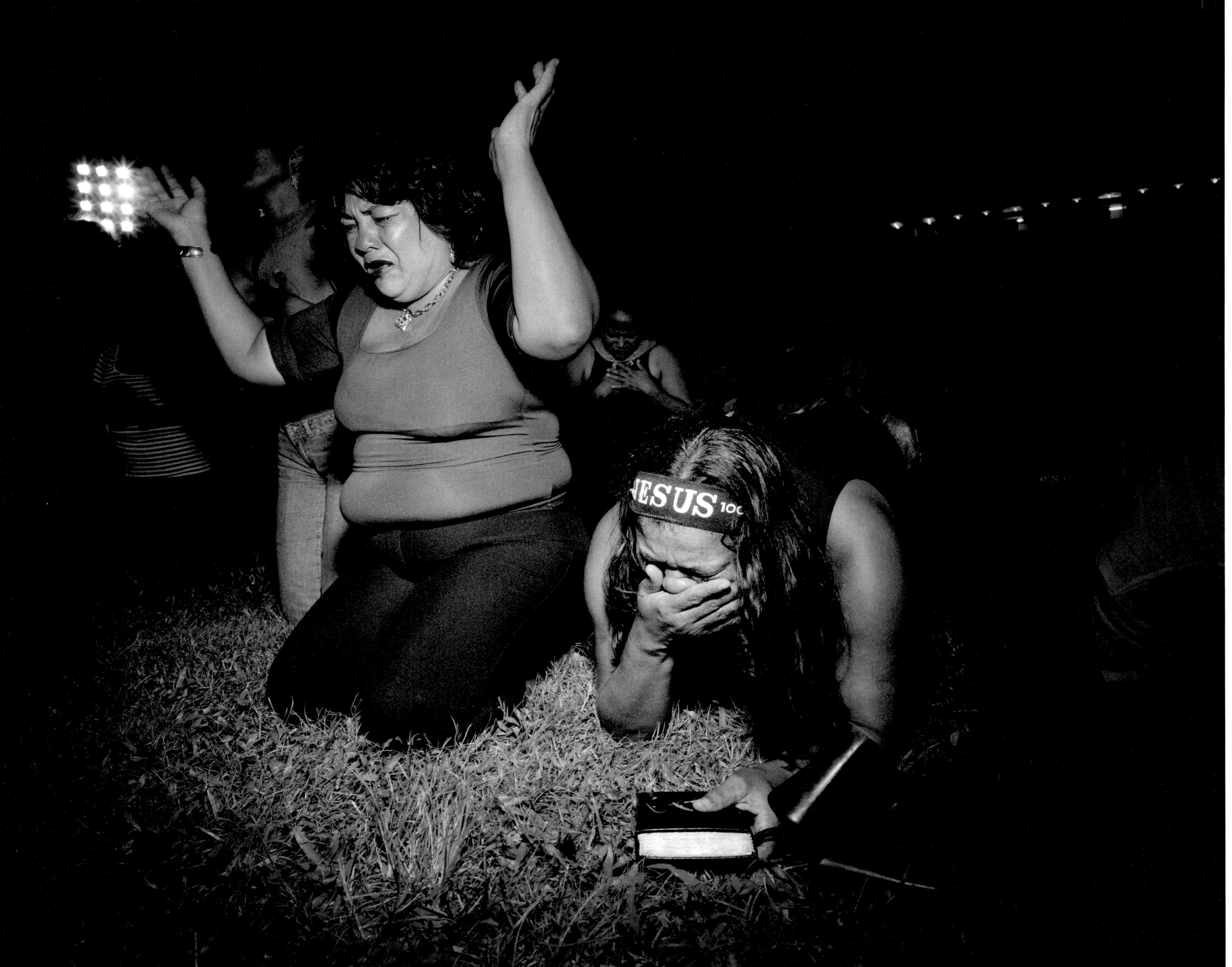
ESUS

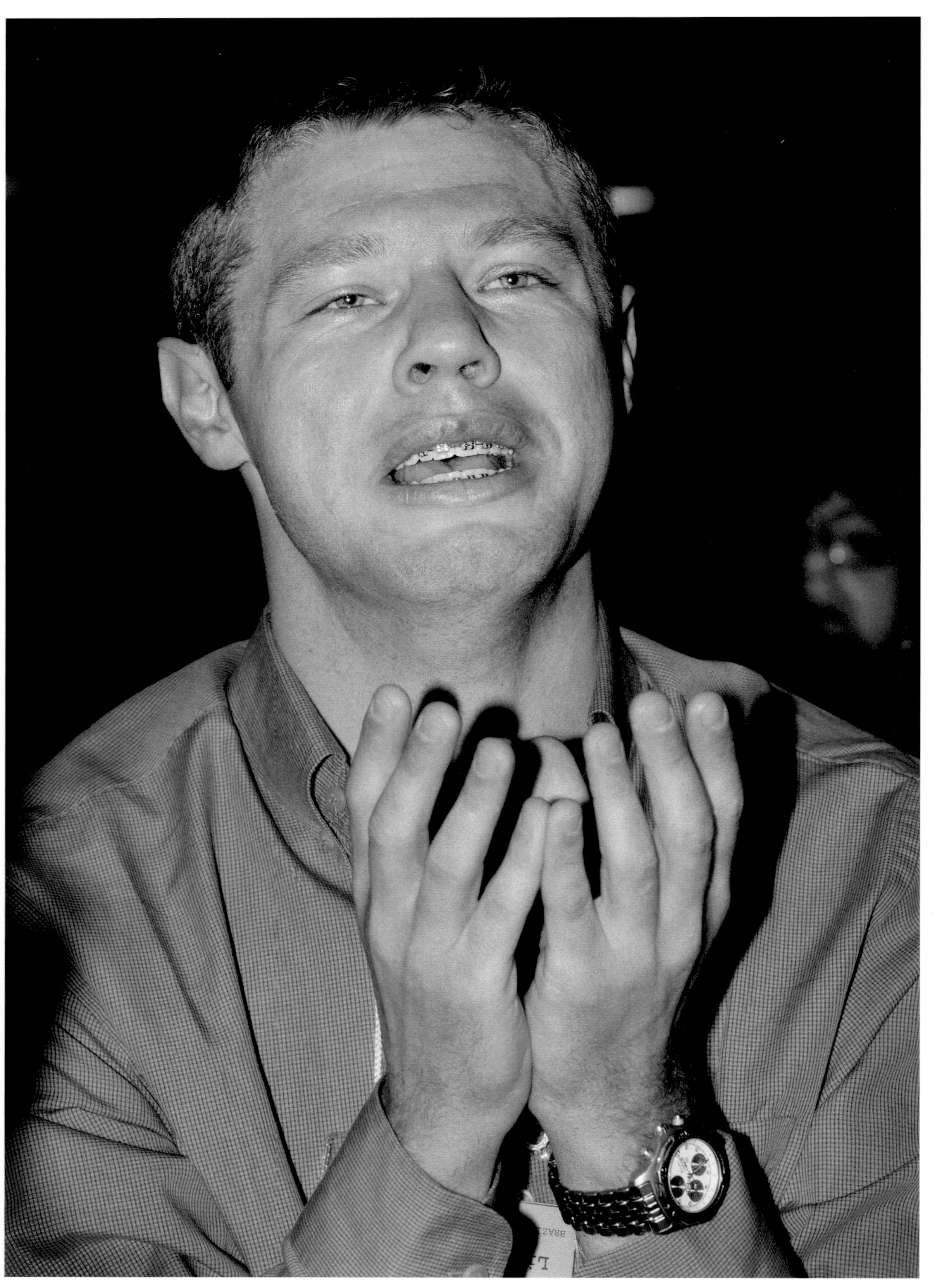

THE FACE OF FORGIVENESS

Salvation and Redemption

Photographs and Testimony by STEVEN KATZMAN

Foreword by A.D. COLEMAN Inspirational Text by BILL JOHNSON

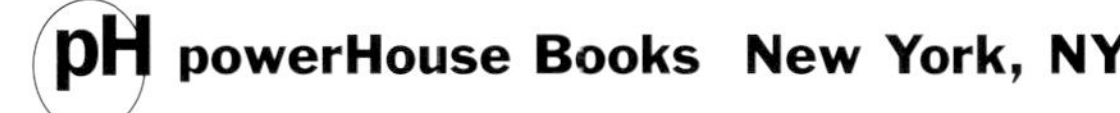
powerHouse Books New York, NY

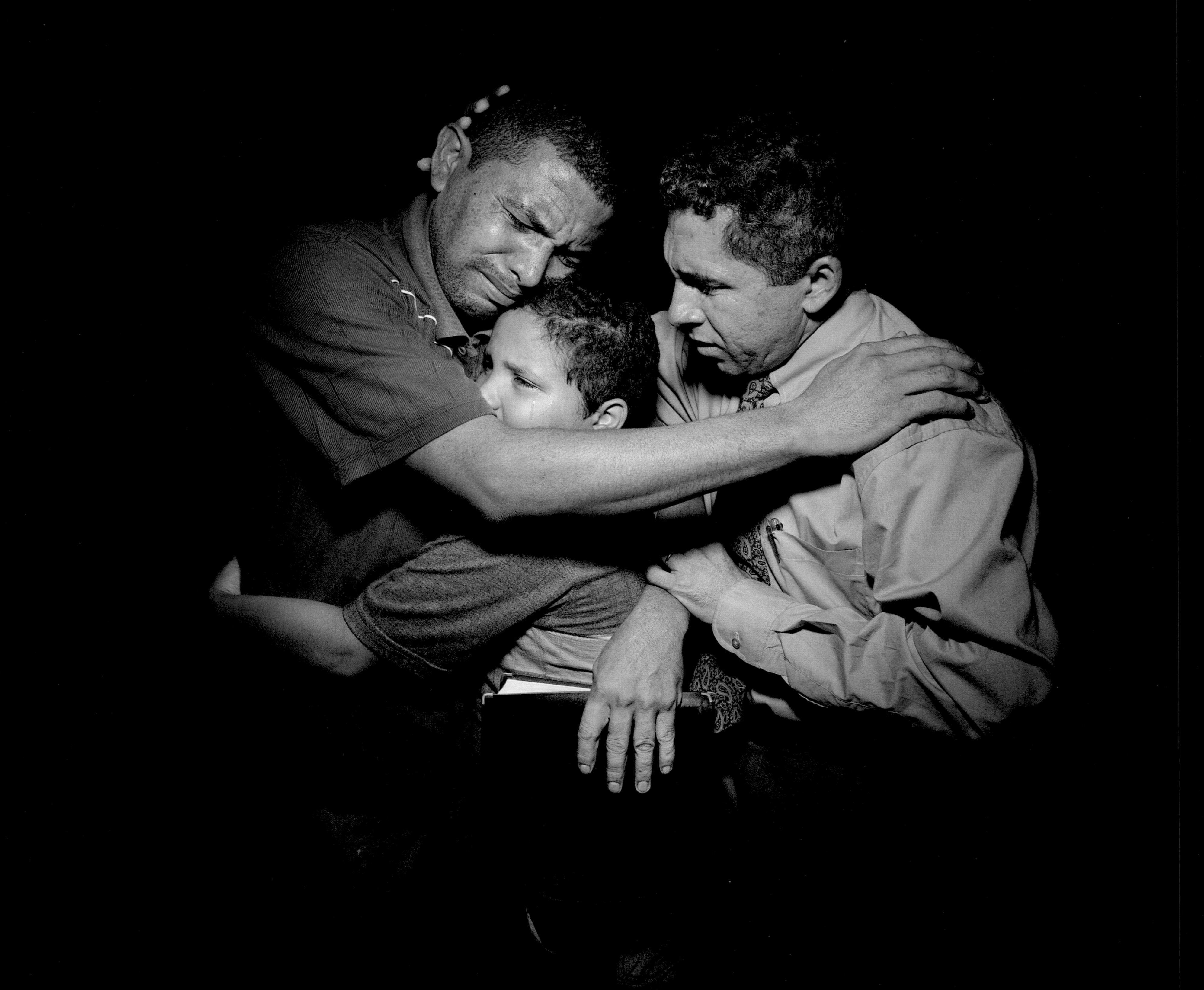

FOR MY FATHER

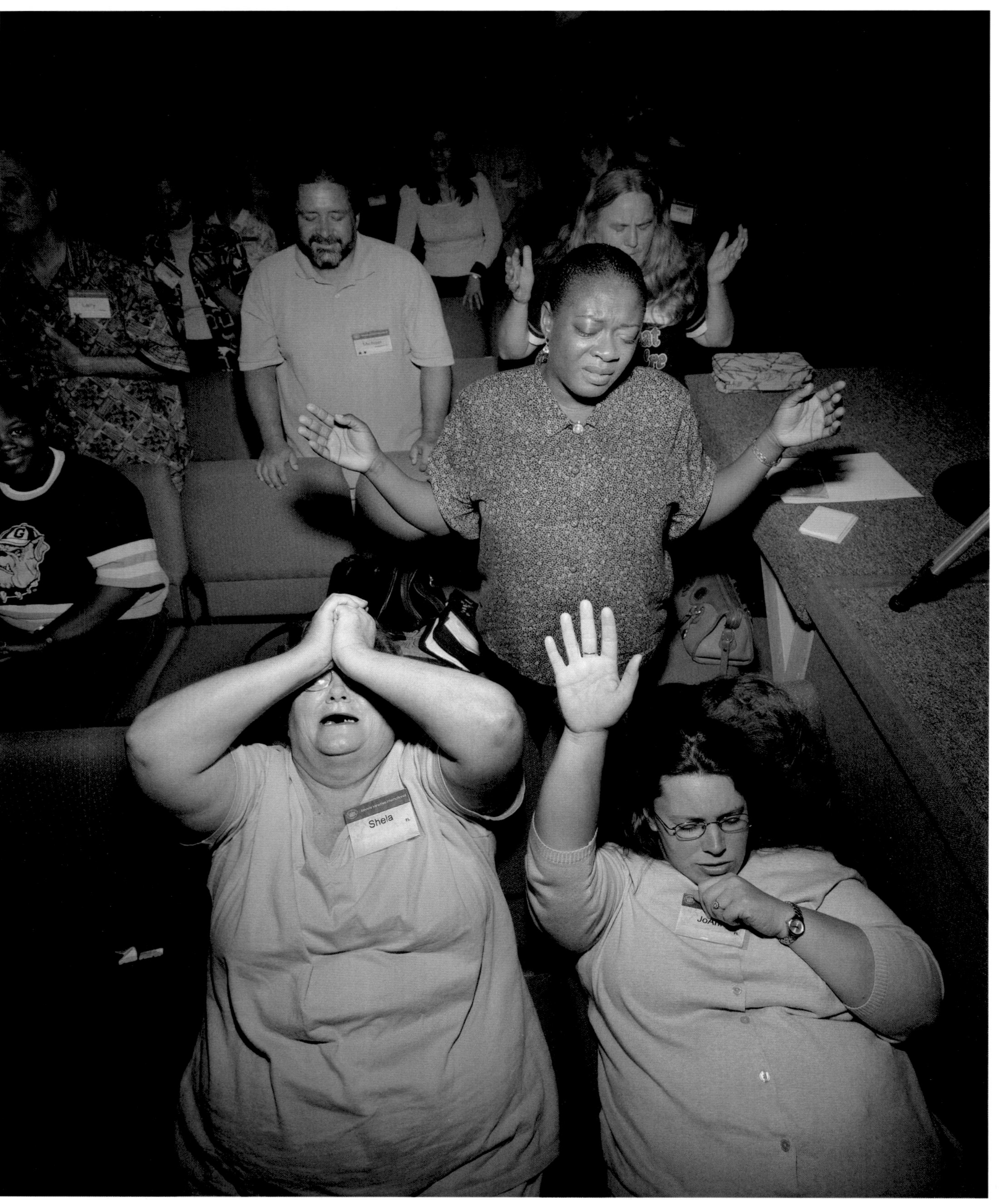
Shela

IN THE FACE OF FORGIVENESS: STEVEN KATZMAN'S EPIPHANIES

FOREWORD BY A.D. COLEMAN

If God had a face what would it look like?
And would you want to see
if seeing meant that
you would have to believe
in things like heaven and in Jesus and the saints
and all the prophets?
—Joan Osborne, "One of Us"

Photographers have photographed believers in all the world's major religions and many of its minor ones while engaged in the act of worship. Often they have done so as outsiders to those creeds, with attitudes ranging from the respectful and curious to the skeptical or even critical. But more than a few of those photographers grew up within a particular faith whose practice and practitioners they subsequently described in images. No doubt some of them remained followers of those belief systems, so it seems safe to assume that while a number of them may have lapsed in their faith, or paid only lip service to it thereafter, others surely sustained their convictions to the point where we would consider them devout.

Therefore we can say that religions have been photographed, as it were, from the inside. However, I can think of no photographer who has given us a firsthand account in words and images of his own spiritual crisis and conversion—especially to a religion with which he had no previous connection, and against which he had decided prejudices. No photographer, that is, until Steven Katzman.

Raised by atheist Marxists, I grew up assuming the nonexistence of God. That didn't stop me from coming to love plain chant, Bach's *St. Matthew's Passion*, and Black gospel music, both raw (the Rev. Gary Davis) and polished (the Golden Gate Quartet). While I was in my teens my family joined the Unitarian Church in New York, where we found an ethical community, a center of social activism, and what struck me as a benign, mild ecumenism that left one praying, as the old joke has it, "To Whom It May Concern." During my undergraduate days at Hunter College in New York I wrote a one-act play celebrating the death of God that, published in the school literary magazine, nearly got censorship imposed on the entire City University of New York system.

Thereafter I took my own atheism for granted until my forties, when a certain interior radicalism started me questioning all of my assumptions, including that one. I concluded that, even for a skeptic, active disbelief per se didn't seem necessary at all times—and found that I could live comfortably without forming or holding an opinion on many open questions, among them the existence of one or more deities.

I also came to terms with and began to acknowledge certain ideas or beliefs that had developed in me by degrees, among them the conviction that forces outside myself and others—some version of what Alcoholics Anonymous refers to as "a Power greater than ourselves"—impinged on human behavior, that the concept of karma pertained to our personal experience, and that the energy of the individual consciousness could neither be created nor destroyed, but somehow continued on through a process that bore some relationship to reincarnation.

This led me eventually to adopt a Buddhist practice, which engages me with a belief system that includes certain acts of faith but doesn't exactly qualify as a religion, at least not to my way of thinking, as it involves no deity. (The Buddha was simply an exemplary human who discovered his own innate capacity for transcendence.) Within months of commencing my practice, I calmed inwardly and people began to comment on the changes they saw in me. I have since served as an informal counselor to many people on personal and spiritual matters, and—on a professional level—a formal advisor to others. Apparently I have developed some ability to mediate in difficult situations and to assist people in finding their own true paths.

I say this because writing about *The Face of Forgiveness*, Steven Katzman's act of bearing witness, necessarily involves addressing not just the human spirit but acts of faith, the evidence of things not seen, even the possibility that God might exist—whether as the all-powerful, omniscient Being that the conventional wisdom assumes or else, in Joan Osborne's words, as "one of us . . . .Just a slob like one of us, just a stranger on the bus, trying to make his way home." This book tells us what Katzman believes, while implicitly asking what we believe, proposing that we put those cards on the table.

So it seems important to position myself in relation to what Katzman describes, to outline my own spiritual course, just as he clearly feels it mandatory to tell us, in his accompanying text, how he came to make these images and what happened to him in the process. I went through something much less dramatic, more like a sea change, but I understand the implications of such a shift. I don't share Katzman's particular convictions, but I don't disbelieve a word of what he has to say. And, as a writer, I know an authentic voice when I hear one.

As it happens, that 1995 lyric of Joan Osborne's serves as the theme song for the TV series "Joan of Arcadia," which astonishes me not only because it is extraordinarily popular on network TV but also because I've found myself drawn to watch it regularly. Its premise—that confused teenagers (or at least Joan Girardi, its eponymous heroine) may be on a mission from God—bemuses me. But I find the show's greatest value in its portrayal of blundering, flawed, vulnerable, wounded, everyday people engaged in a search for meaning, attempting to figure out the right thing to do in mostly ordinary if not always easy situations, and striving to treat each other decently and lovingly.

In short, it's about the way that those I think of as fundamentally good people, whether known to me or not, try to live their lives everywhere on this planet, regardless of their religious persuasion. By that I don't suggest that I consider their faith, or conscious acts of agnosticism or atheism, irrelevant. You can use almost any belief system as a weapon with which to injure yourself or as an excuse to harm others. Or you can use it as a reflecting pool to show you the trace of the sacred in your own poor slob's face. Christian, Jew, Muslim, Hindu, Buddhist, agnostic, atheist—anyone can do either, which is all I mean by "regardless." In my experience, what you choose to believe matters less than how you apply it to your existence on earth.

The people Katzman shows us surely qualify as pilgrims, seekers of enlightenment, and he renders them with all his considerable skill as a photographer at moments in which they have surrendered themselves to a possibility, the instant of each one's act of faith. You can't photograph faith itself, of course. Photographs describe the light that bounces off the surfaces of objects, nothing more, and both faith and revelation remain private, invisible inner experiences.

You can photograph people testifying, feeling the spirit—but that's not the same thing. The outward appearance of a spiritual experience inevitably becomes more open to interpretation. If we decontextualized Katzman's electrifying images and recaptioned them, presenting his subjects variously as attendees at a James Brown or Tom Jones or Britney Spears concert, customers at a comedy club, victims of a tragedy, or subjects of a hallucinogenic drug experiment, they'd lose none of their visual power. But their meaning, and our understanding of them, would shift dramatically.

So our reading of what these pictures signify depends to a great extent on what Katzman tells us he underwent at the Brownsville Assembly of God in Pensacola, Florida in 1999, and thereafter through 2004. His riveting account of entering this environment as a documentary photographer pursuing a sociological project and exiting it transformed, perhaps permanently, by his encounter with an energy both terrifying and rapturous turns his photographs into what detectives call "trace evidence"—insufficient in itself to fully prove the case, but corroborative of other evidence, supportive of a specific interpretation of the events.

Typically, in a documentary project such as Katzman initially intended to create, the photographer interviews selected subjects of his or her images, transcribing and editing their statements to allow those represented to speak for themselves. This empowers them, by giving them voice, while at the same time distancing the photographer from the situation, casting him or her in the relatively detached role of translator, facilitator, or intermediary.

Katzman, clearly, will have none of this. Or perhaps I should say that whatever has possessed him won't allow it, won't permit him to stand aside, pretending to impartiality and noninvolvement. In a superficial reading, this results in a seeming disconnect between the pictures—which employ conventional tropes of ostensibly and even clinically objective modernist documentary photography—and Katzman's intensely subjective, highly emotional, first-person confessional narrative, entirely uncharacteristic of the "artist's statement" that normally accompanies such a suite of photographs.

Katzman makes a point of mentioning several times the importance to him of using strobe flash for his images. I'm inclined to take that strobe—and, by extension, the pictures he made with it—metaphorically rather than literally. Like Diogenes with his lantern, searching for an honest man, Katzman behaved with his camera and strobe as if he could discover and expose (first for himself, then for us) the essence of revelation merely by putting a bigger bulb in the socket. Unlike Diogenes, he wasn't making a philosophical point, but behaving in a way we might call presumptuous.

Katzman aspired to produce in his photographs a visual analogue of what he calls "the throng of lost souls being blinded by His light." Powerful images result from this, pictures that suggest how we might appear as motes in an omniscient God's eye, but they don't take you inside the individual's encounter with the divine—because they can't. How could a mere photograph convey the actual presence, the immanence, of the Holy Spirit?

Yet if one approaches these pictures not as factual, scientific proof but as a form of this photographer's testament to his own ambition, epiphany, and conversion, they take on different, deeper, autobiographical resonances. When Katzman states, "I was the lost soul in my photographs. . . .I realized that I was no longer a stranger shooting from the outside. I was now. . .on the inside looking out," his images and text recombine in a much different and more potent configuration, as manifestations of his own personal search for salvation. Think of them as self-portraits, each one an aspect of Katzman's own yearning for the state of grace, and they fit exactly with his words, merge with them perfectly.

Here's what I take away from this: Katzman can show you his intense, charged photographs of religious ecstasy manifest in the faces and bodies of human beings, with whom he so closely identifies. As one who now has undergone it himself, he can tell you in his own eloquent, convincing words how that actually feels—especially what it means to a nonbeliever (perhaps like yourself) who, to his utter astonishment, totally without warning, found himself swept away. But, no matter how finely wrought and persuasive, Katzman's representations constitute mere reports, not the event itself as it registers in a receptive heart, mind, soul. Someone or something taught Steven Katzman a lesson, and he's passing it along. His true message (or the message of whatever force speaks through him here):

You cannot have this experience at some remove; it happens firsthand, hands-on, or not at all. But it does happen. It happens to others. It happened to him. It could happen to you.

MARCH 2005

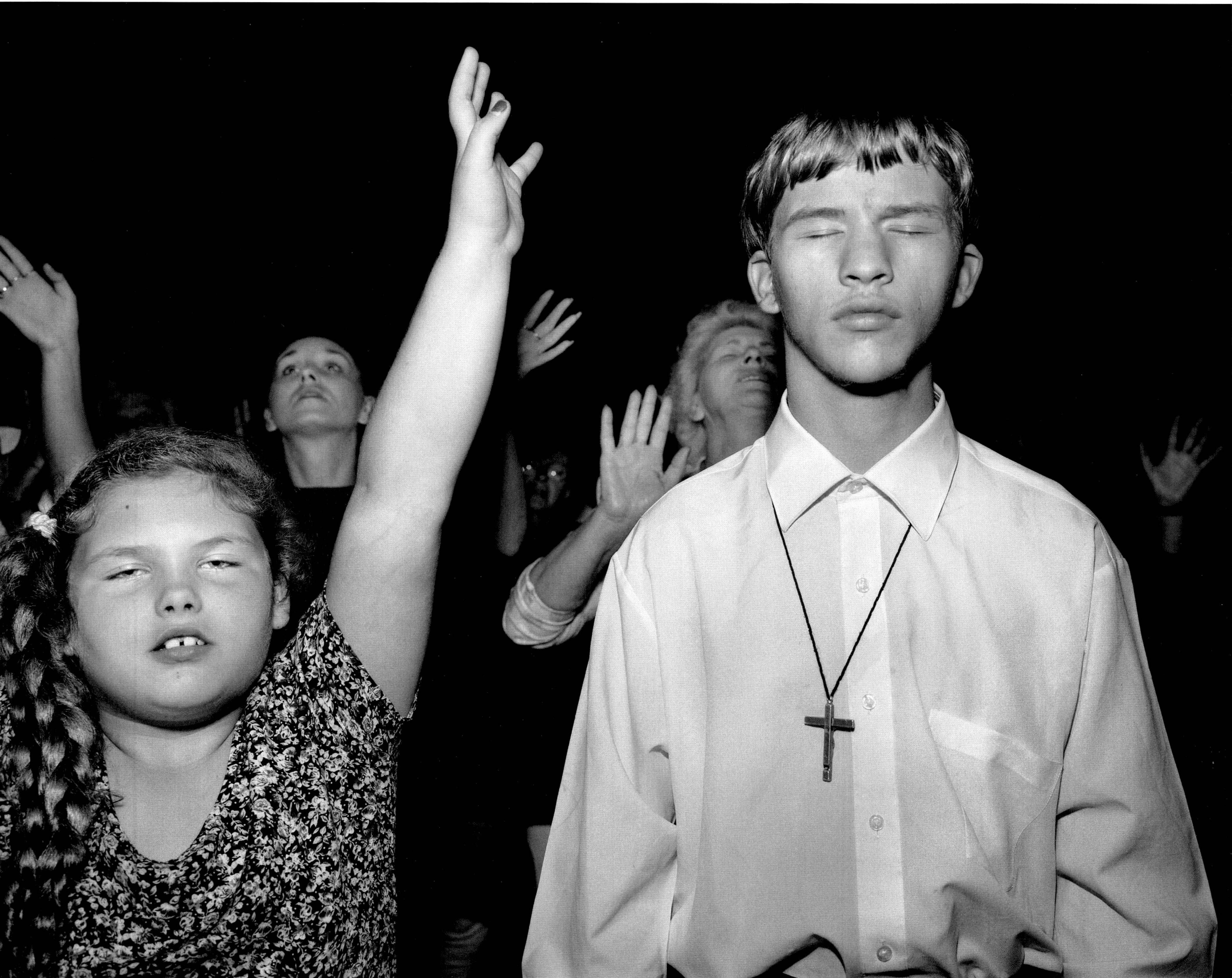

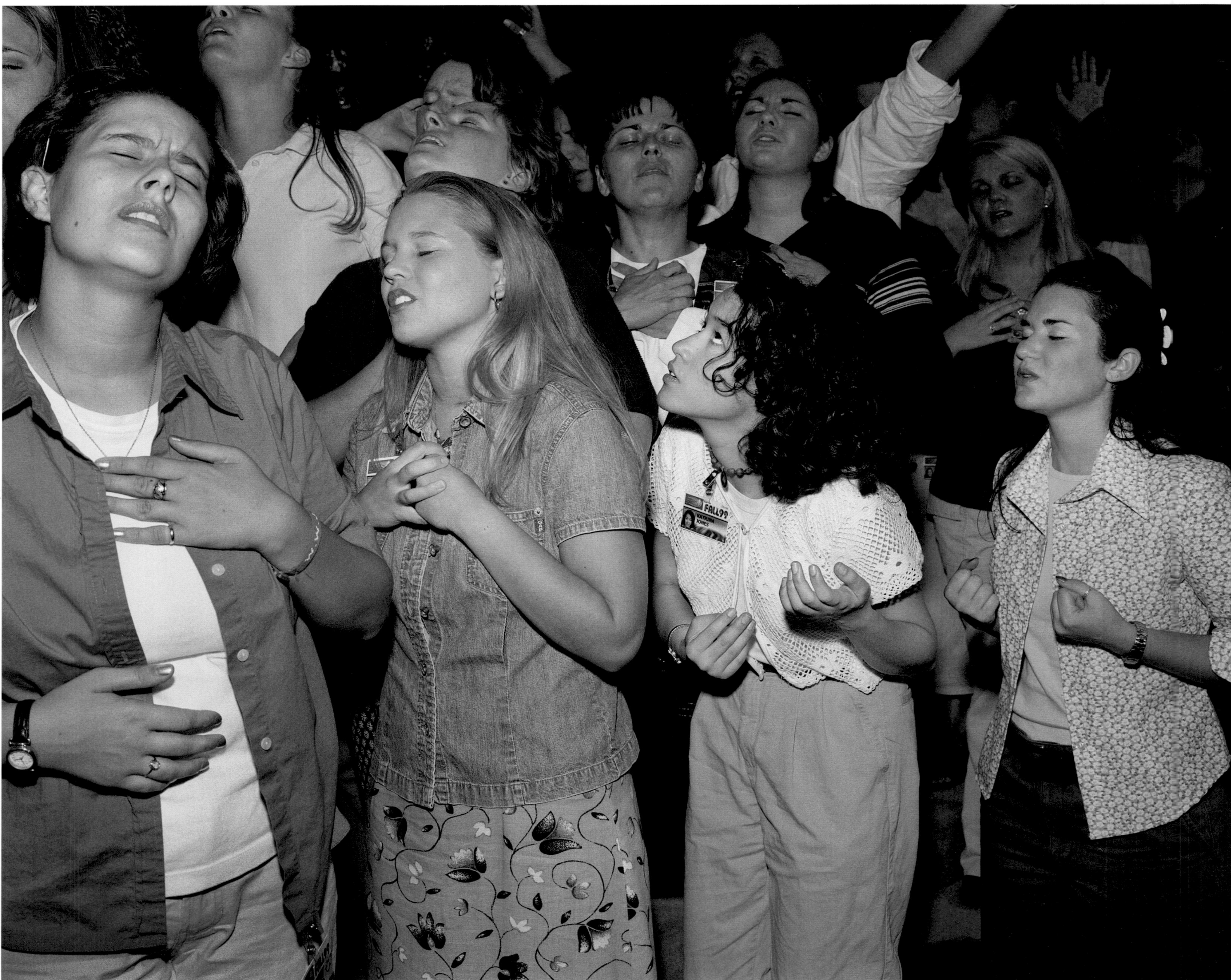
FALL99
KATRINA
JONES

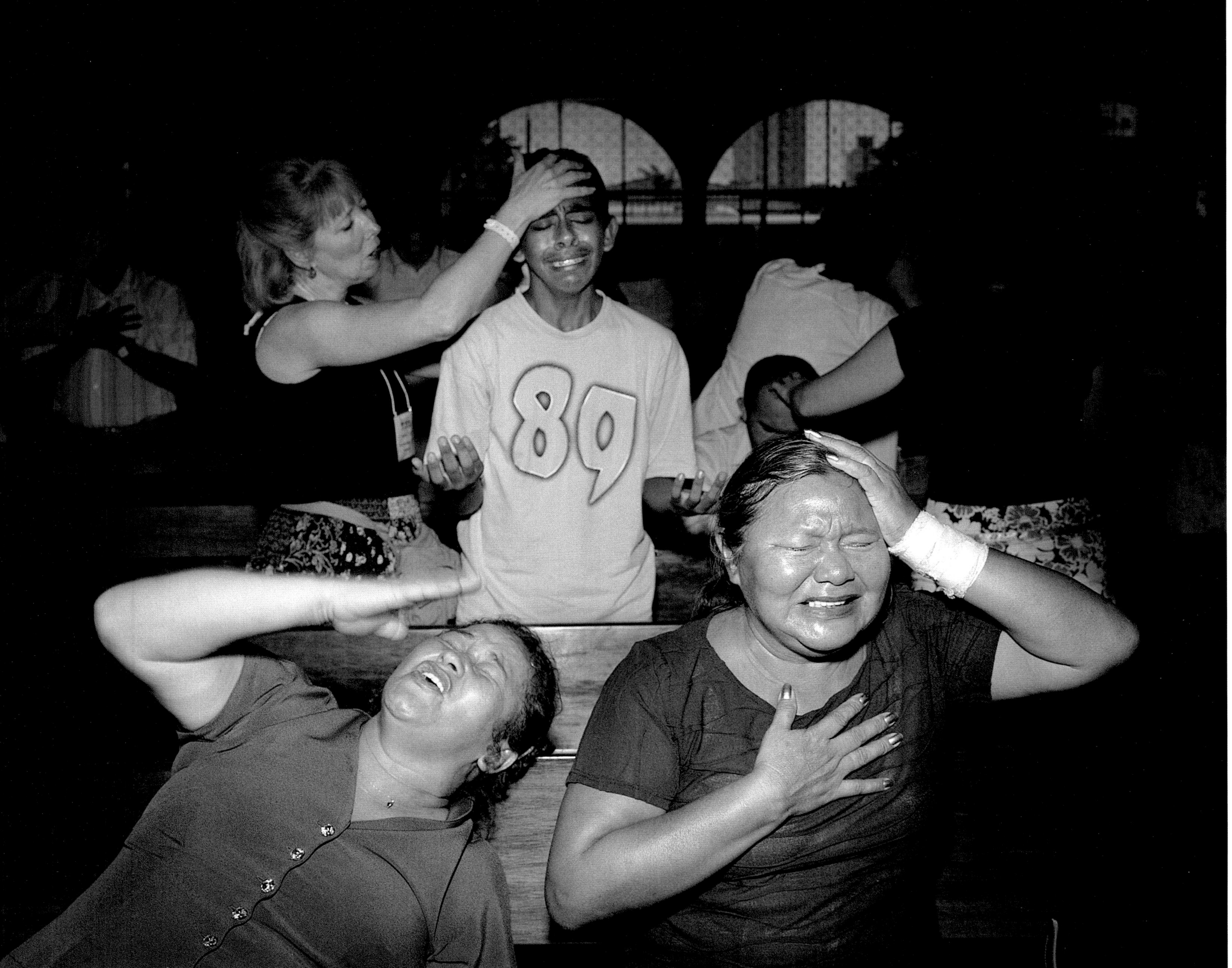
89

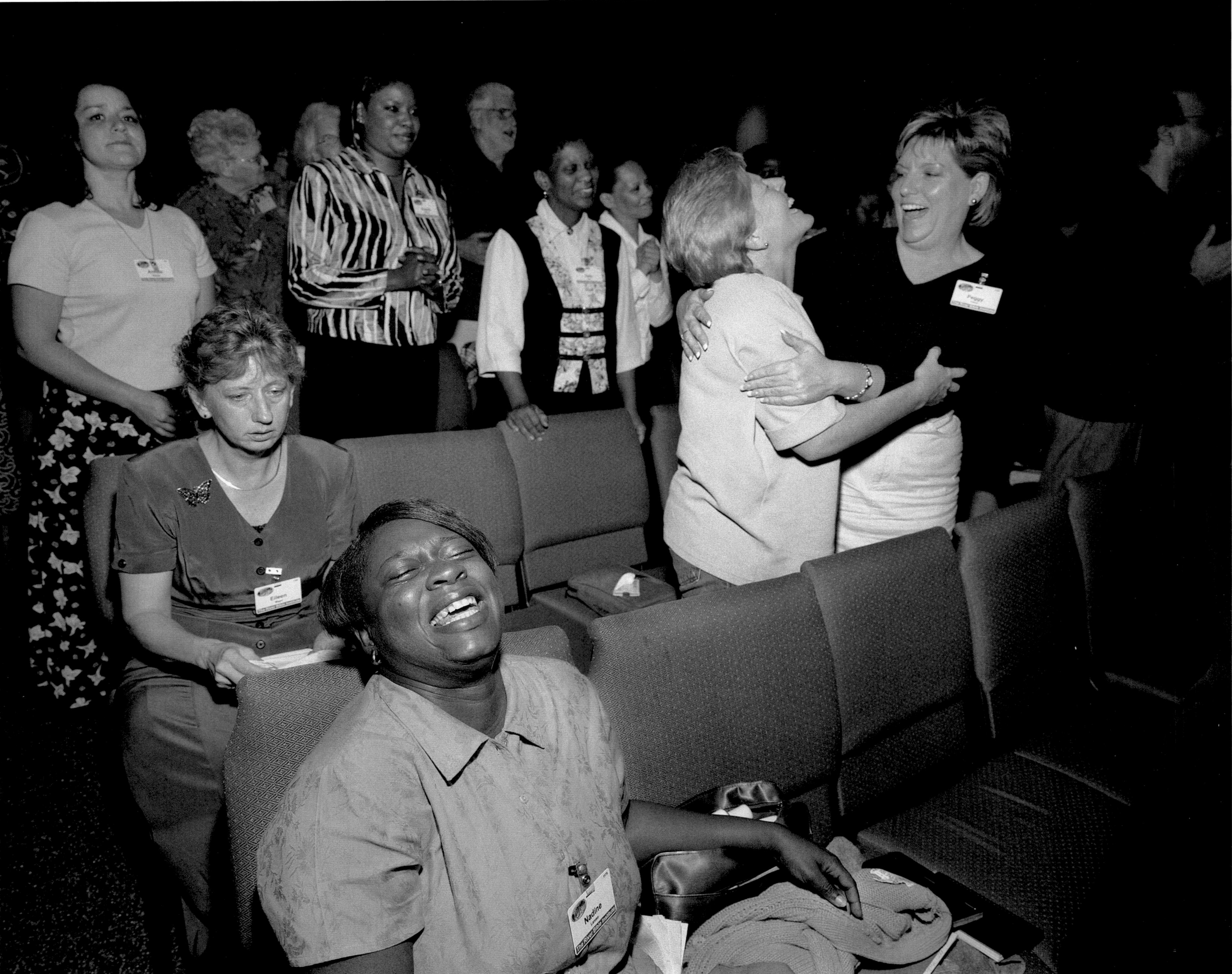
Peggy
Eileen
Nadine

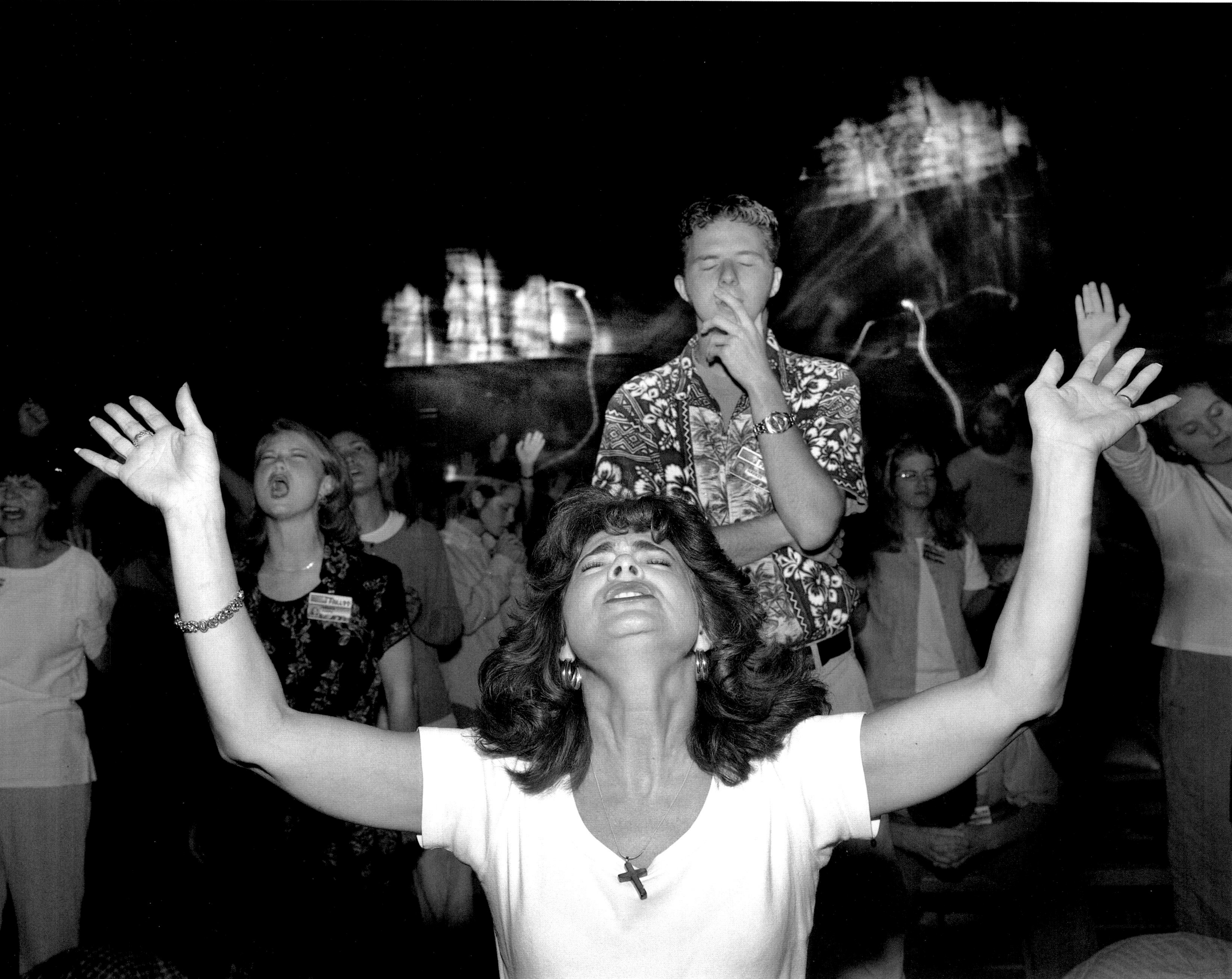

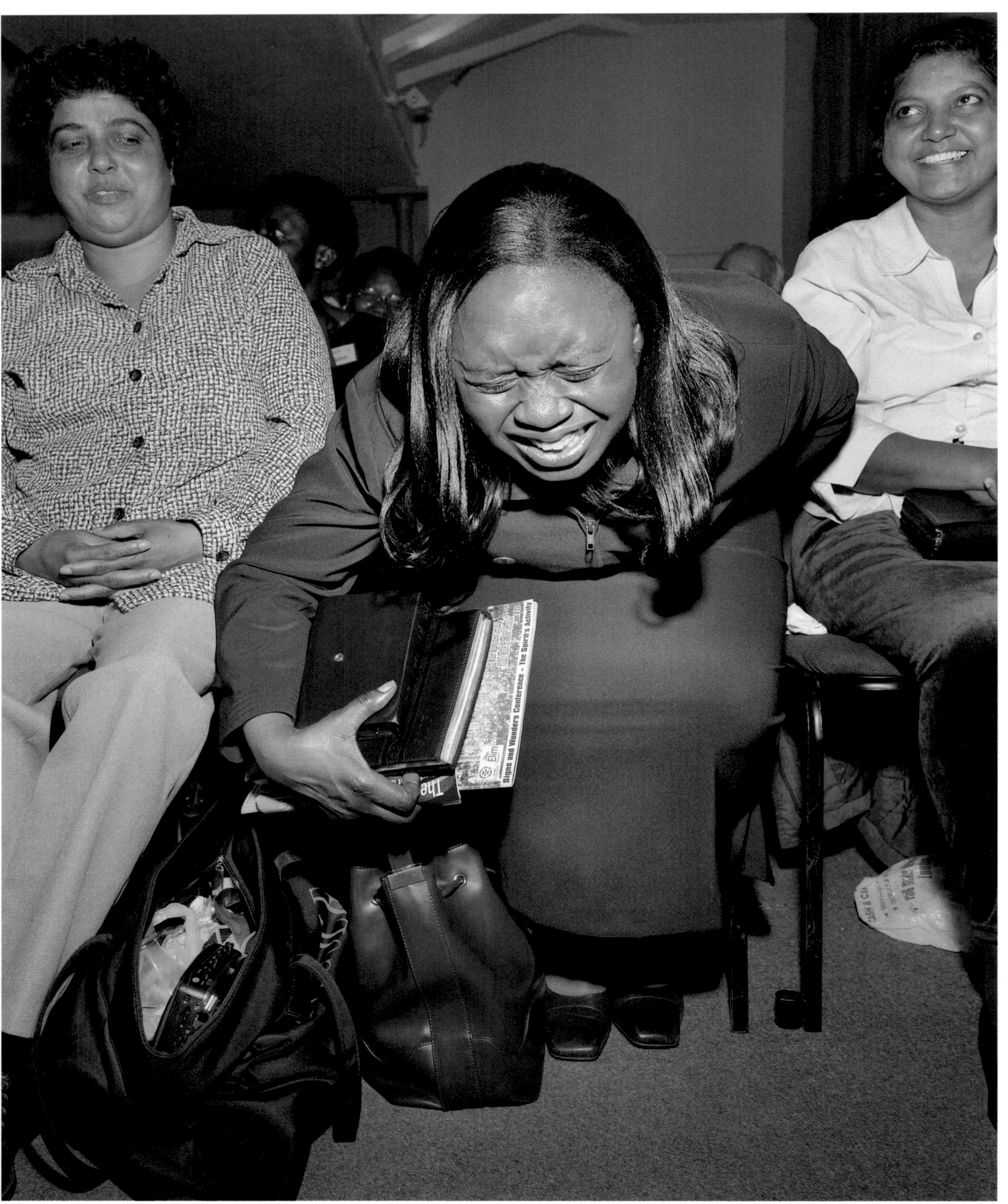
Signs and Wonders Conference - The Spirit's Activity
Elim
The

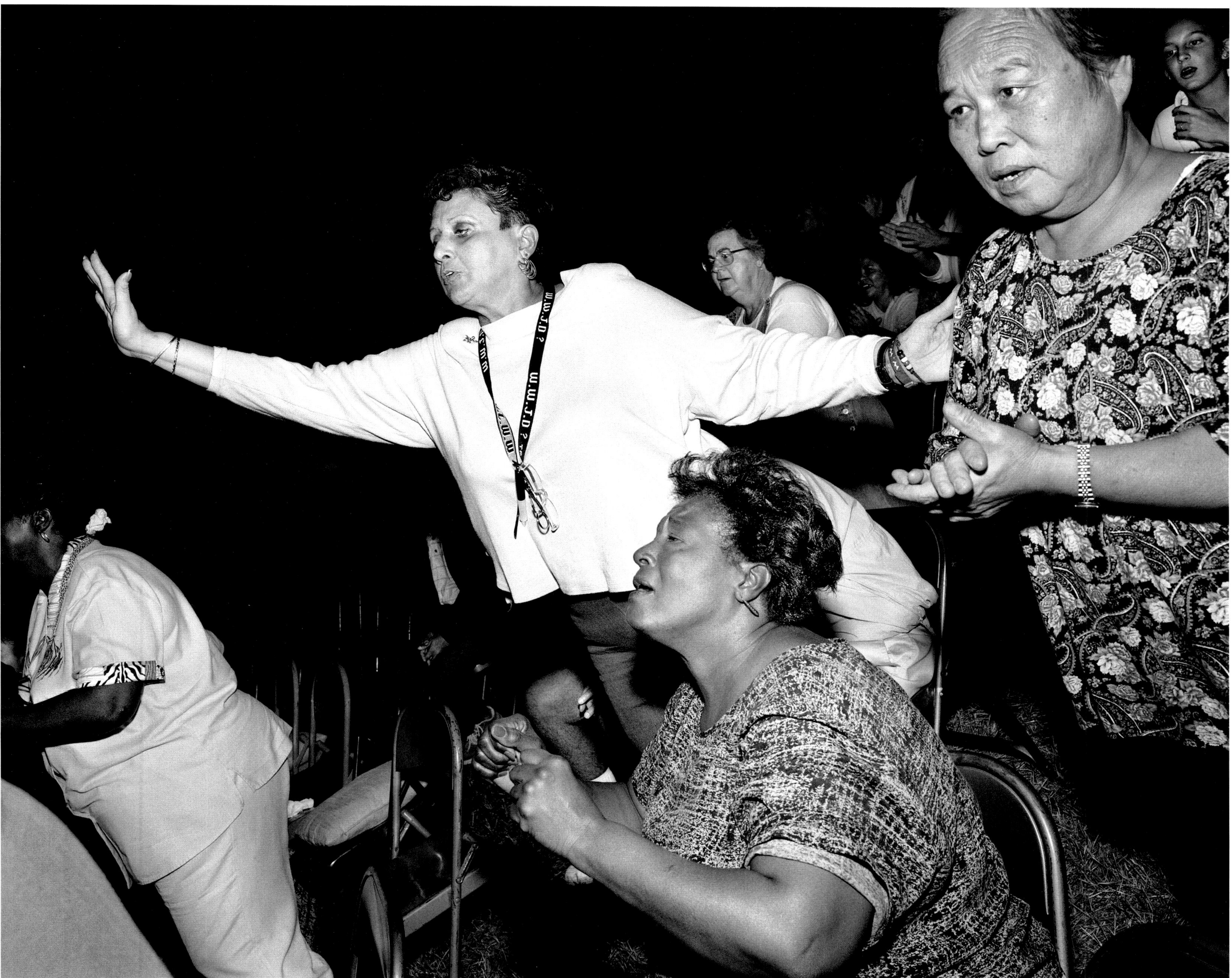
W.W.J.D.?

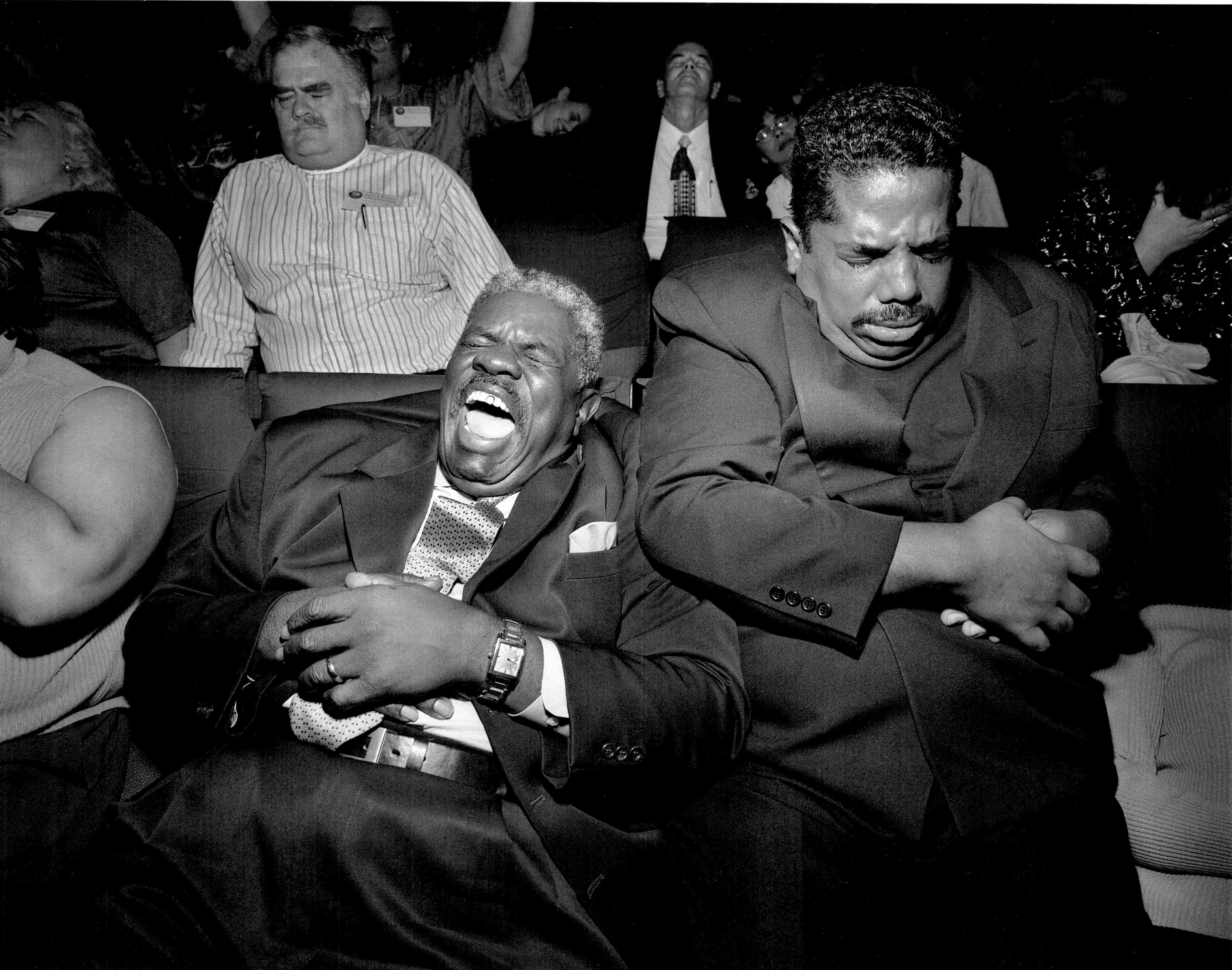

THE SOURCE OF FORGIVENESS

BY BILL JOHNSON

ABOUT GOD

God is extravagant—radically generous, joyous beyond description, loving to the point of suffering. His passion goes beyond the boundaries of our comprehension. Yet, in the same measure He loves, He also hates. He hates whatever attempts to destroy us—His anger is always aimed at that what interferes with love.

A STORY OF ROMANCE

There was much in existence before we were created. All things were made for God's pleasure. But one thing was missing—there was nothing in all that He had made that was created in the likeness of God Himself. God is love. And love must give. And so, humankind was made.

The worlds were framed by God's voice—He spoke things into being. In His desire for intimacy He created humankind in His likeness. There's no pleasure in the servitude or friendship of robotlike beings, so Adam and Eve were given the ability to choose whom they would serve.

They were placed into God's ultimate expression of beauty and peace: the Garden of Eden. Chaos existed outside the garden. It needed the order and blessing from the influence of God's delegated ones—Adam and Eve. They became the key to the restoration of planet earth that God had desired.

They were placed in the garden with a commission from God. He said, "Be fruitful and multiply; fill the earth and subdue it."[1] The Heavenly Father knew that as they and their children lived under His loving rule, they would extend the boundaries of His government until the entire planet was like His garden of blessings. The greater the number of people in a right relationship to God, the greater the impact of their leadership. This process of growth and increase was to continue until the entire earth was covered with the glorious rule of God through humanity.

A project of restoration was needed because Satan had previously rebelled against God and was then cast out of heaven. He, along with the portion of angels under his charge, exercised dominion over the earth. Everything outside of the garden needed to be subdued because it was under the influence of the prince of darkness.[2] God could have destroyed the devil and his host with a single word. Instead, He chose to defeat the powers of darkness through His delegated ones—those made in His image who were lovers of God by choice.

God, the creator of all, placed Adam and his descendants in charge of the planet: "The heaven, even the heavens, are the LORD'S; but the earth He has given to the children of men."[3] This honor was given to us out of God's love; and love always chooses the best. We were created in God's image, *for intimacy*, that His dominion might be expressed through love. The stage was set for all the powers of darkness to fall as humanity exercised its godly influence over creation. But instead, man sinned, rejecting the glory and lordship of God for which we were destined.

PERFECTION REQUIRED

God is perfectly holy and just, and does not tolerate sin. Therefore He declared that all who sin must die. God's perfection requires such an outcome. The effect of Adam and Eve's sin was immediate—the ones who had enjoyed perfect union with God were now estranged from Him. The shame they felt for their sin caused them to hide. For the first time they realized they were naked. Adam and Eve gave up their position of rulership when they ate the forbidden fruit. In that one act humanity became the slave and possession of the evil one. All that Adam owned, including the title deed to the planet, the authority to rule, and even the lives of his descendants, became part of the devil's spoil. Although they continued to live, sickness, disease, and death entered the world. They were now eating of the crop they had planted—the fruit of their choices. They had removed themselves from the realm of God's blessing, placing themselves under the curse of the evil one.

Satan didn't come into the Garden of Eden and take control of Adam and Eve. He couldn't because he had no authority. Since man was given the keys of dominion over the planet, the devil would have to get authority from them. The suggestion to eat the forbidden fruit was simply the devil's effort to get Adam and Eve to agree with him in opposition to God. Once they did so, they gave their authority to Satan to rule the world. Thus he began to *kill, steal, and destroy.*[4] The Apostle Paul said, "You are that one's slaves whom you obey."[5] Rebellion against God was what the devil was hoping for.

Yet the God of love was prepared for humankind's rejection. He positioned Himself to redeem humankind from Satan's slavery and the grip of sin. Jesus would come to reclaim all that was lost. But the cost for such a purchase was higher than we could imagine—He would have to pay with His own life.

The word *redeem* means to *buy back*. God had already planned for the risk involved in creating people with the freedom to choose whom they would serve. The Father was prepared to offer Jesus, His only son, as a sacrificial offering in the place of man.

PERFECTION FOUND

Jesus became a man in order to meet the requirements of the purchase—the purchase price was the life of a sinless man. Jesus would have to live without sin, yet face every temptation known to mankind. God *put on* human flesh, and lived with the restrictions that belong to humanity. From that place of humility He lived in absolute obedience to God, without any sin. He became the perfect sacrifice.

His life was filled with ridicule and mockery, but He took no revenge. On His way to the cross He was beaten with a whip in which pieces of metal were tied to leather straps, bringing Him very close to death. Yet they wanted to keep Him alive to experience the horrendous suffering of the cross. The cross in itself was the most gruesome way known for a man to die. He was nailed to a cross between two thieves. But the greatest of all His sufferings was the moment He was separated from God the Father. In all eternity, that had never happened. According to the scriptures, He became wholly identified with us to the point that He actually became sin,[6] and God rejects all sin! The weight of the sin of all of humanity was placed upon Him. He died bearing the consequences for our sin.

Jesus became a curse so that we wouldn't have to bear the curse. He took upon Himself what I deserved that I might inherit what He deserved. But this provision of God could not be forced upon anyone. In the same way that humanity departed from God, they would have to return—through their freedom to choose. Faith, the yielded expression of the heart, would be the only way for this wonderful provision of the Lord to be applied to an individual's life. And so the declaration of God's provision rings true—"By grace we have been saved through faith."[7]

ROMANCE RESTORED

The Bible states it well: "Greater love has no one than this, that one lay down his life for his friends."[8] Giving His life for us was His invitation to come to Him and receive forgiveness, enjoy restored friendship, and be adopted into His eternal family.

Becoming a Christian is not about church membership or a pledge to uphold a religious creed. It is a personal relationship with God made possible by Jesus Christ. And in that relationship we discover what it was that Jesus made available. The word 'salvation' actually means *saved, healed,* and *delivered. Saved* from sin and eternal death, *healed* from disease and infirmity, and *delivered* from all torment of the devil. These are the things that Jesus made available to people in His earthly ministry, and it is supposed to be offered to people in this day by those who are true followers of Jesus. It is what Jesus paid for.

When Jesus redeemed humanity, He retrieved what humankind had given away. From His place of great victory He declared, "All authority has been given to Me in heaven and on earth. Go therefore...."[9] Knowing that *keys* represent *authority*, it is as though He said: *I got the keys back that you gave away through your sin. I forgive you. Now go use my authority and reclaim people by bringing them the good news of my forgiveness*. Jesus fulfilled the promise to His disciples, "I will give you the keys of the kingdom of heaven."[10] The original plan was never changed; it came into fullness once and for all in the death, resurrection, and ascension of Jesus. We are restored as a people who exercise dominion from a place of intimacy with God. As friends of God we are to learn how to enforce the victory obtained at the cross: "The God of peace will soon crush Satan under your feet."[11]

We were born to rule—rule over creation, over darkness—to plunder hell and declare the good news of God's Kingdom wherever we go. *Kingdom* means: *King's domain*. In the original plan of God, mankind ruled over creation. Now that sin has entered the world, creation has been infected by darkness, namely disease, sickness, afflicting spirits, poverty, natural disasters, demonic influence, etc. Dominion destroys the works of the devil.

Personal transformation is made possible by believing in the redemptive work of Jesus, asking God for forgiveness, and confessing His right to rule over our lives. His invasion of us changes us from the inside out. As a result, we are able to give what we have received in order to see others transformed.[12] If I truly receive power from an encounter with the God of power, I am equipped to give it away. The invasion of God into impossible situations flows through a people who have received power from heaven, and have learned to release it into the circumstances of life.

ABUNDANT LIFE

As we put our faith in Jesus Christ, and receive the salvation made available by His suffering on the cross, we become a child of the King of all Kings. In actuality, we become "citizens of Heaven." But God's desire is not merely to get us into Heaven; rather, His passion is to get His dominion into us, that we might discover our purpose. Simply put, we are to become lovers of God. And from that place of intimacy, we have the privilege and responsibility to destroy the works of the devil by extending the domain of the King. This is the opportunity given to all humankind—all because Jesus received what we deserved, that we might receive what He deserves.

FOOTNOTES

1 Genesis 1:28 NKJV
2 Genesis 1:2
3 Psalms 115:16 NKJV
4 John 10:10
5 Romans 6:16 NKJV
6 Corinthians 5:21
7 Ephesians 2:8 NKJV
8 John 15:13 NASB
9 Matthew 28:18–19 NASB
10 Matthew 16:19 NASB
11 Romans 16:20 NASB
12 See Matthew 10:8

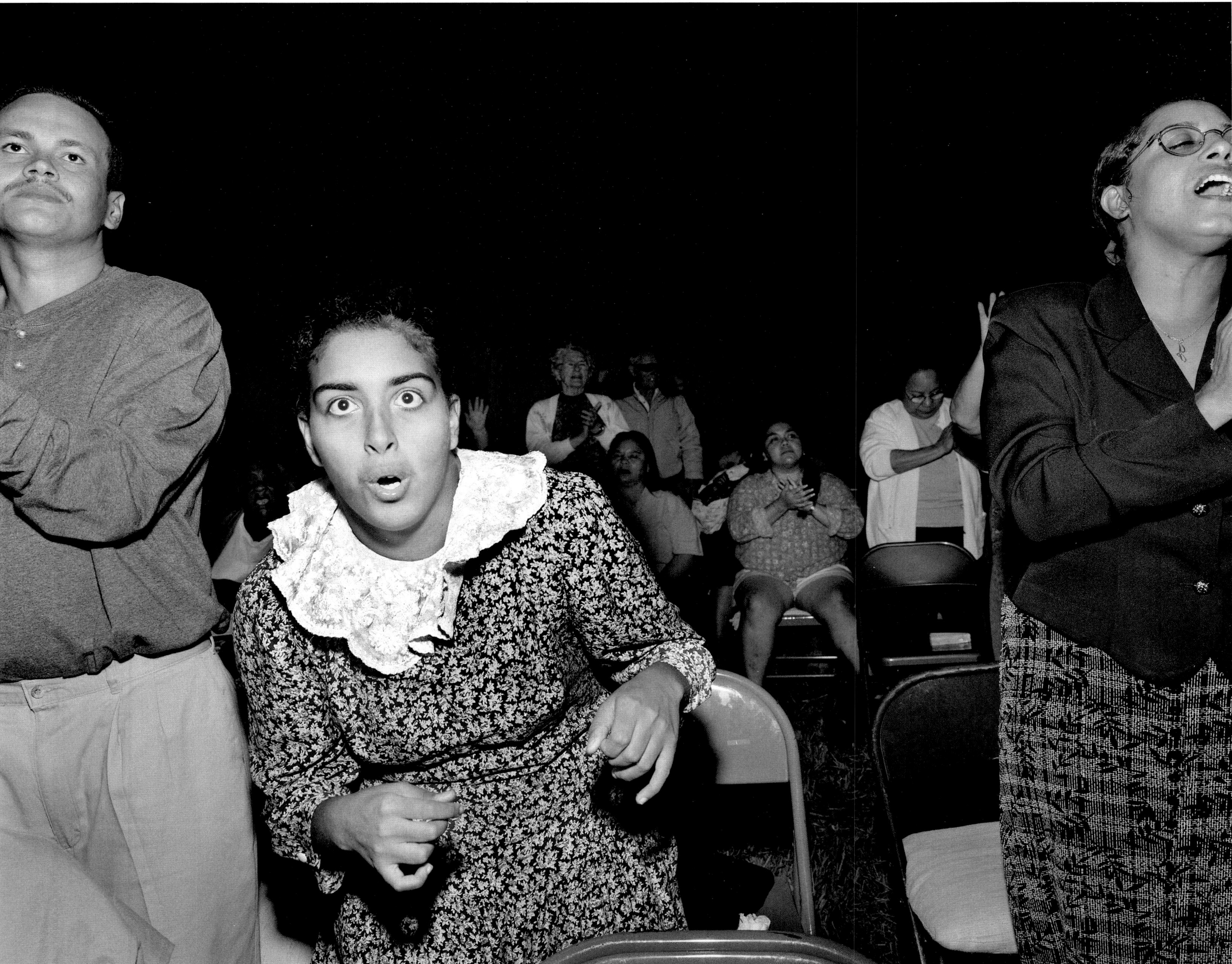

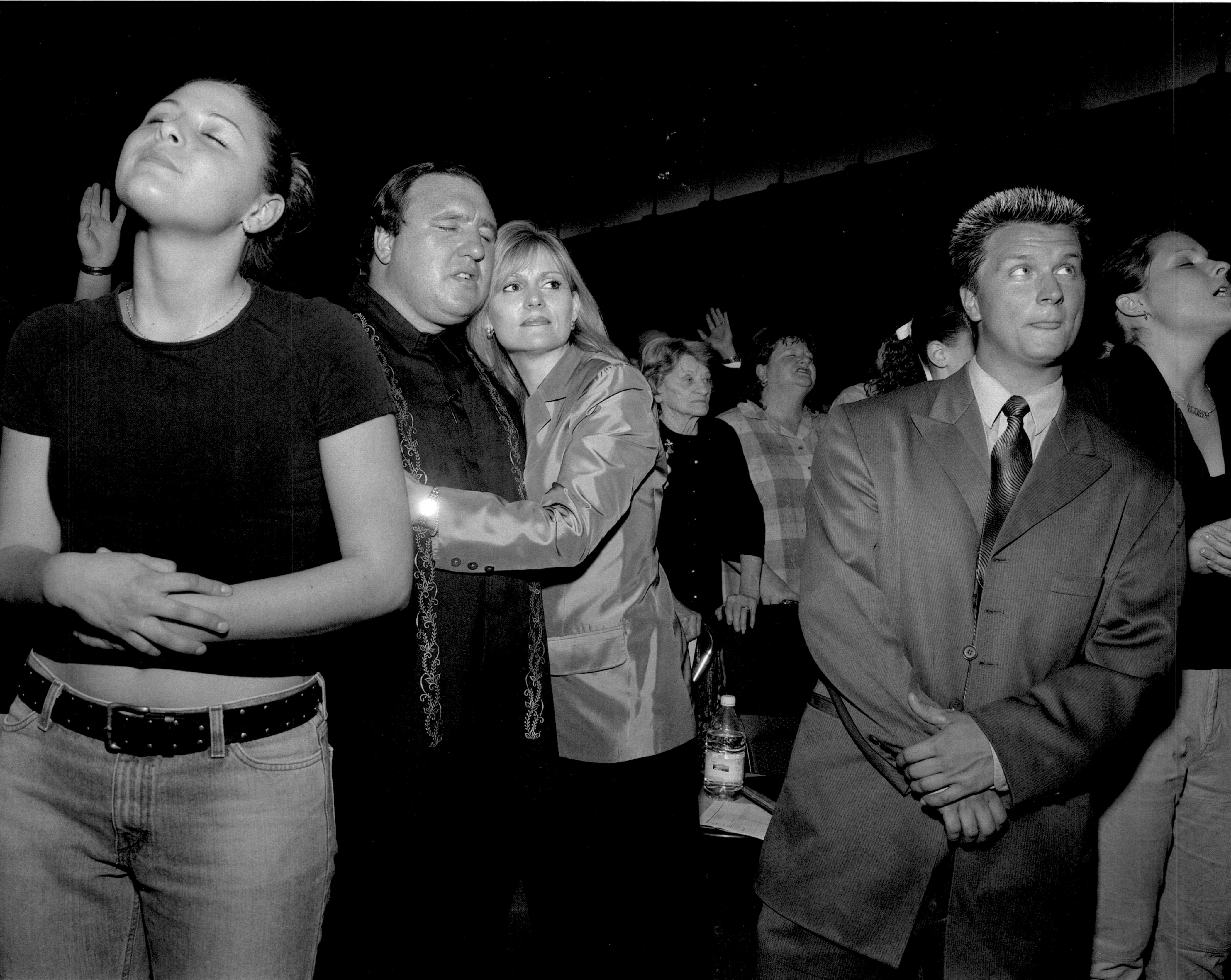

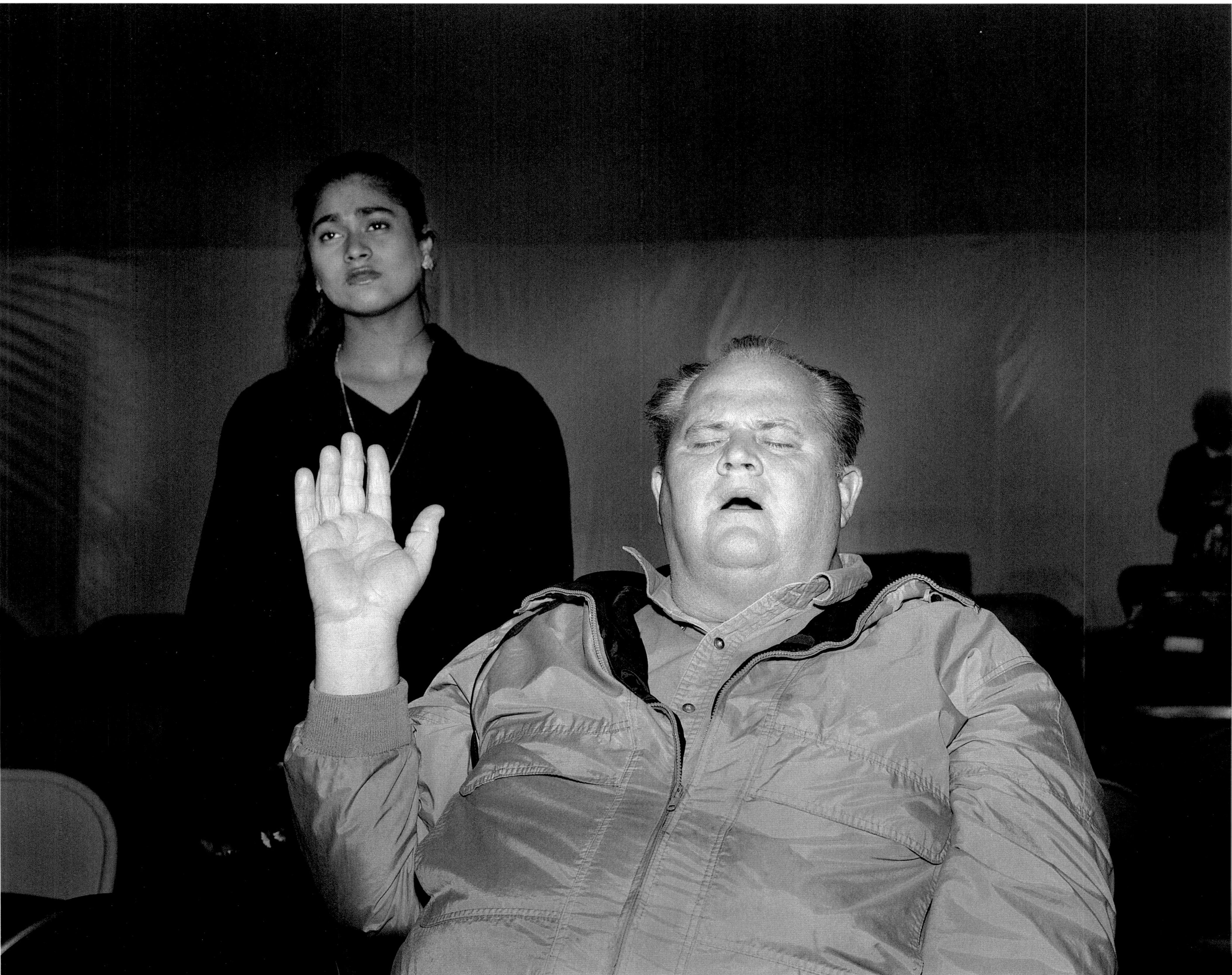

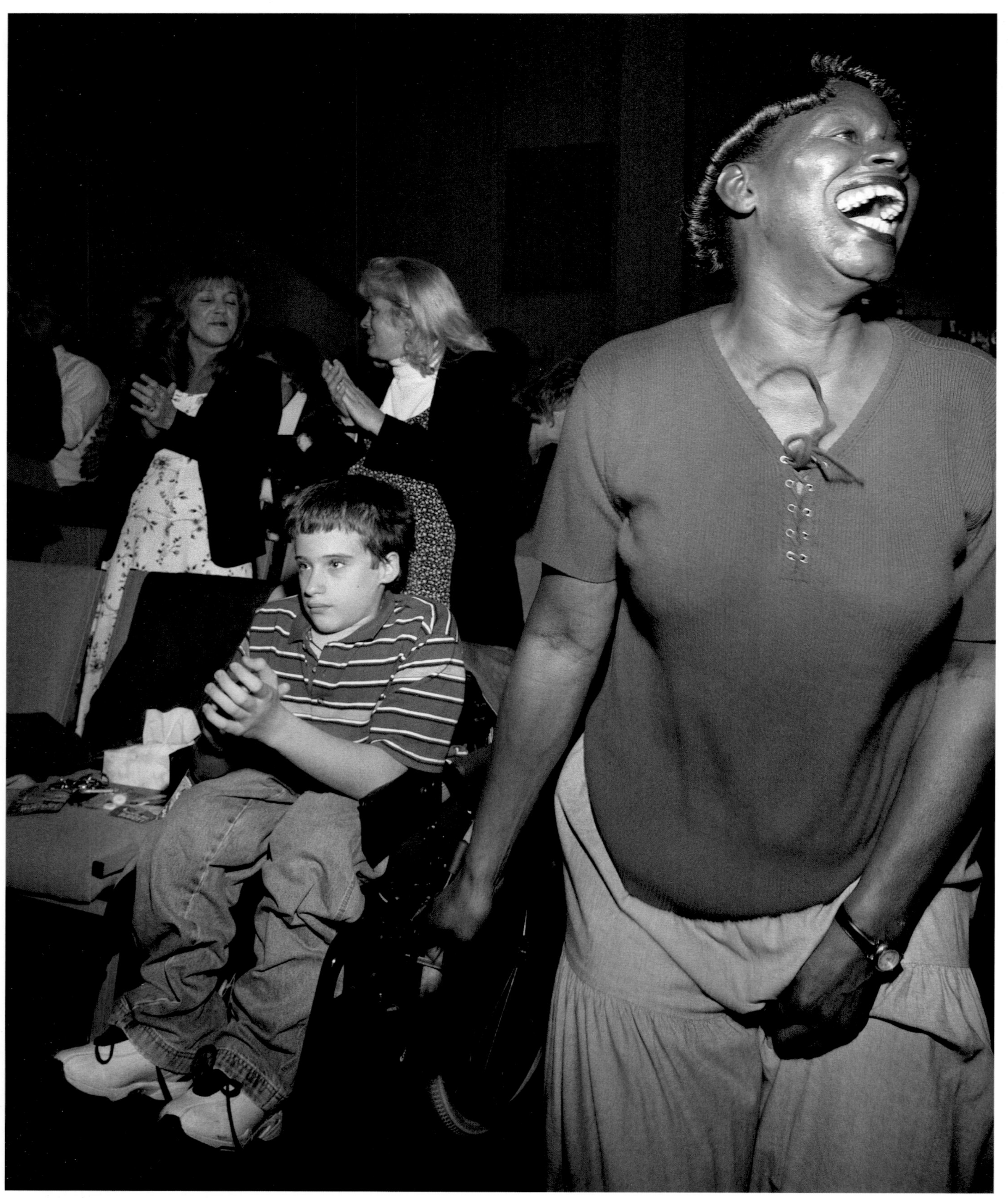

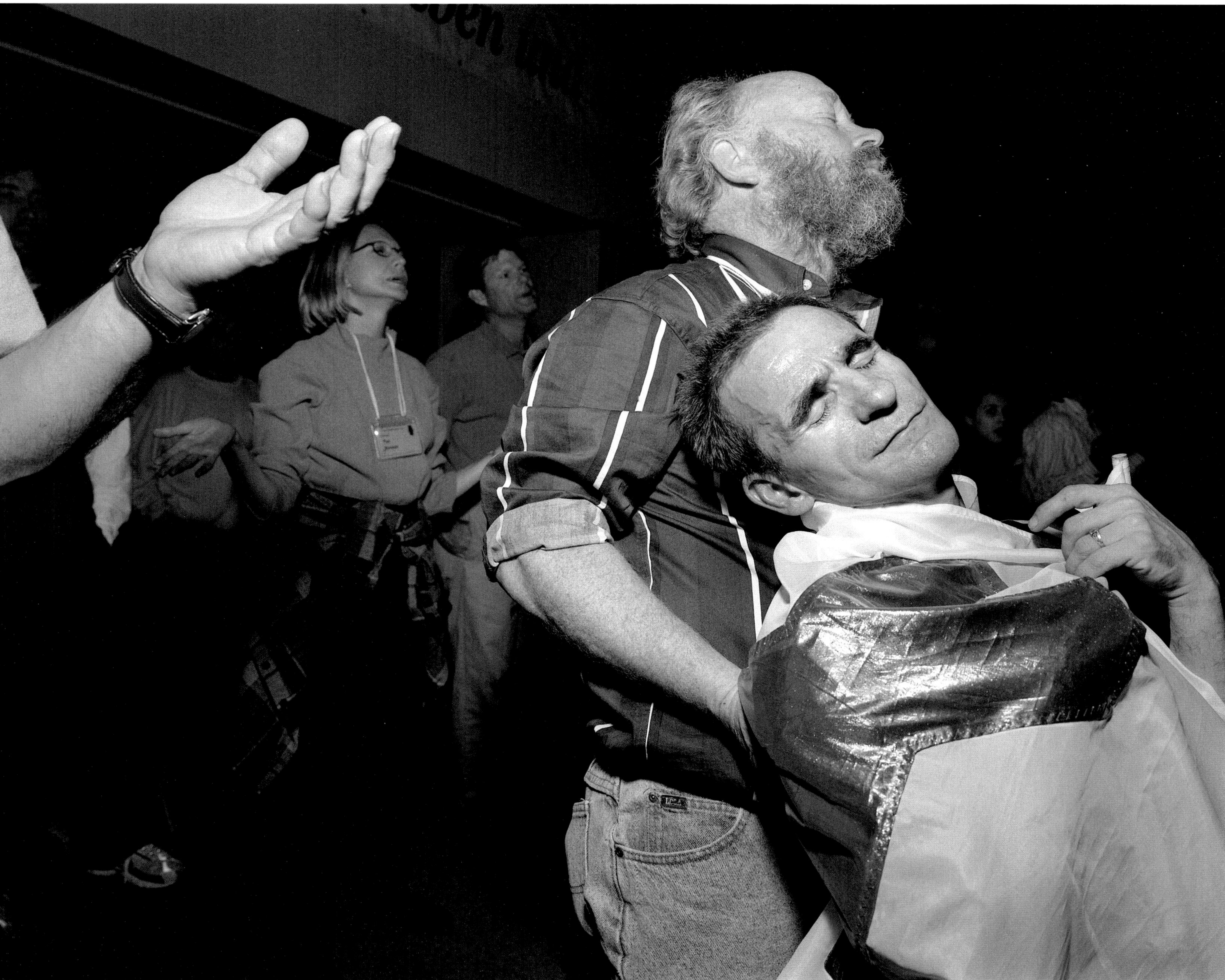

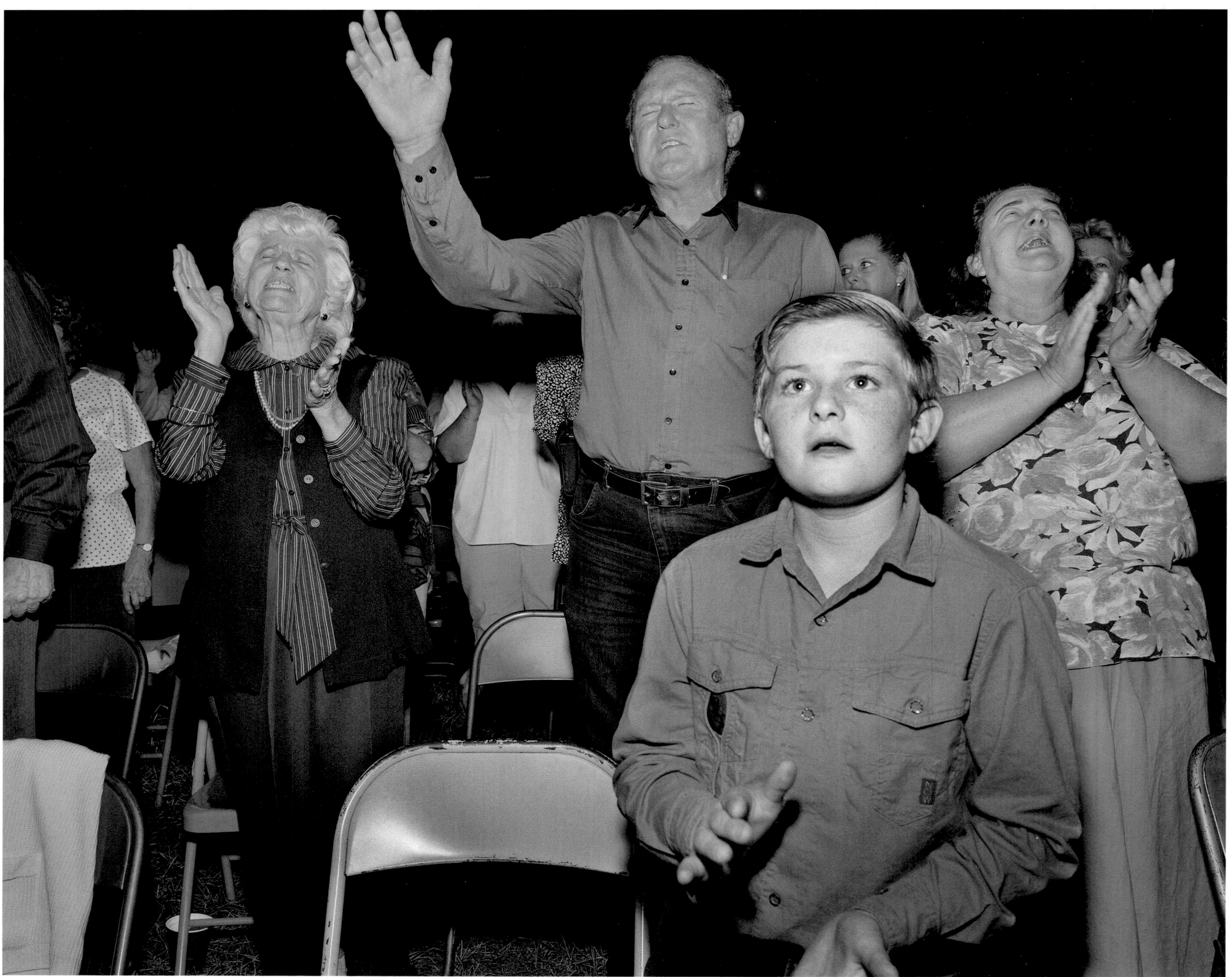

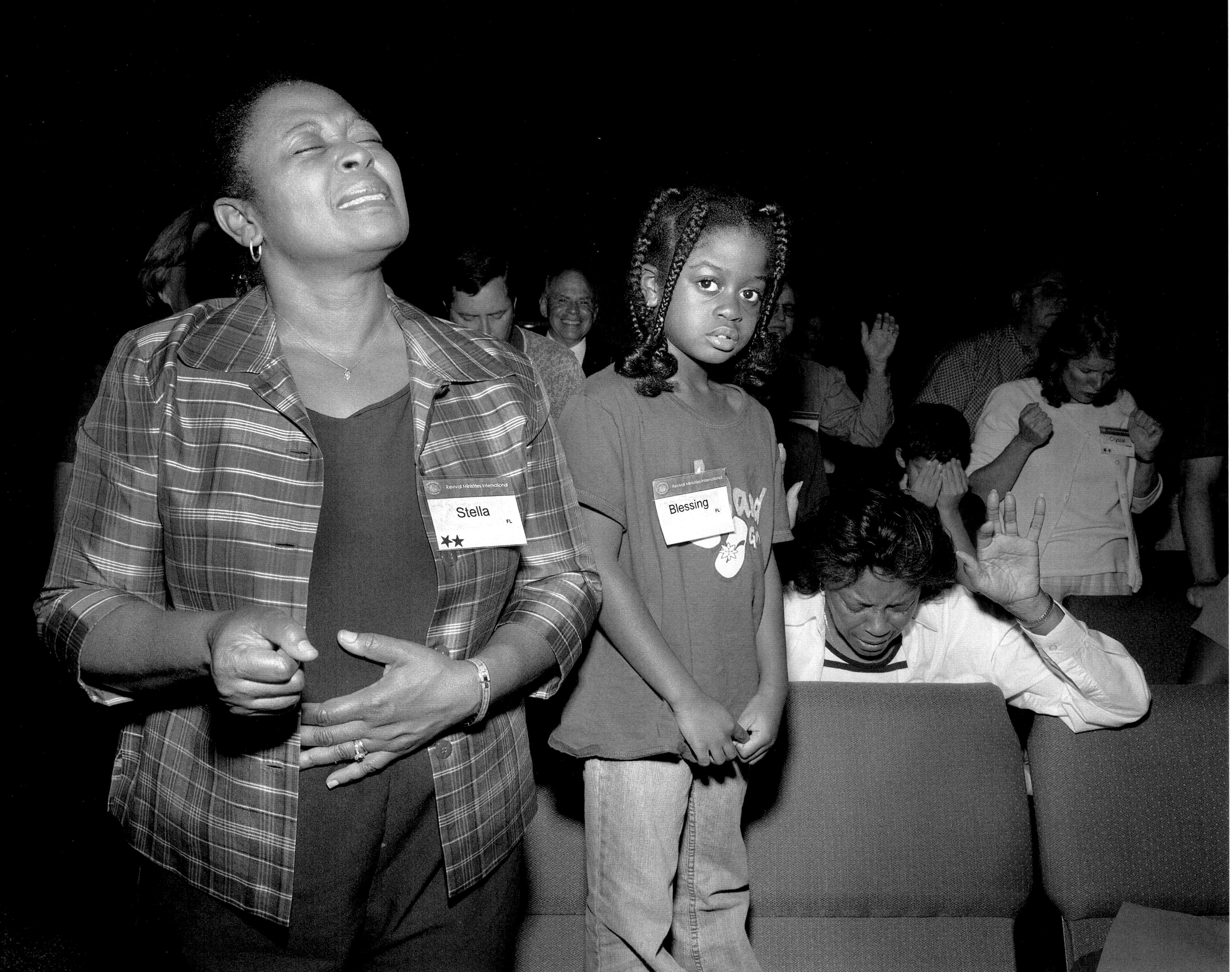
Revival Ministries International
Stella
FL
Revival Ministries International
Blessing
FL

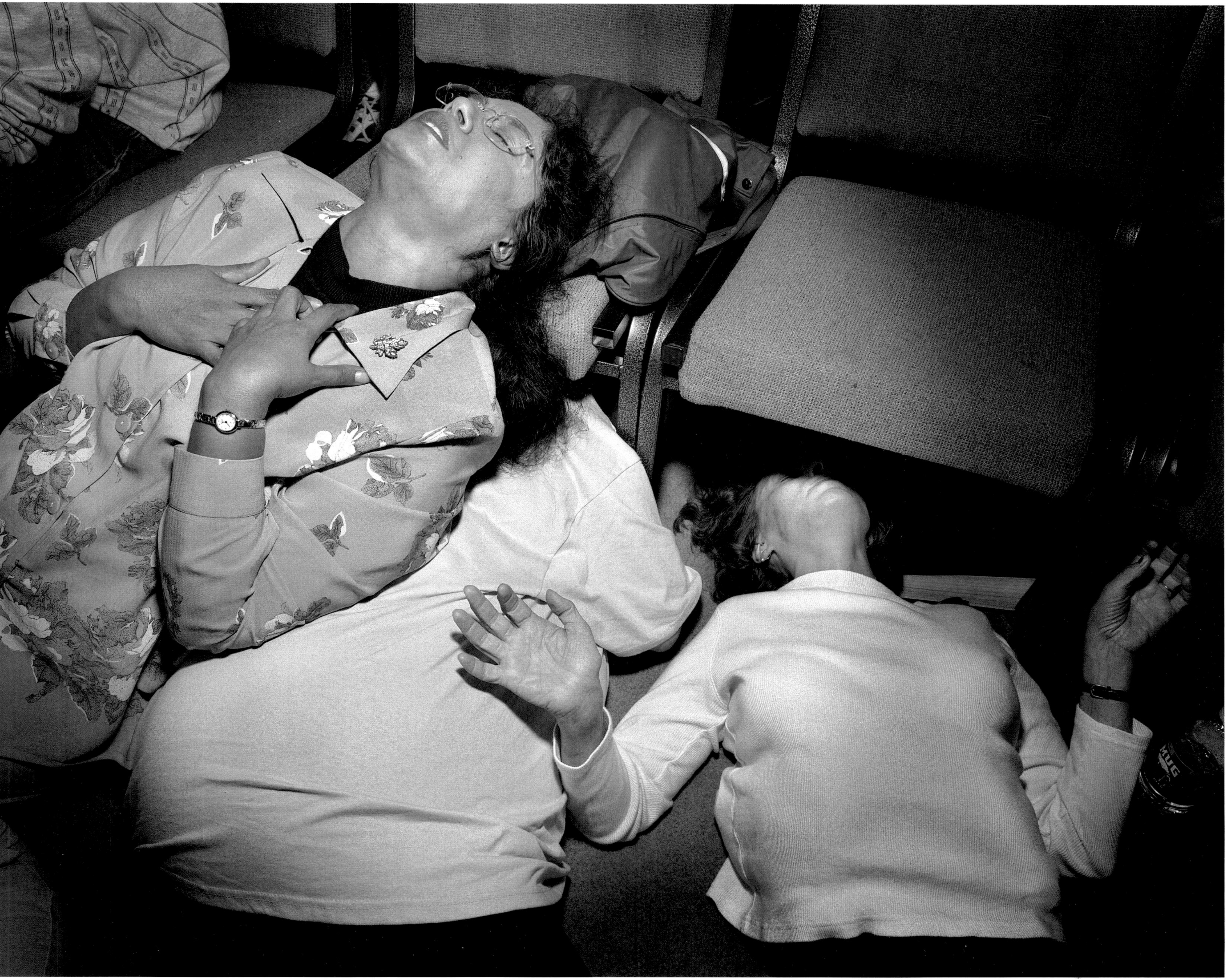

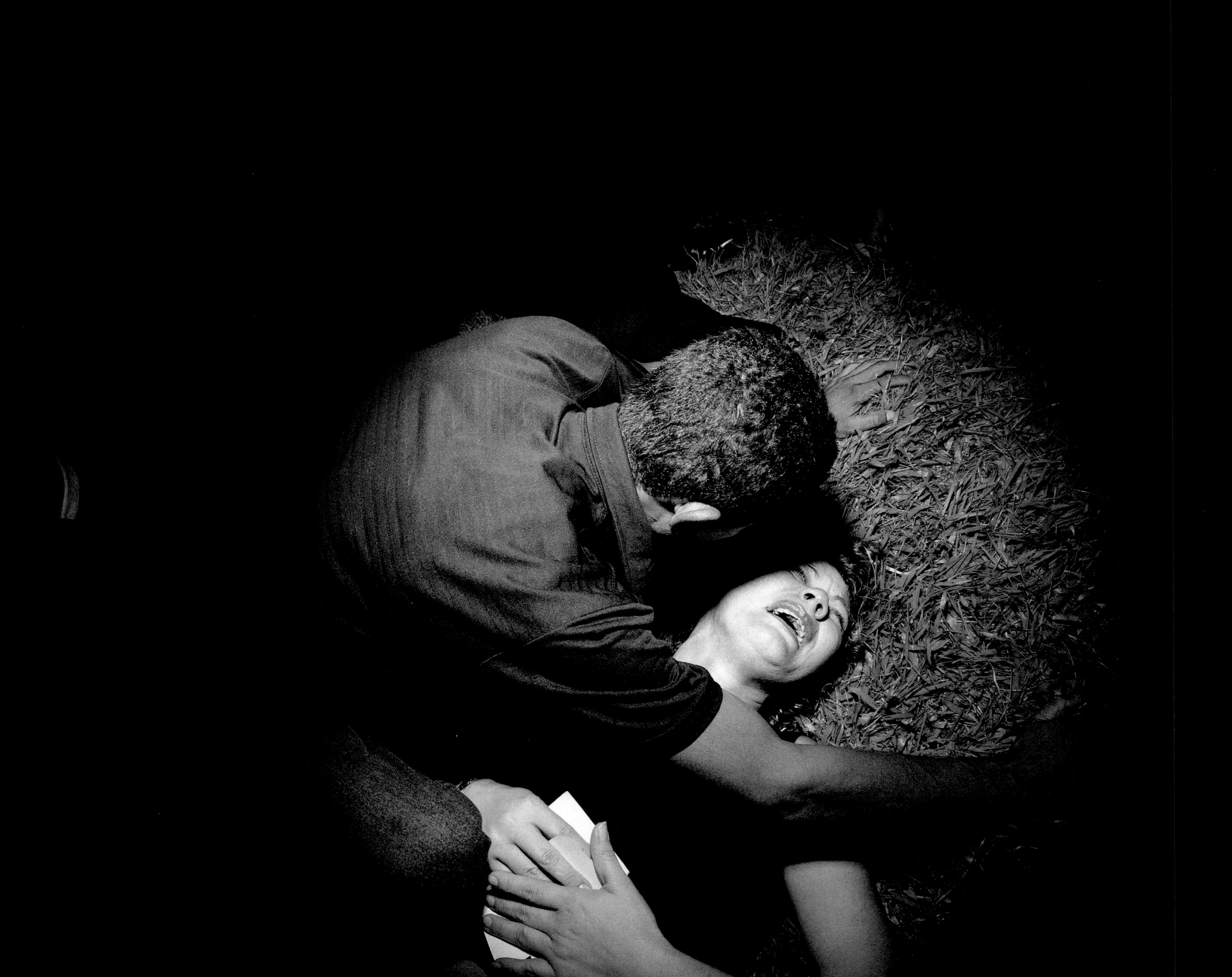

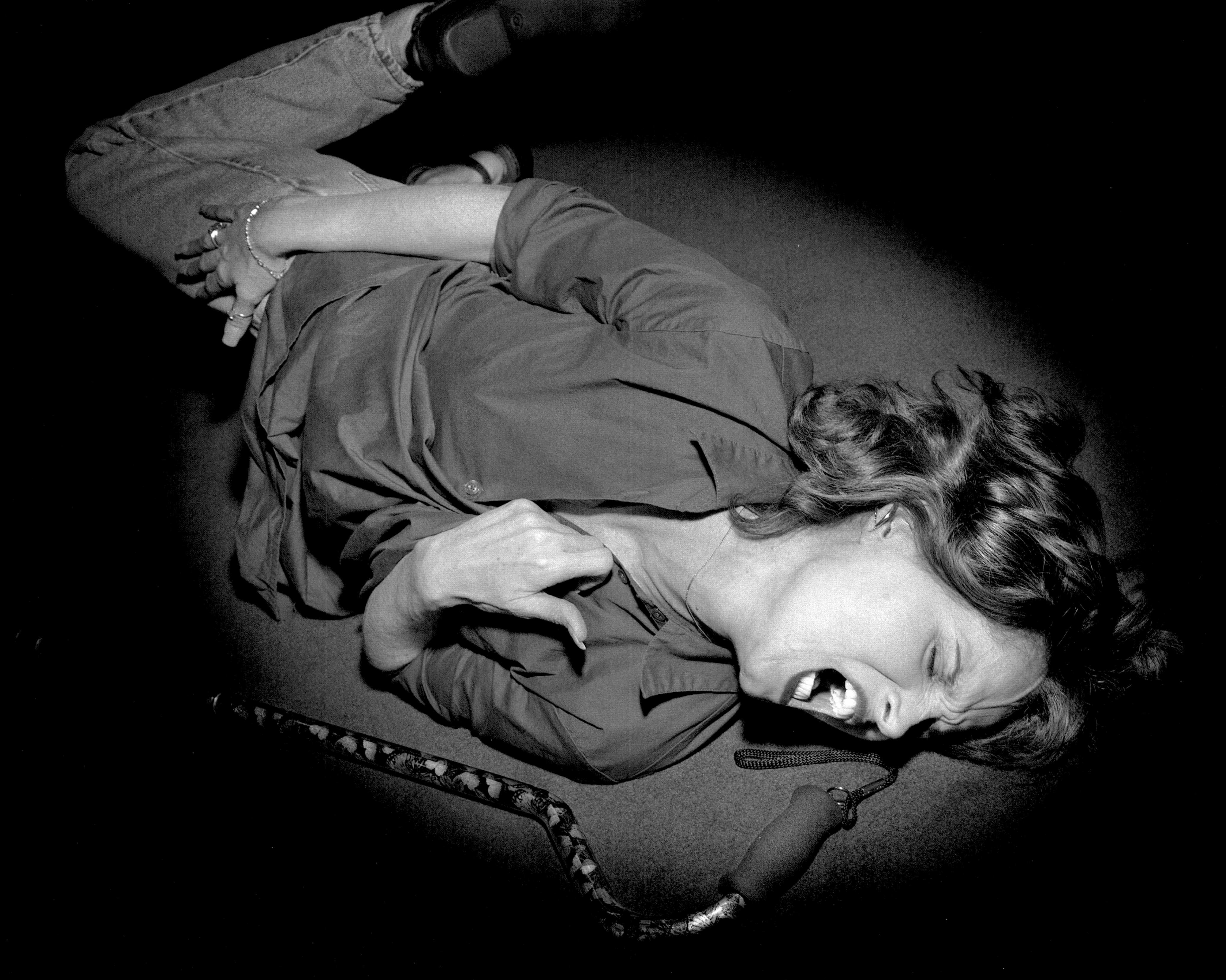

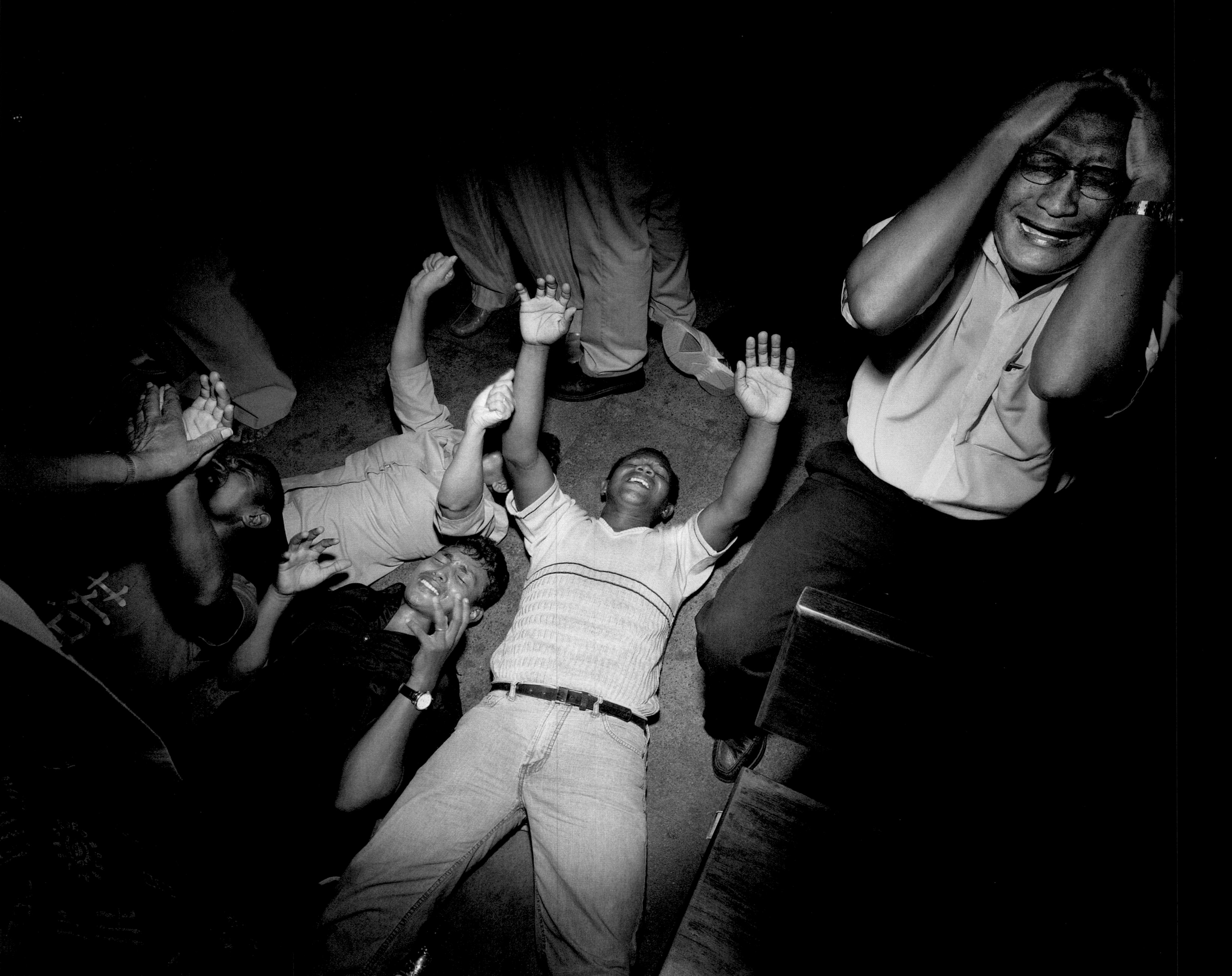

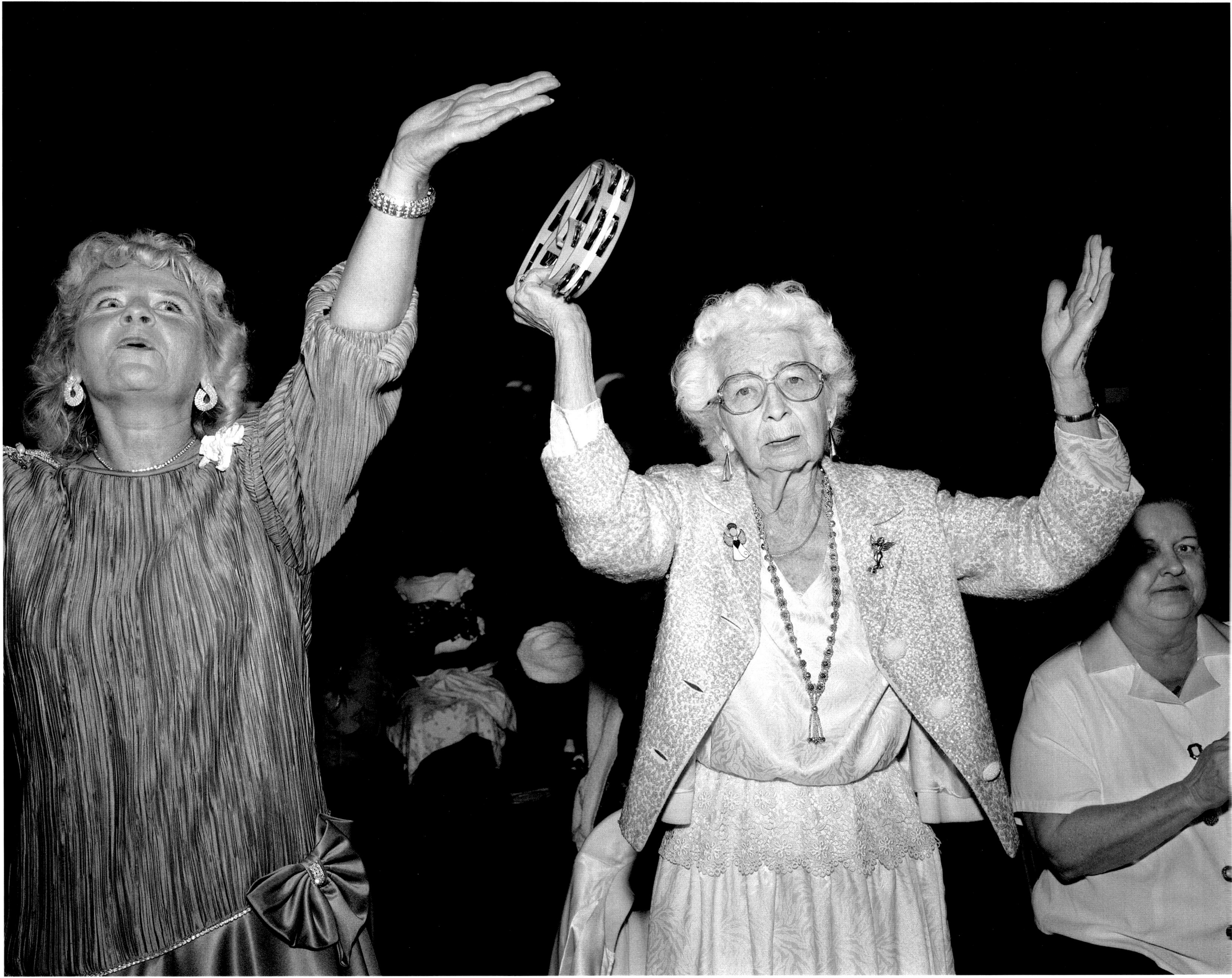

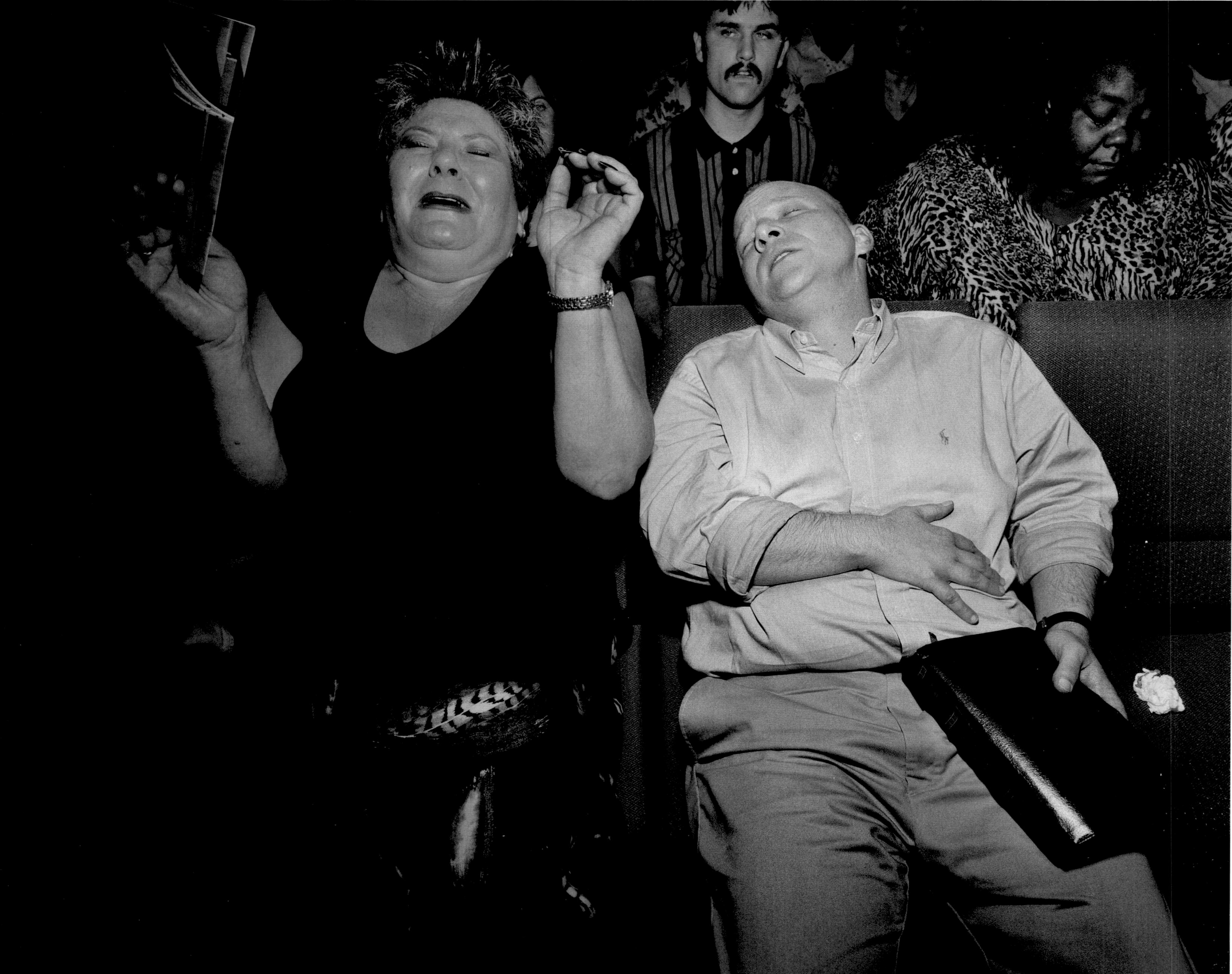

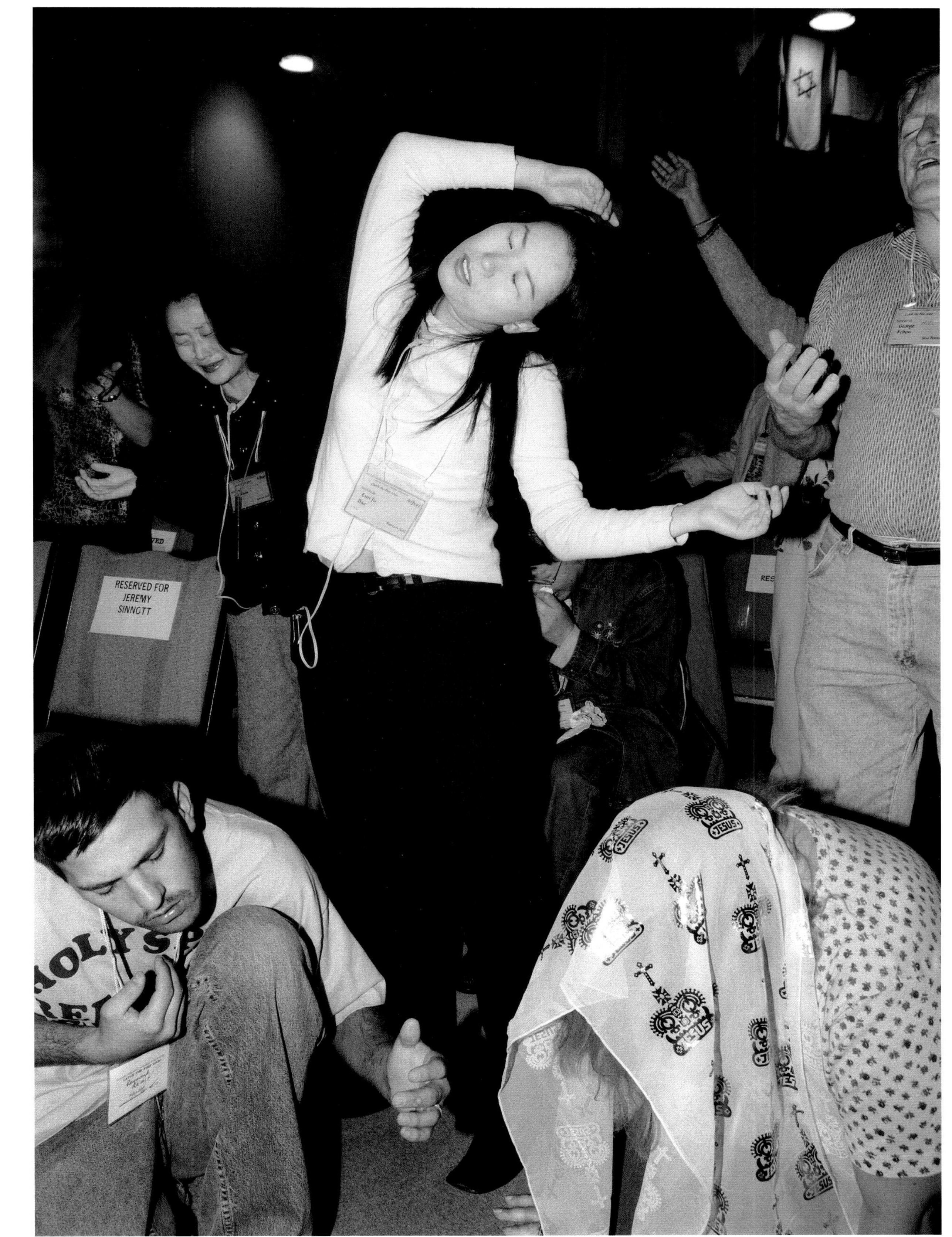
RESERVED FOR
JEREMY
SINNOTT
JESUS

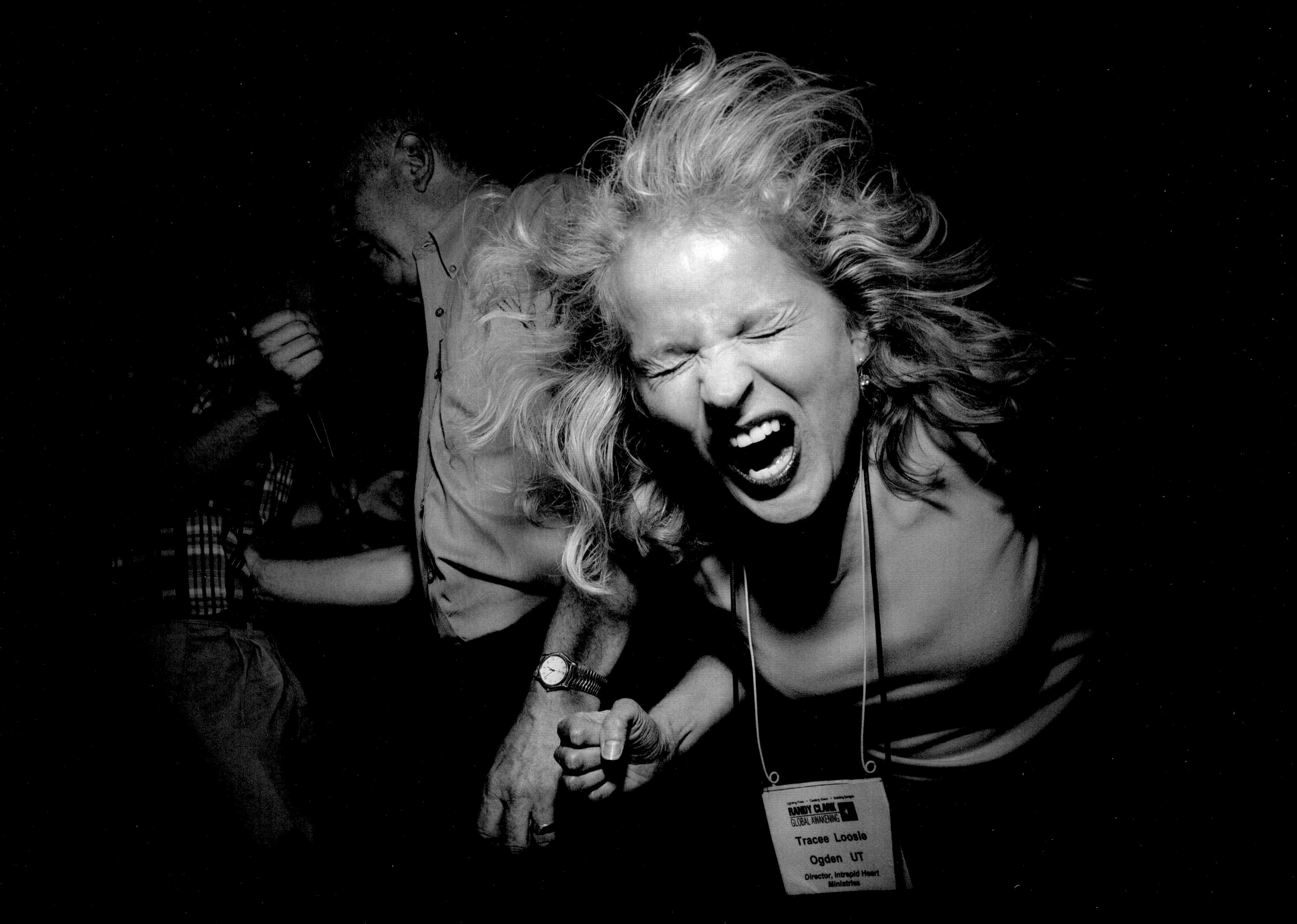
RANDY CLARK
GLOBAL AWAKENING
Tracee Loosle
Ogden UT
Director, Intrepid Heart
Ministries

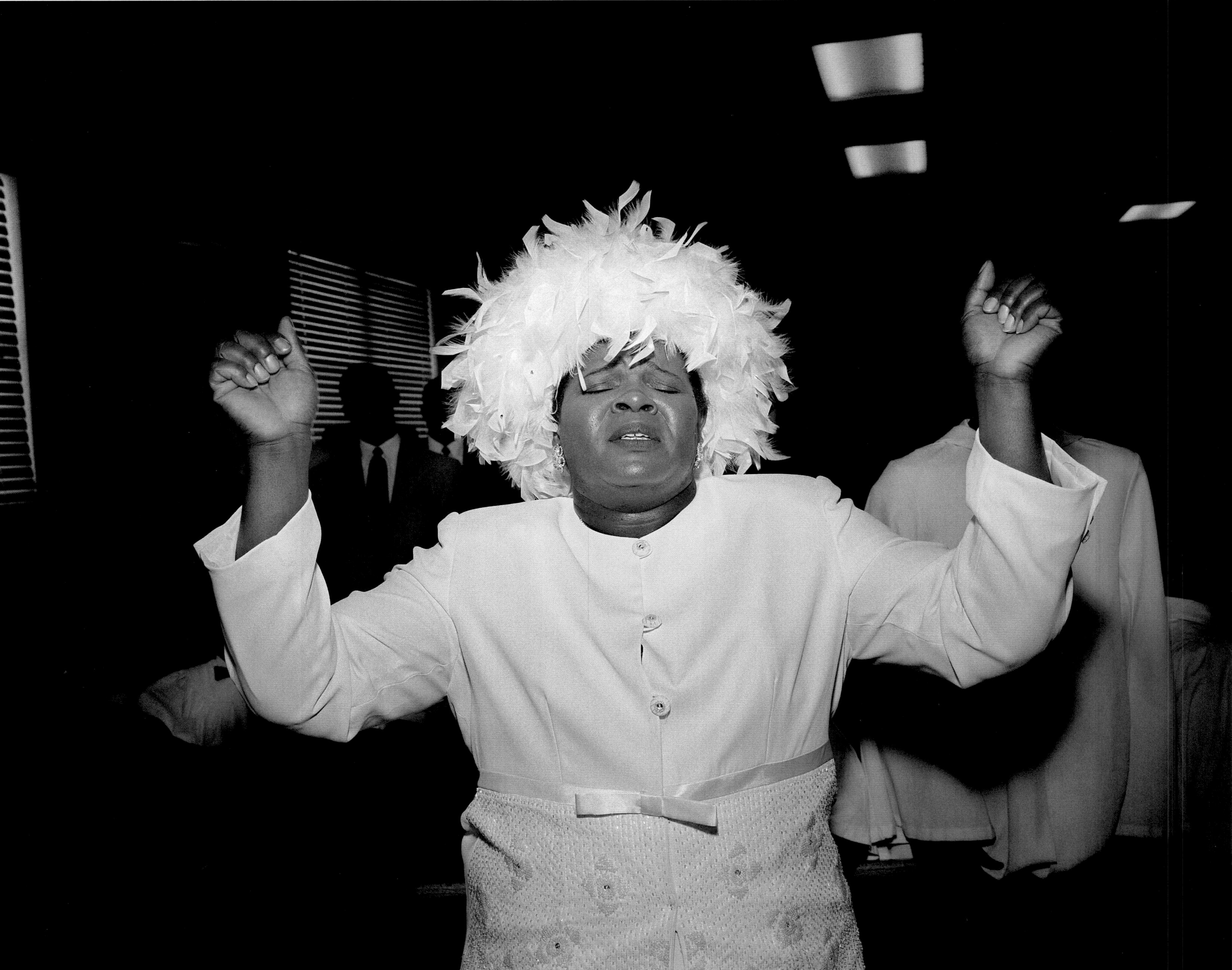

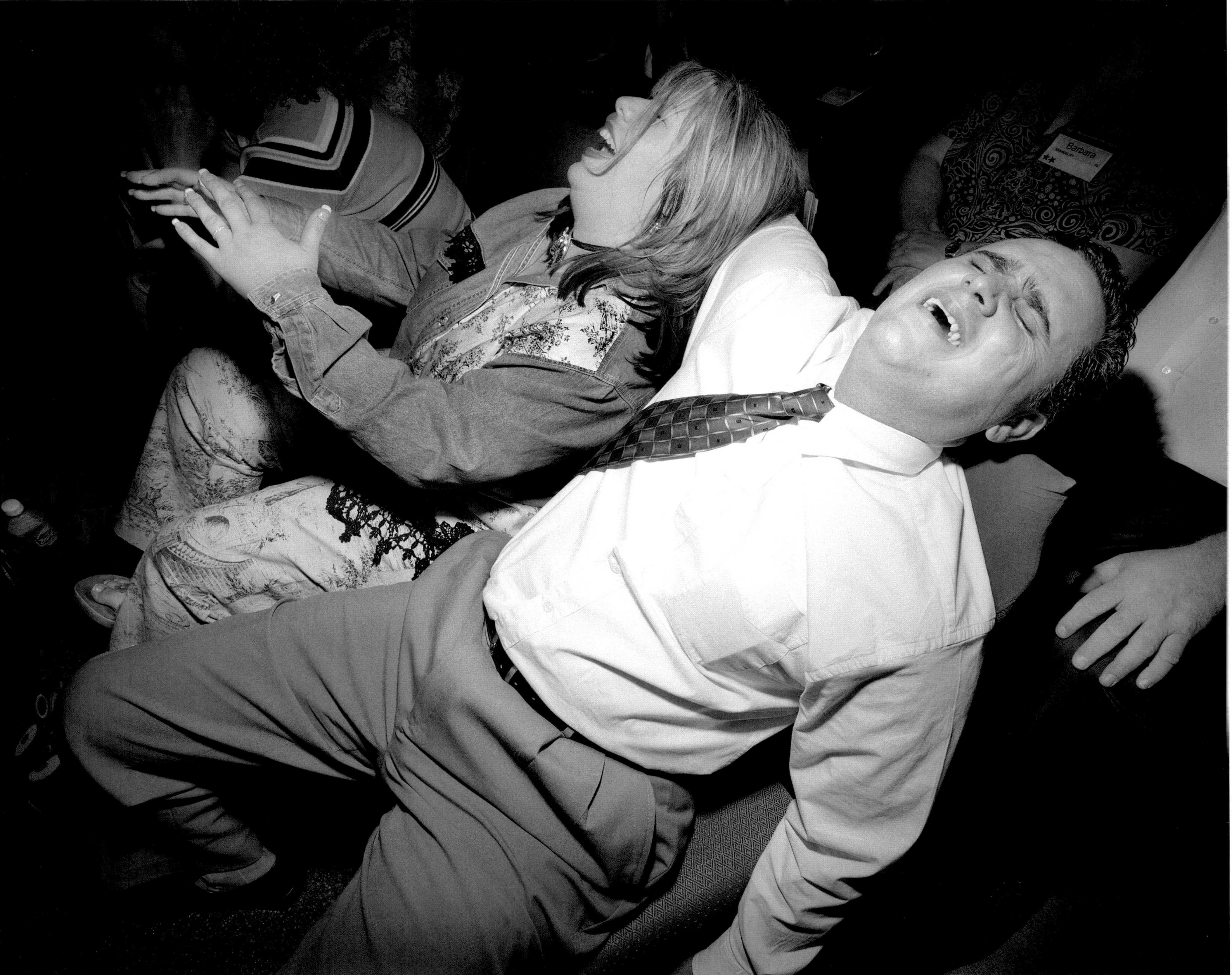
Barbara

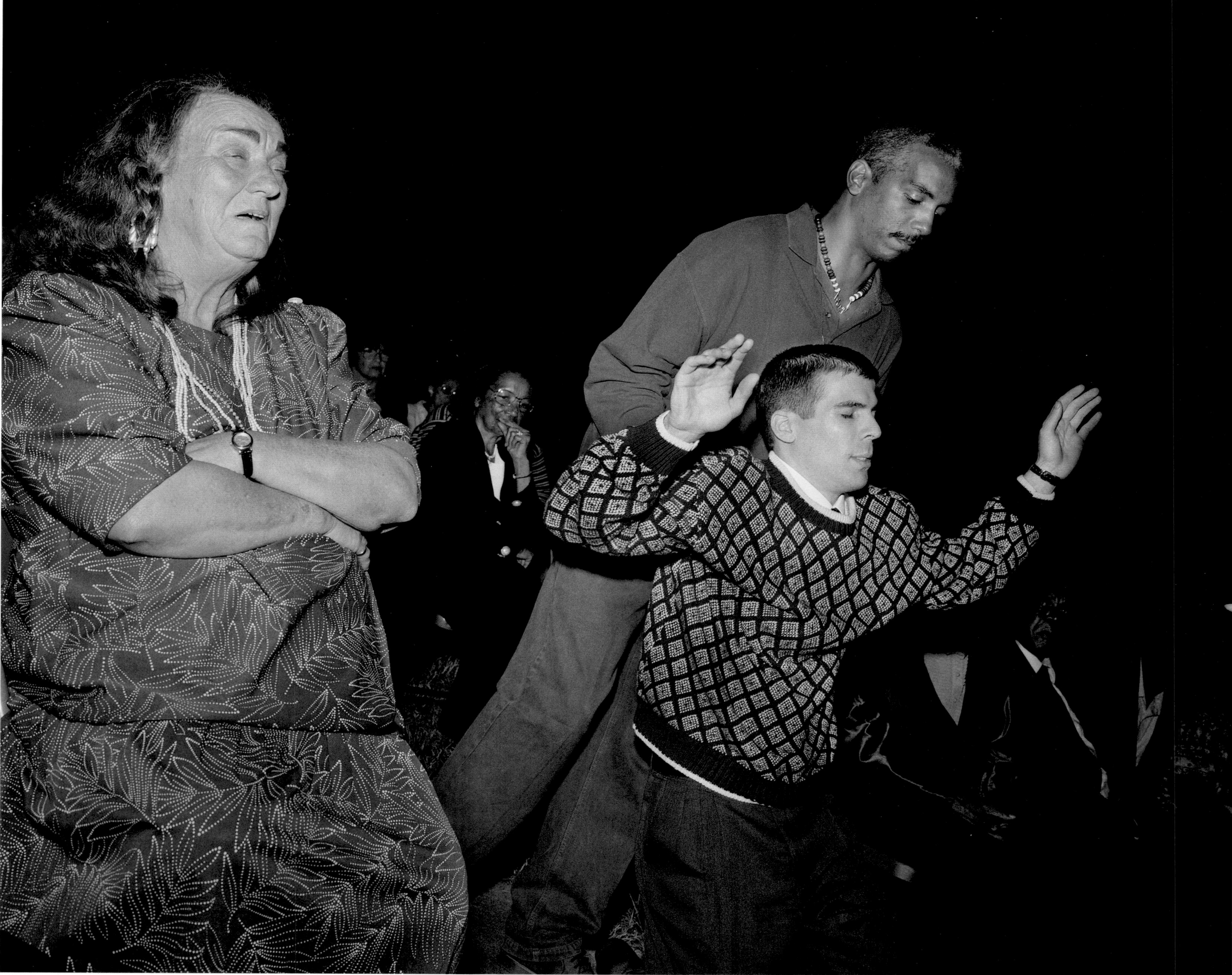

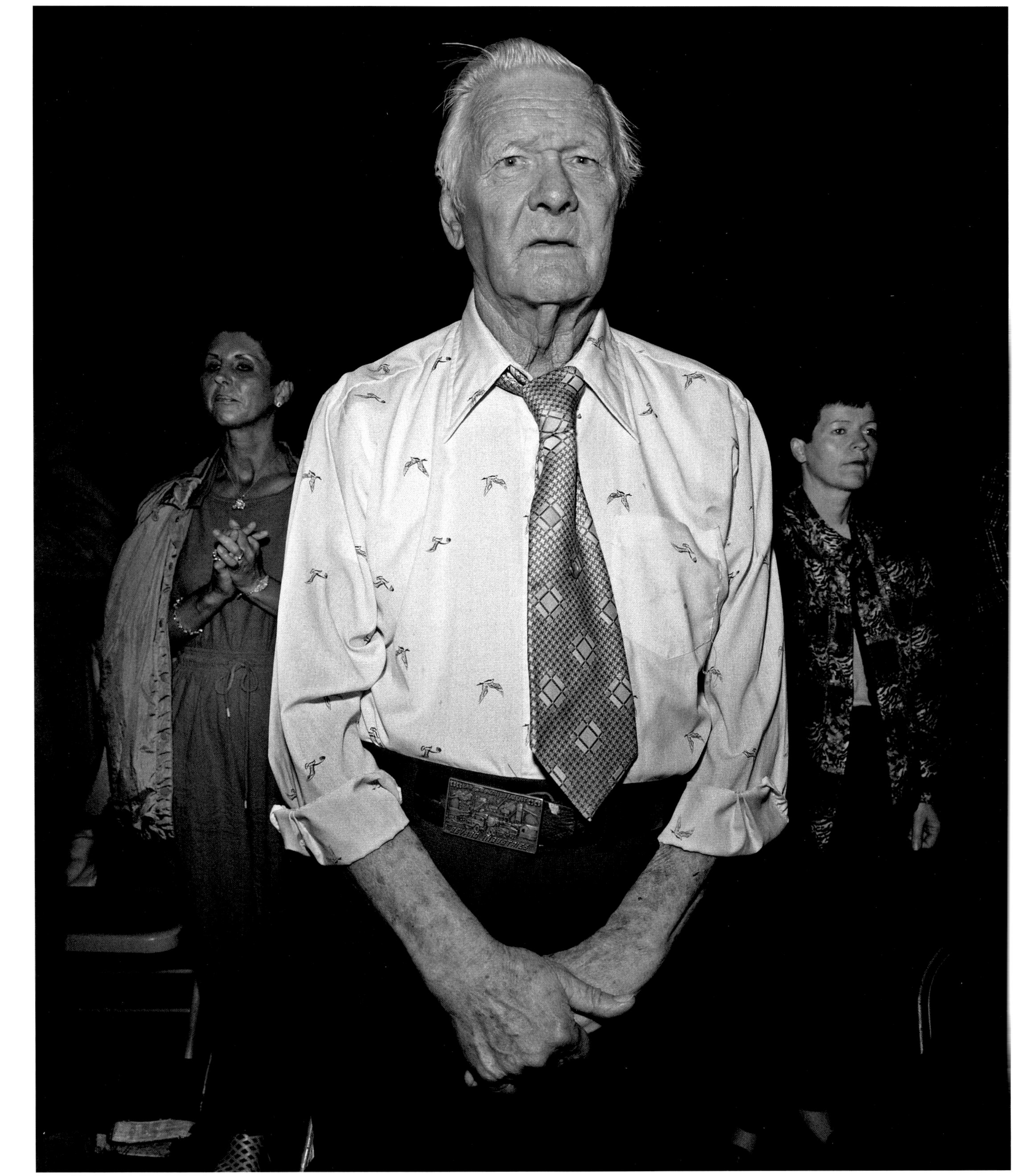

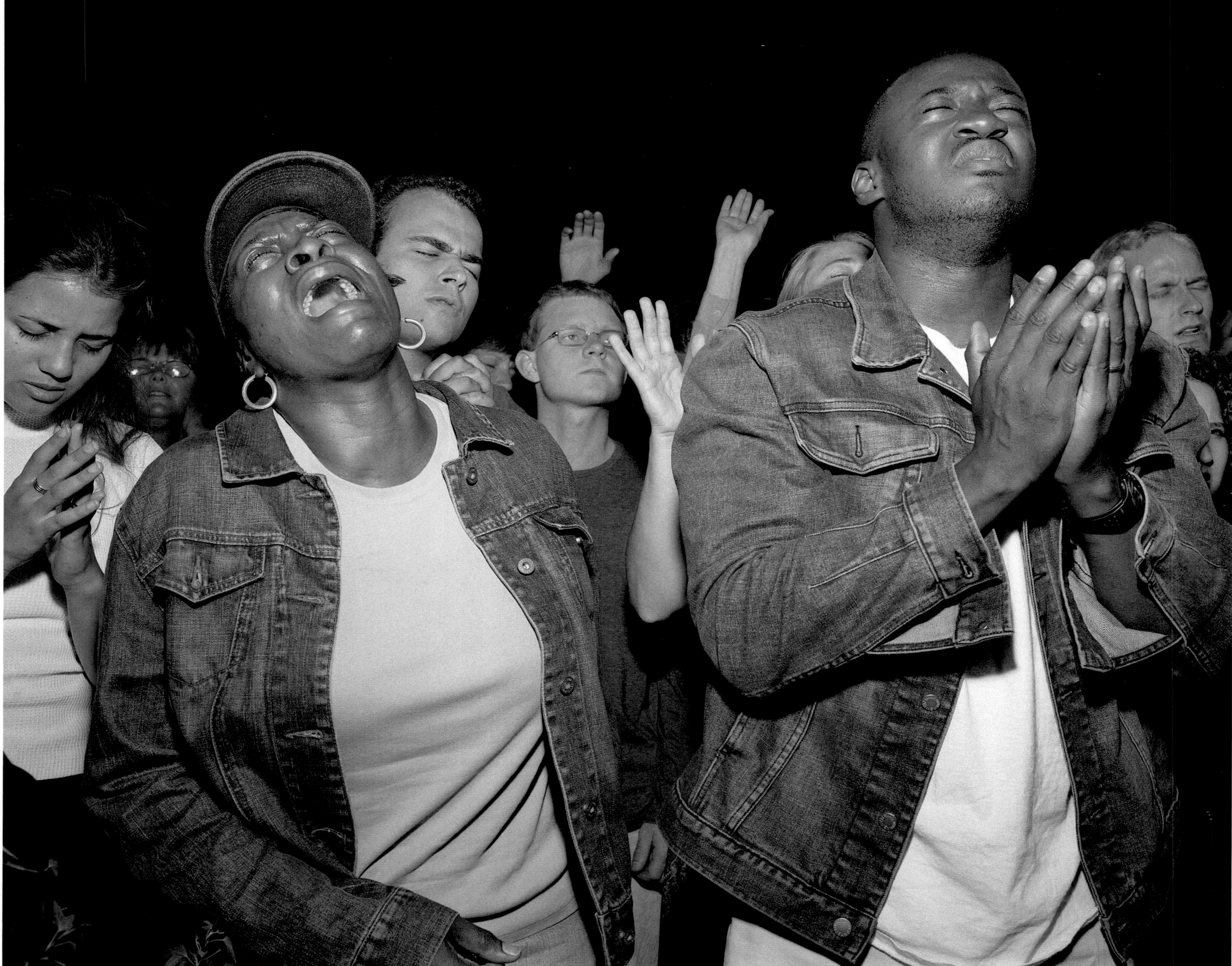

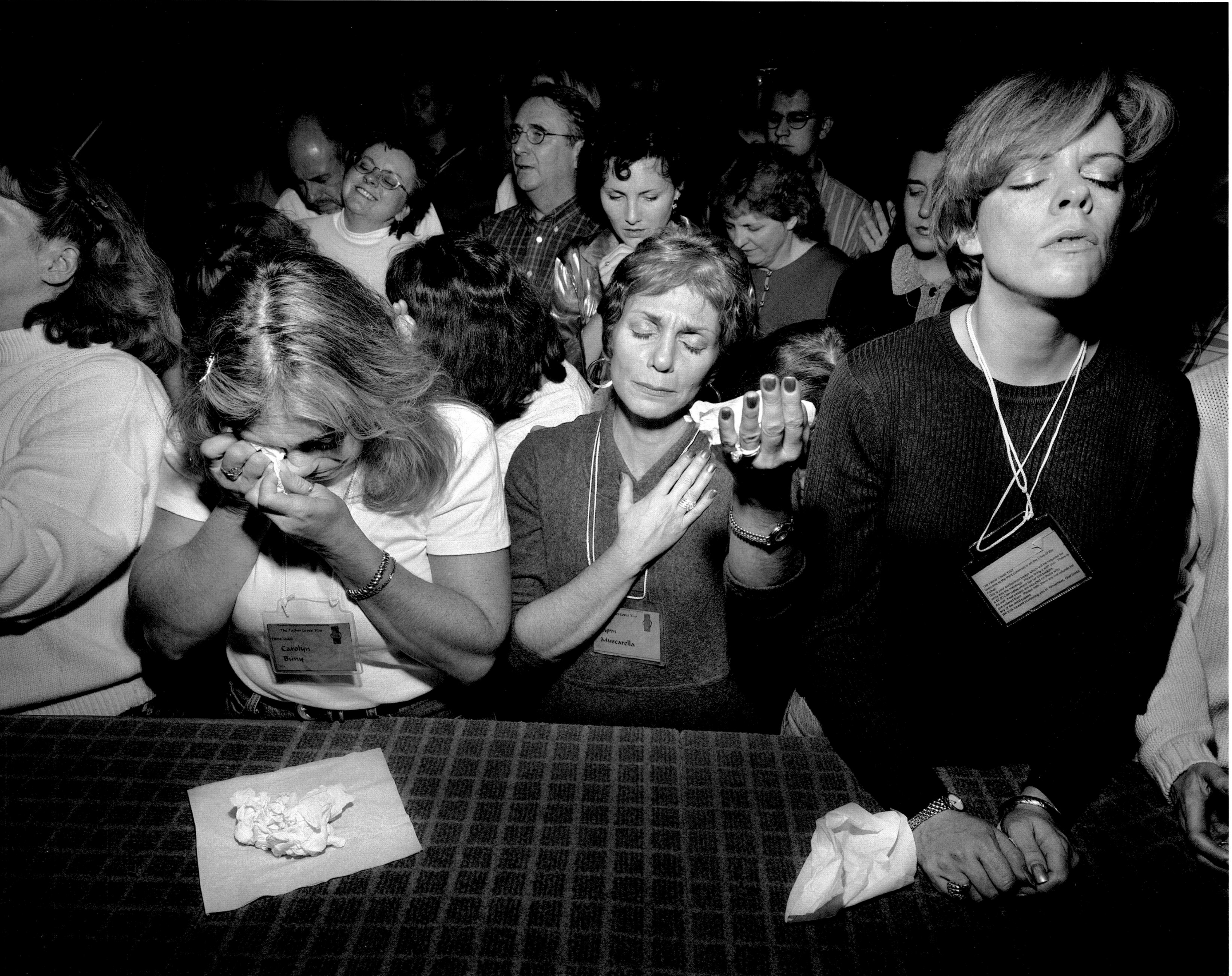
The Father Loves You
Carolyn
Buny
Muscarella

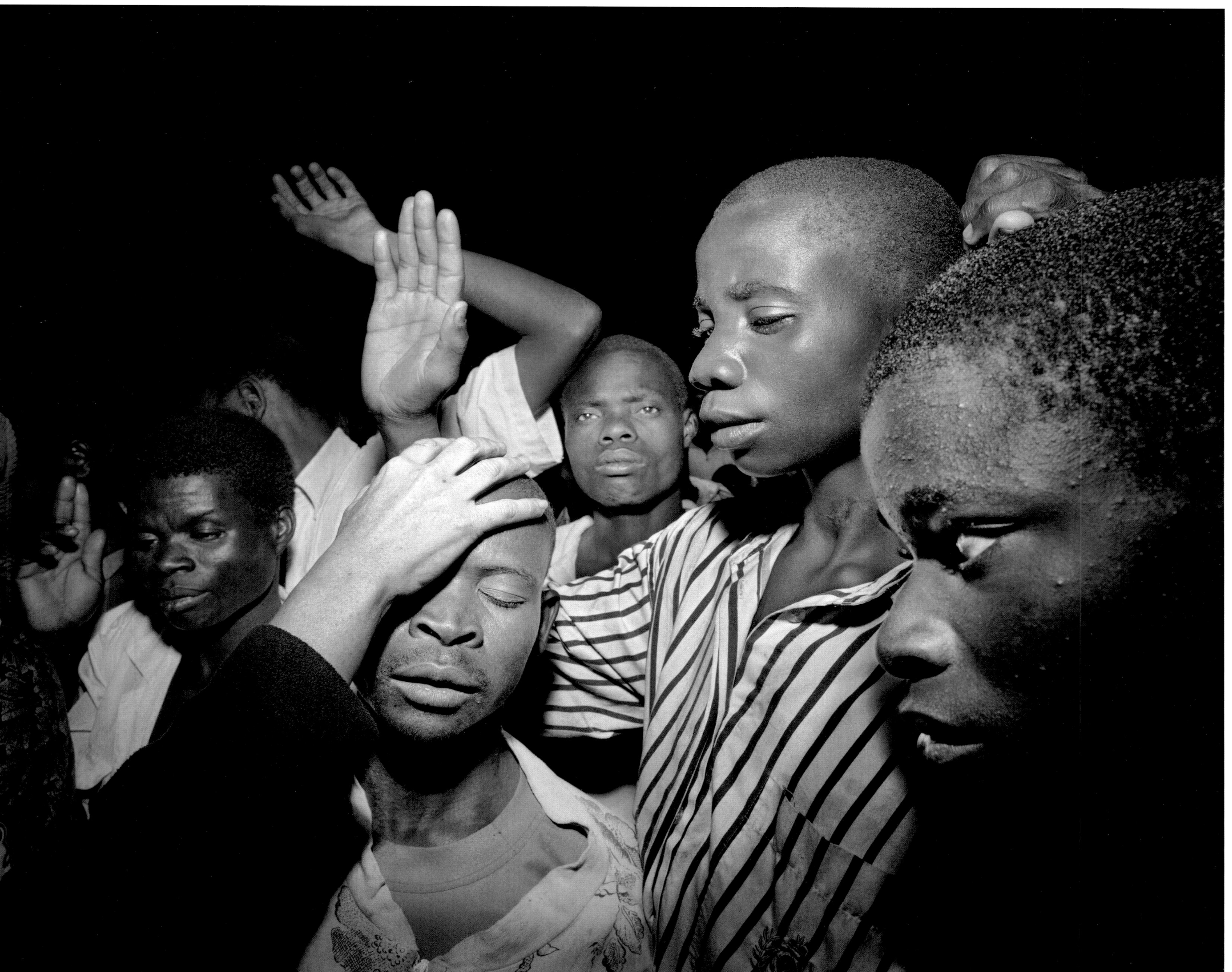

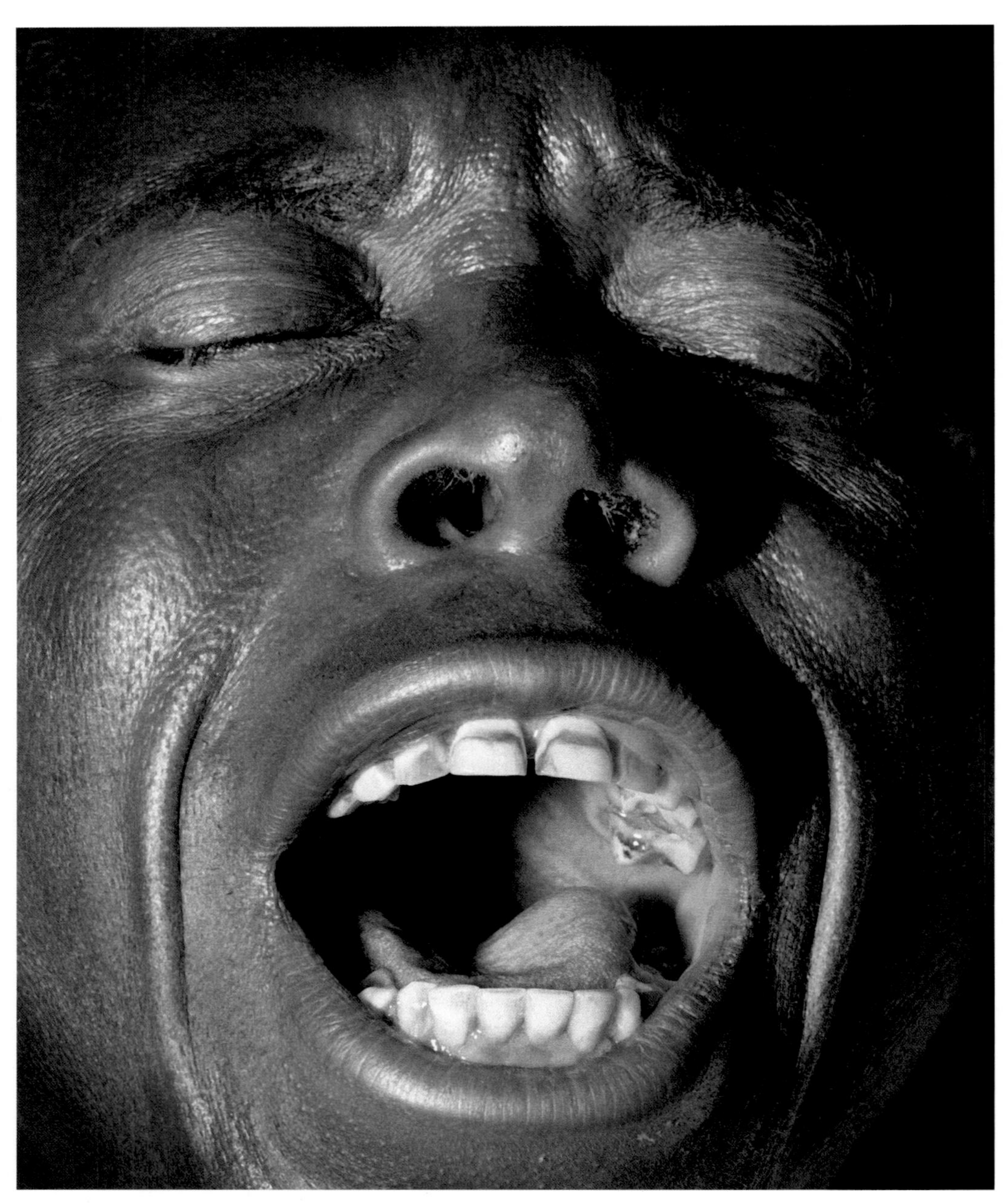

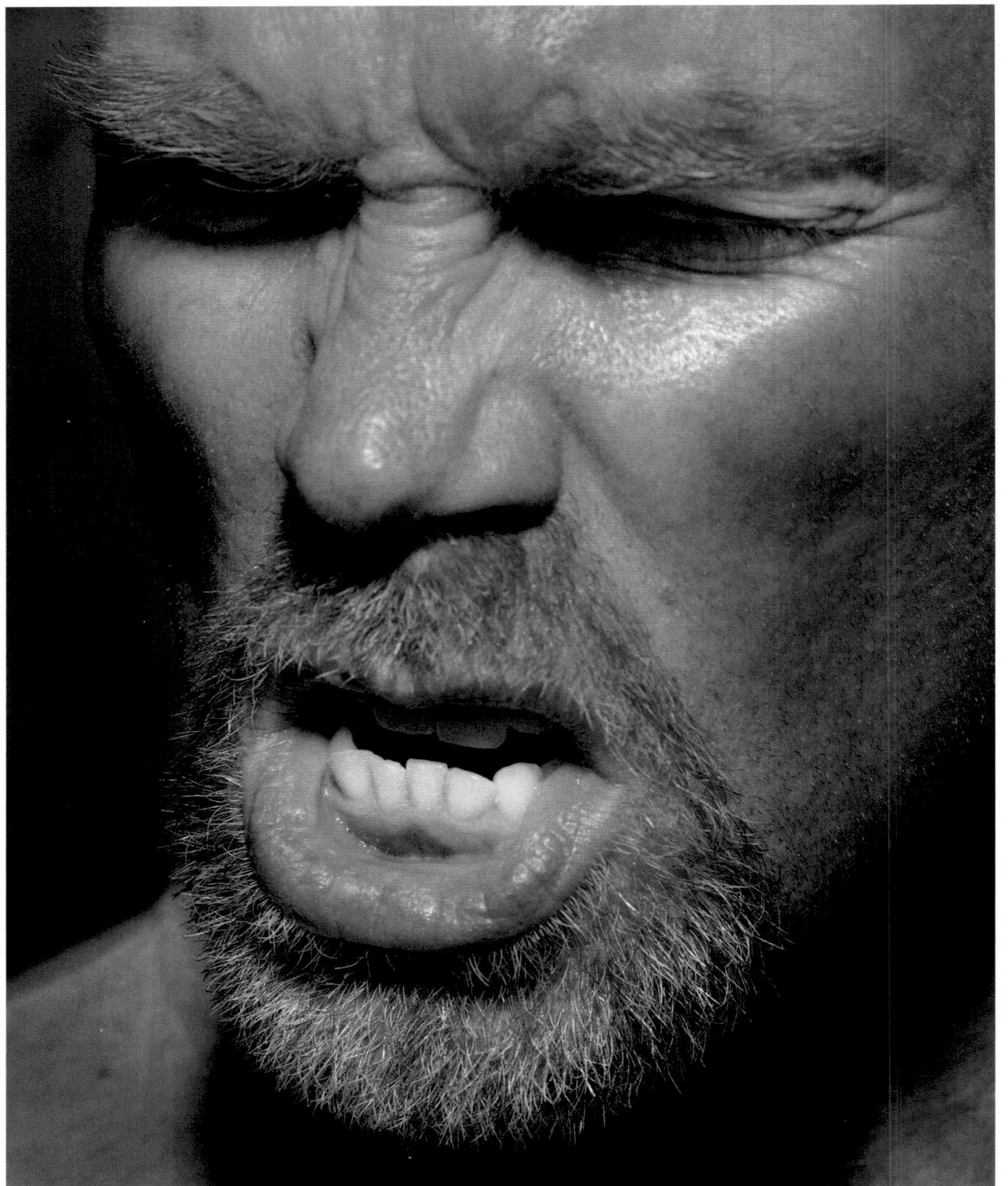

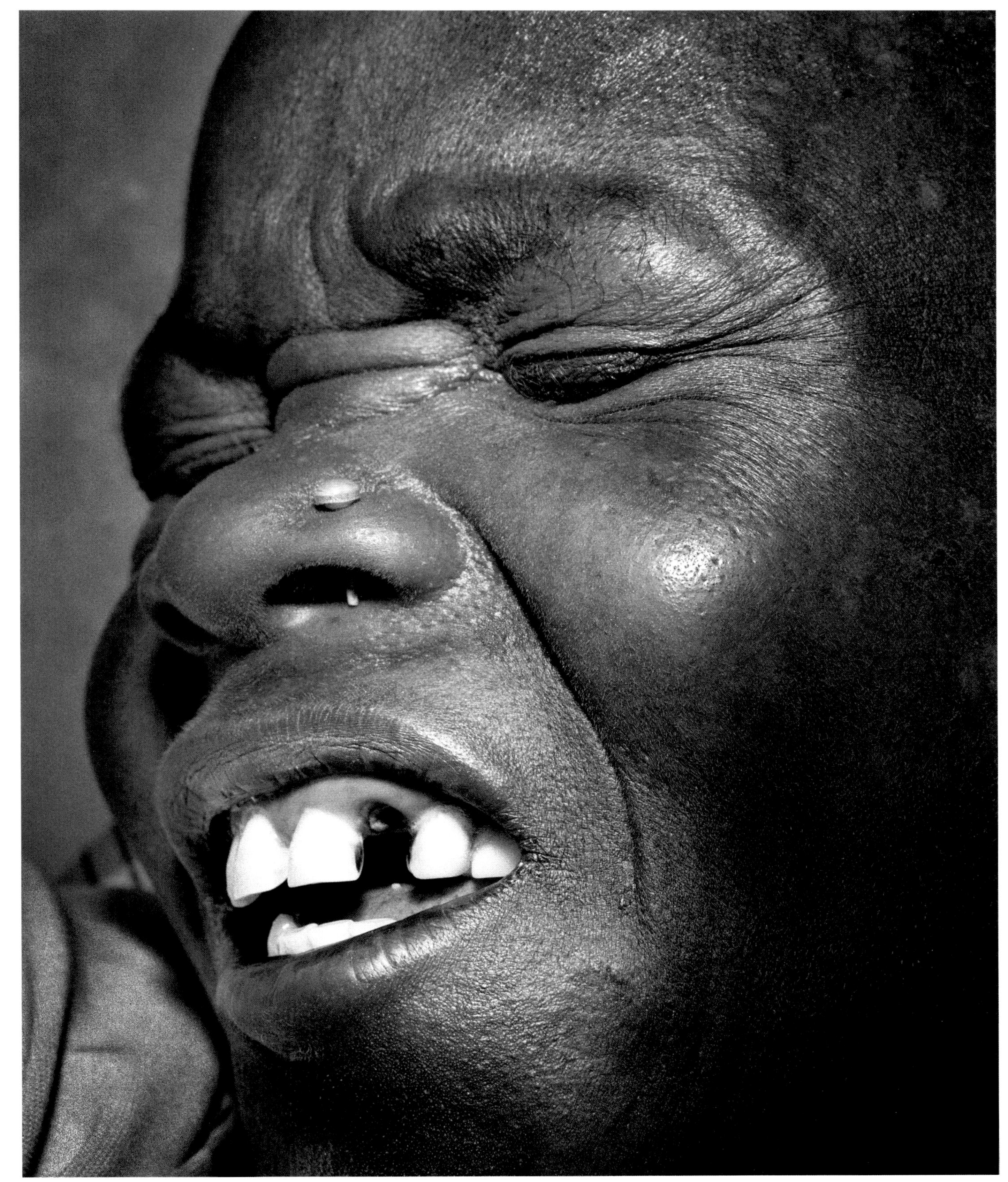

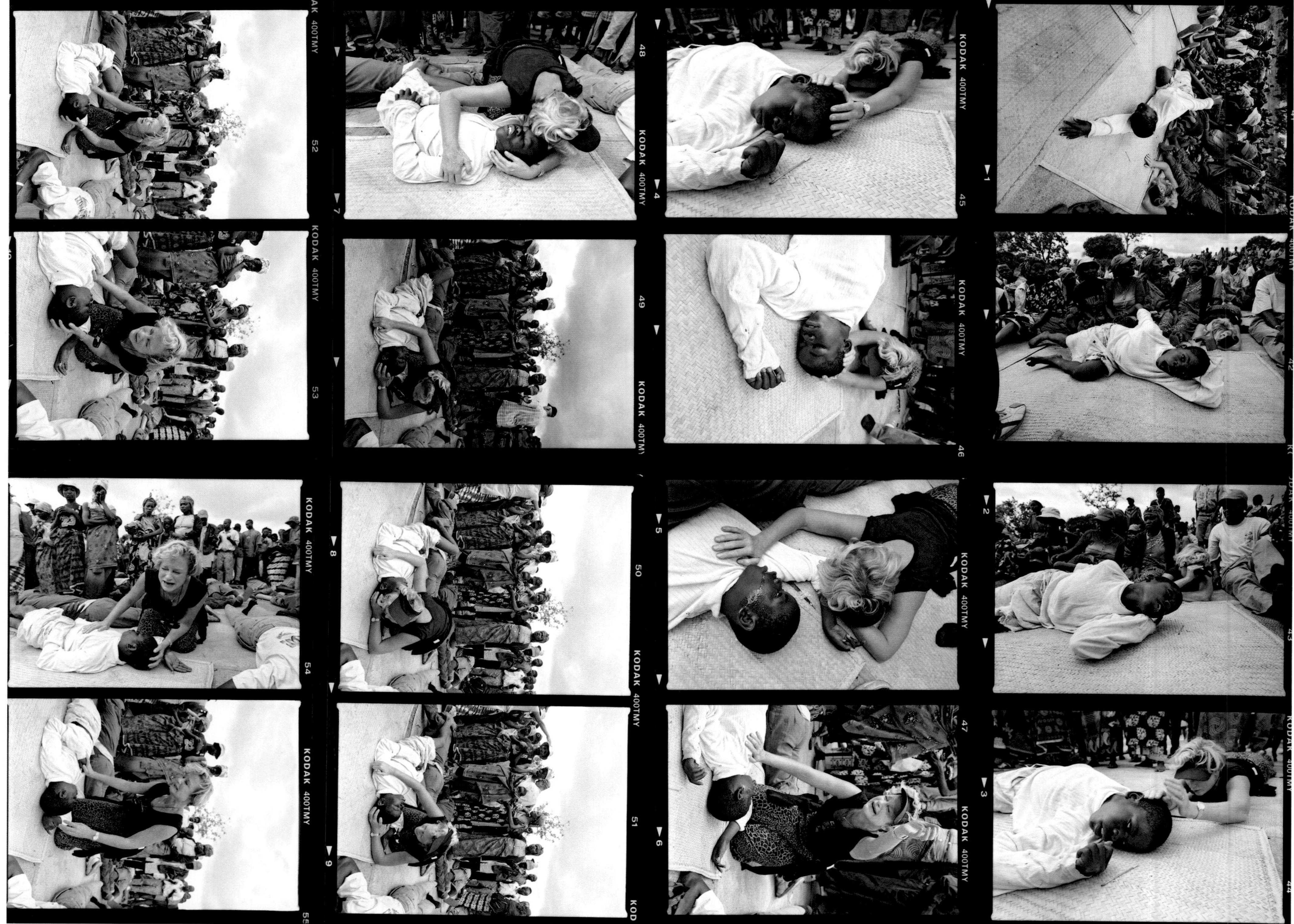

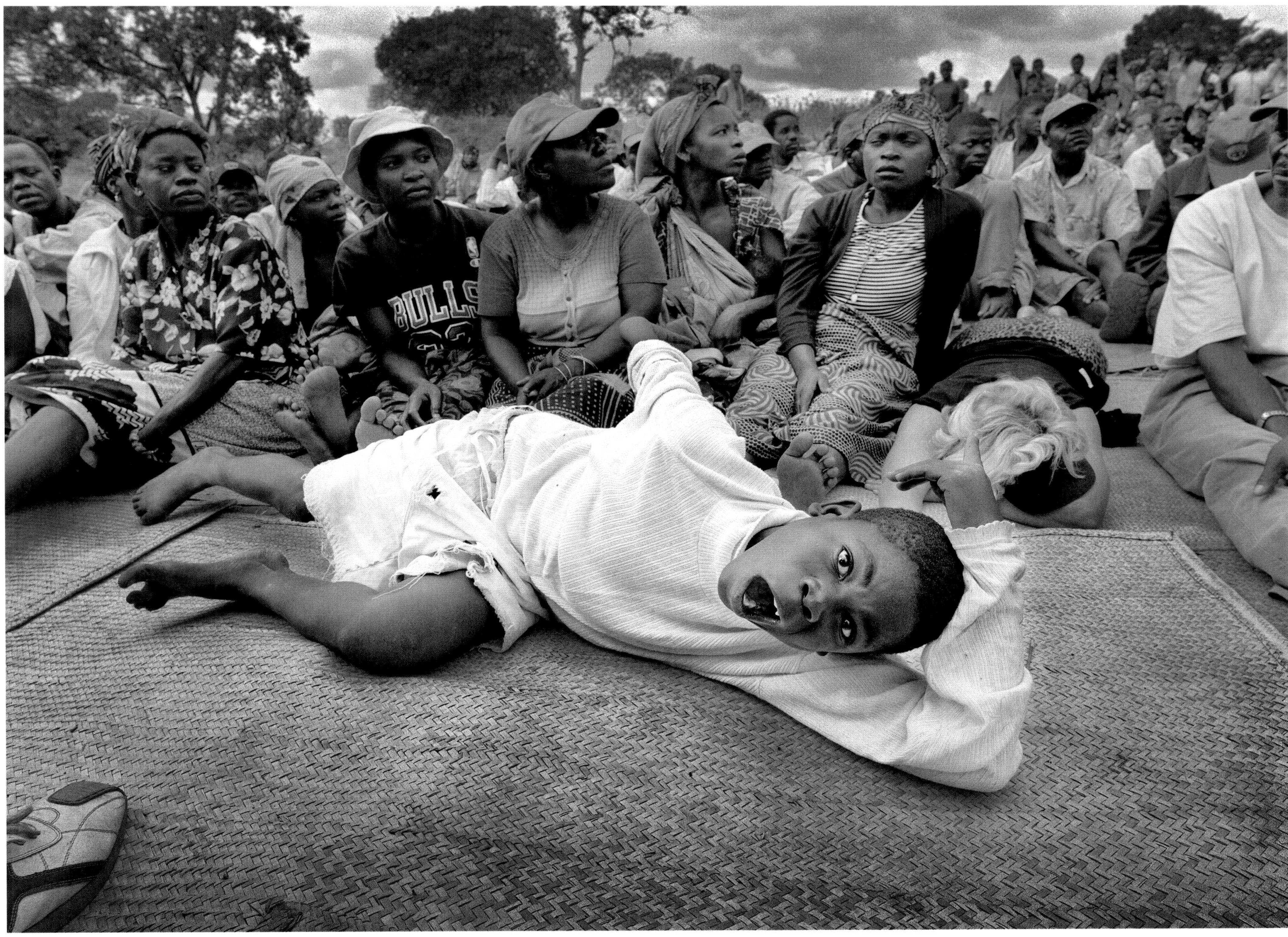
BULLS

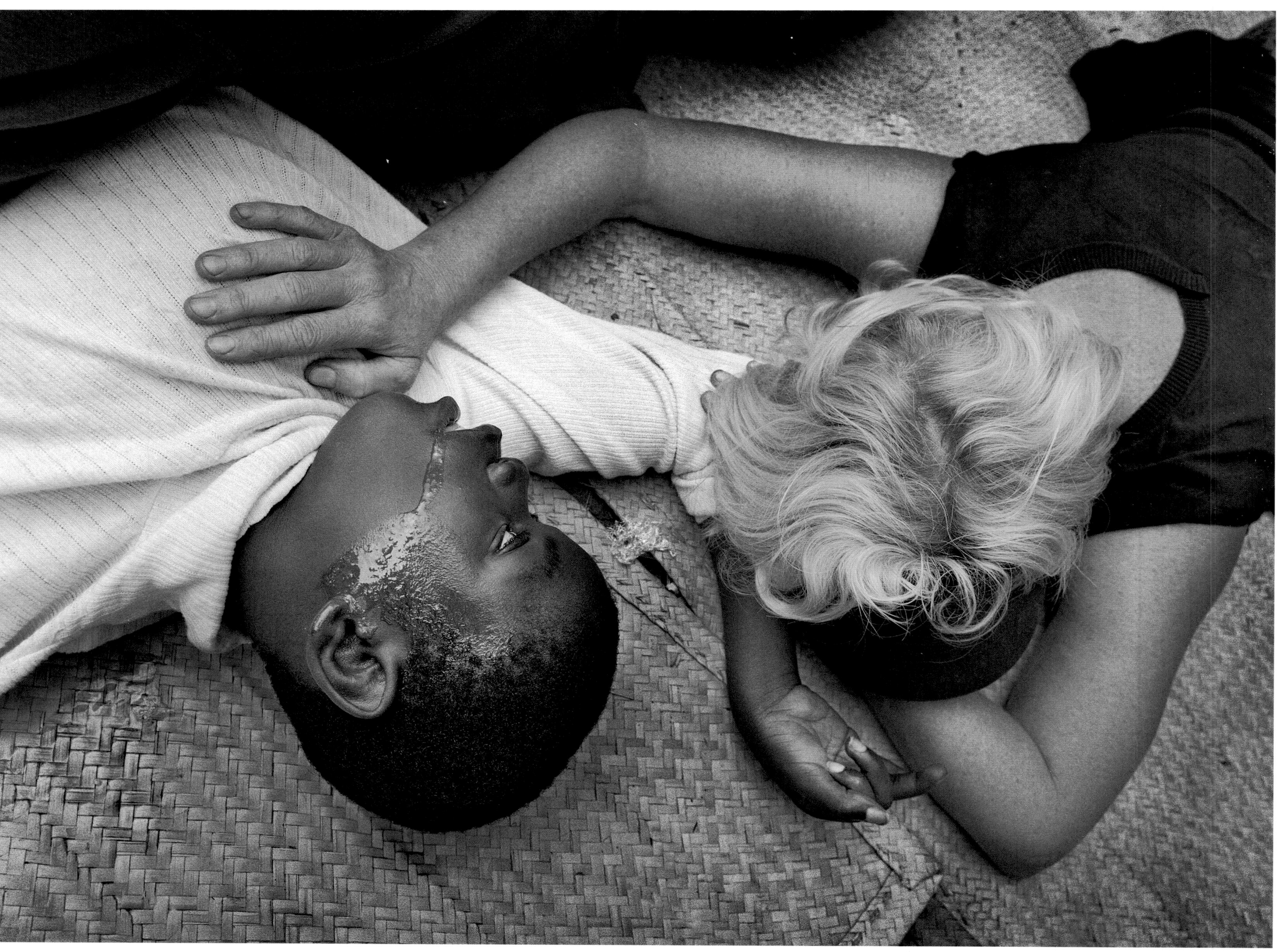

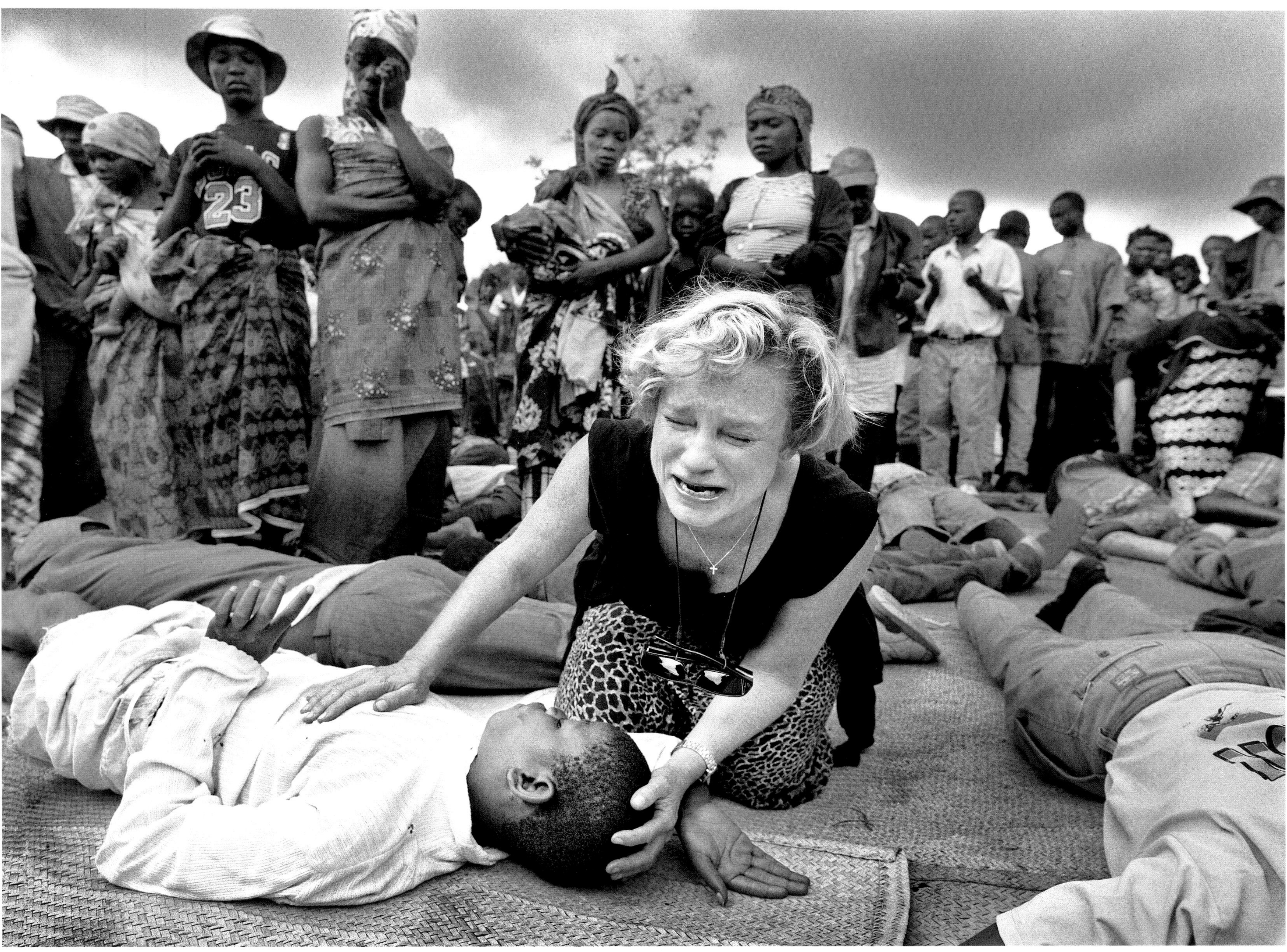
23

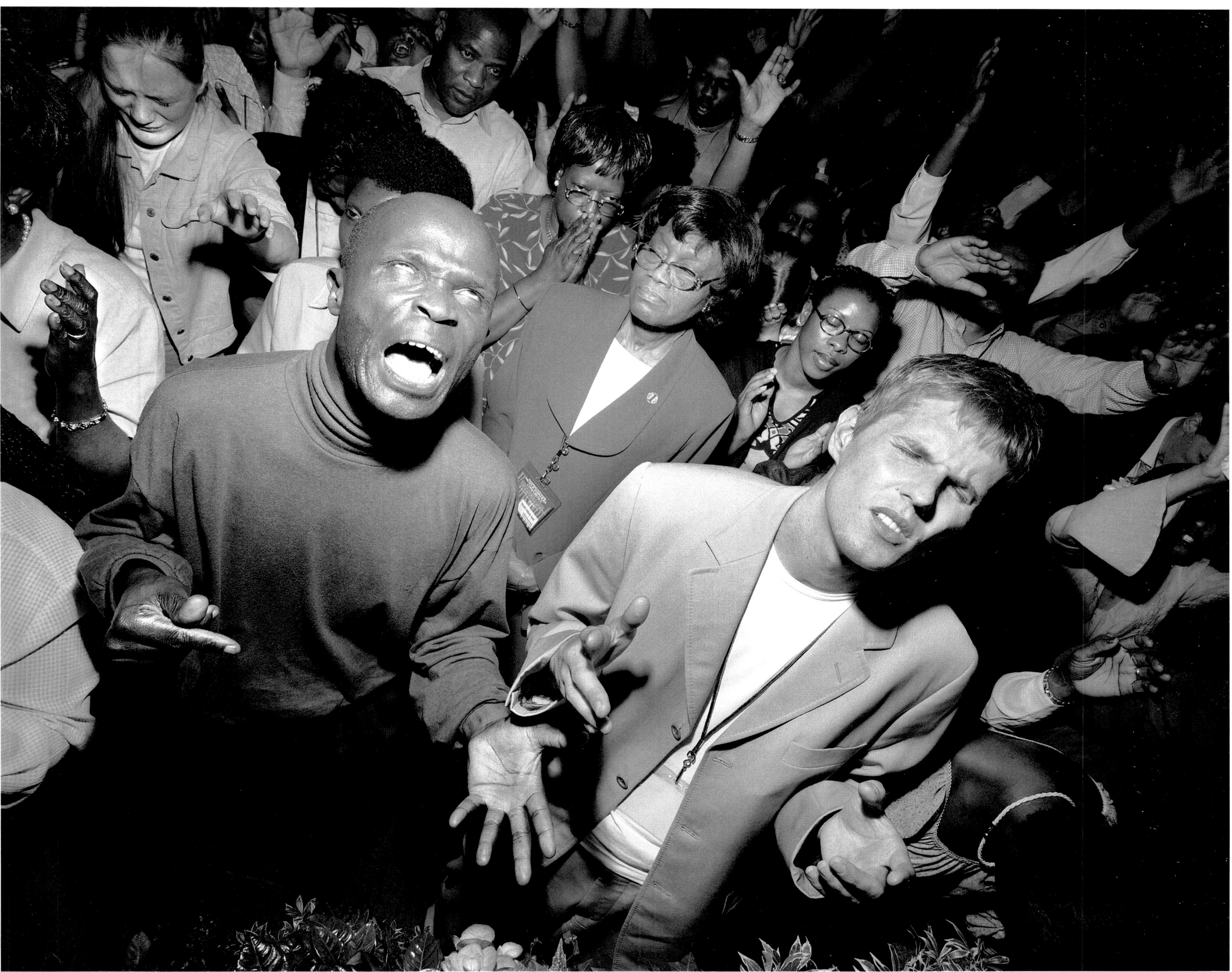

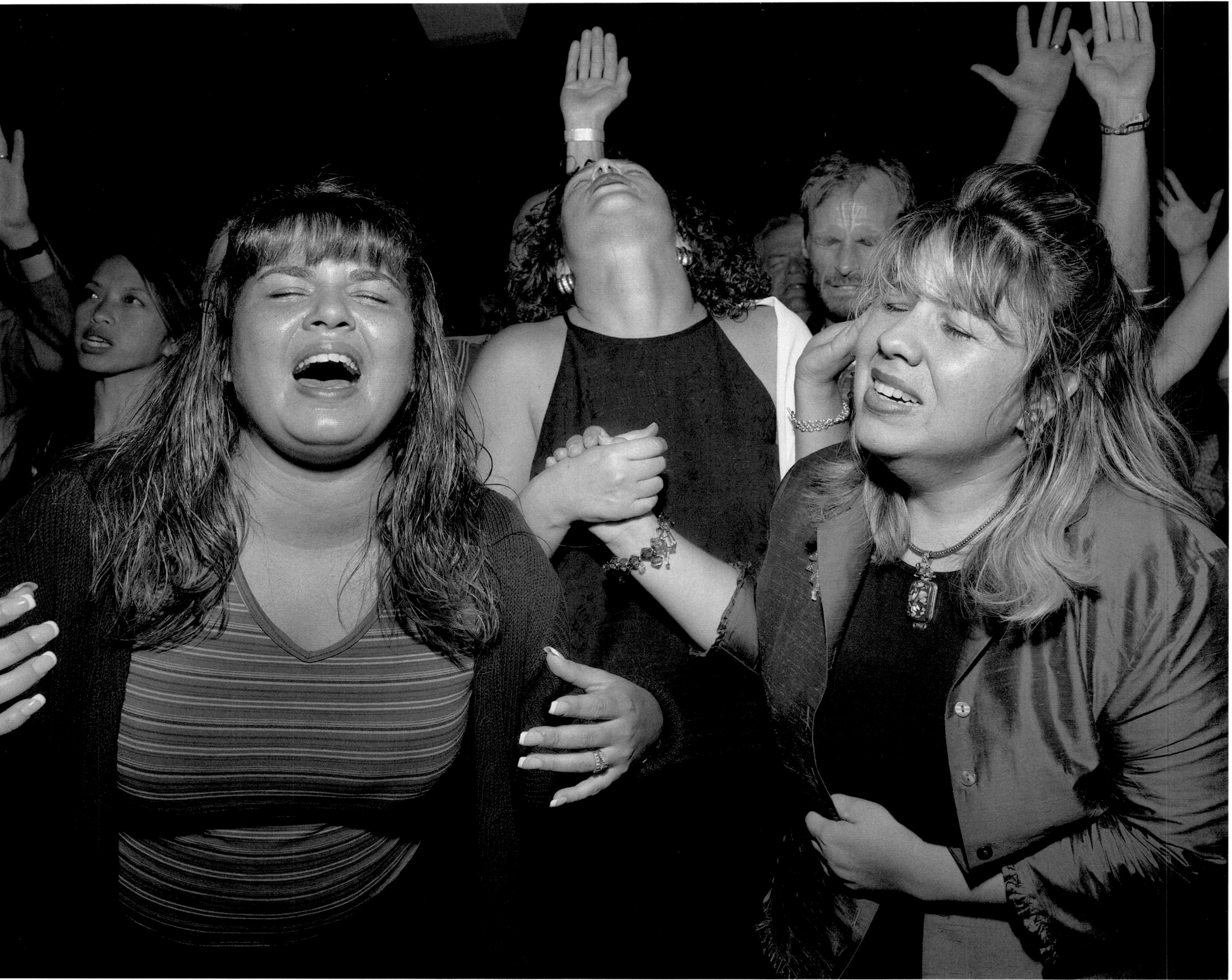

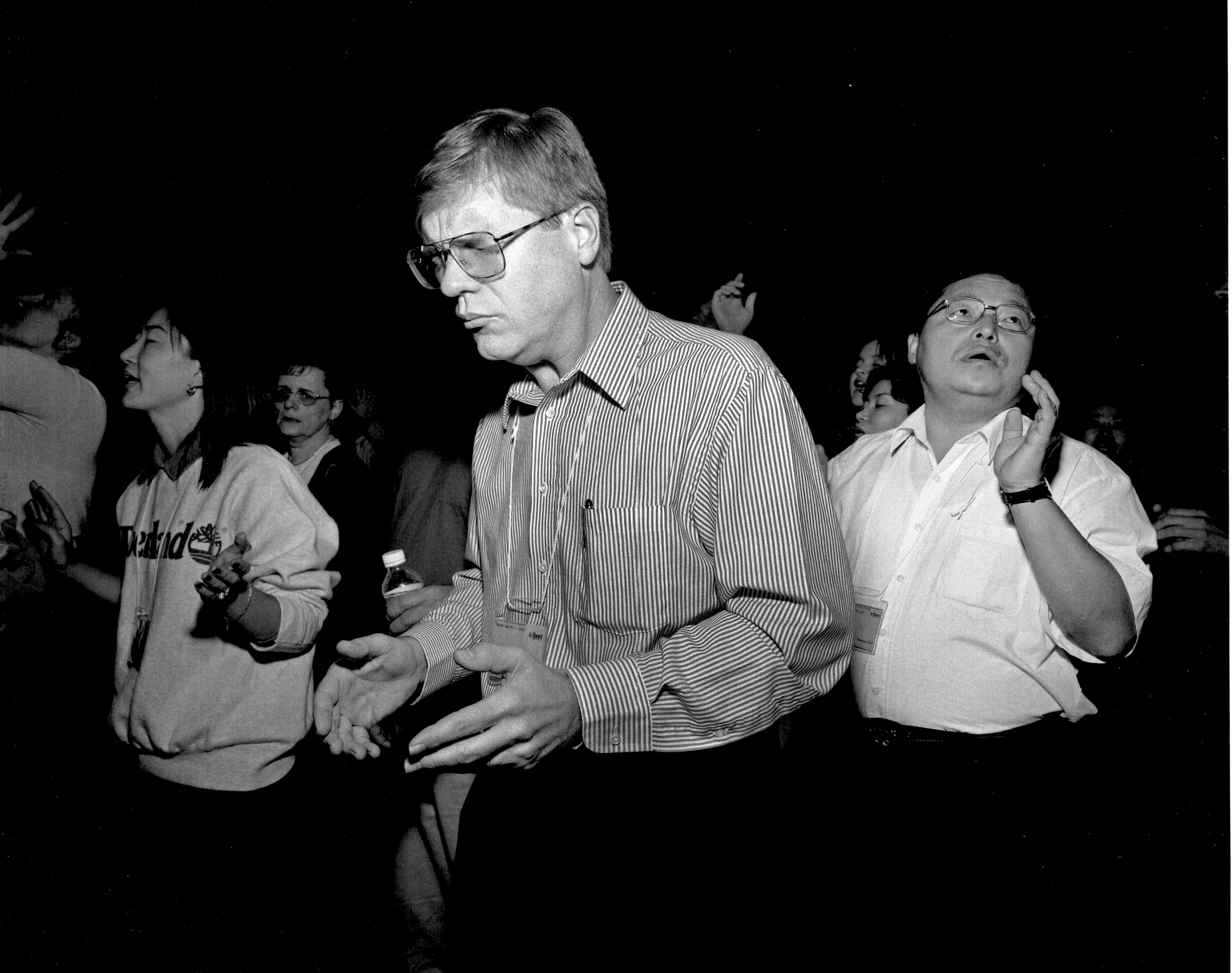

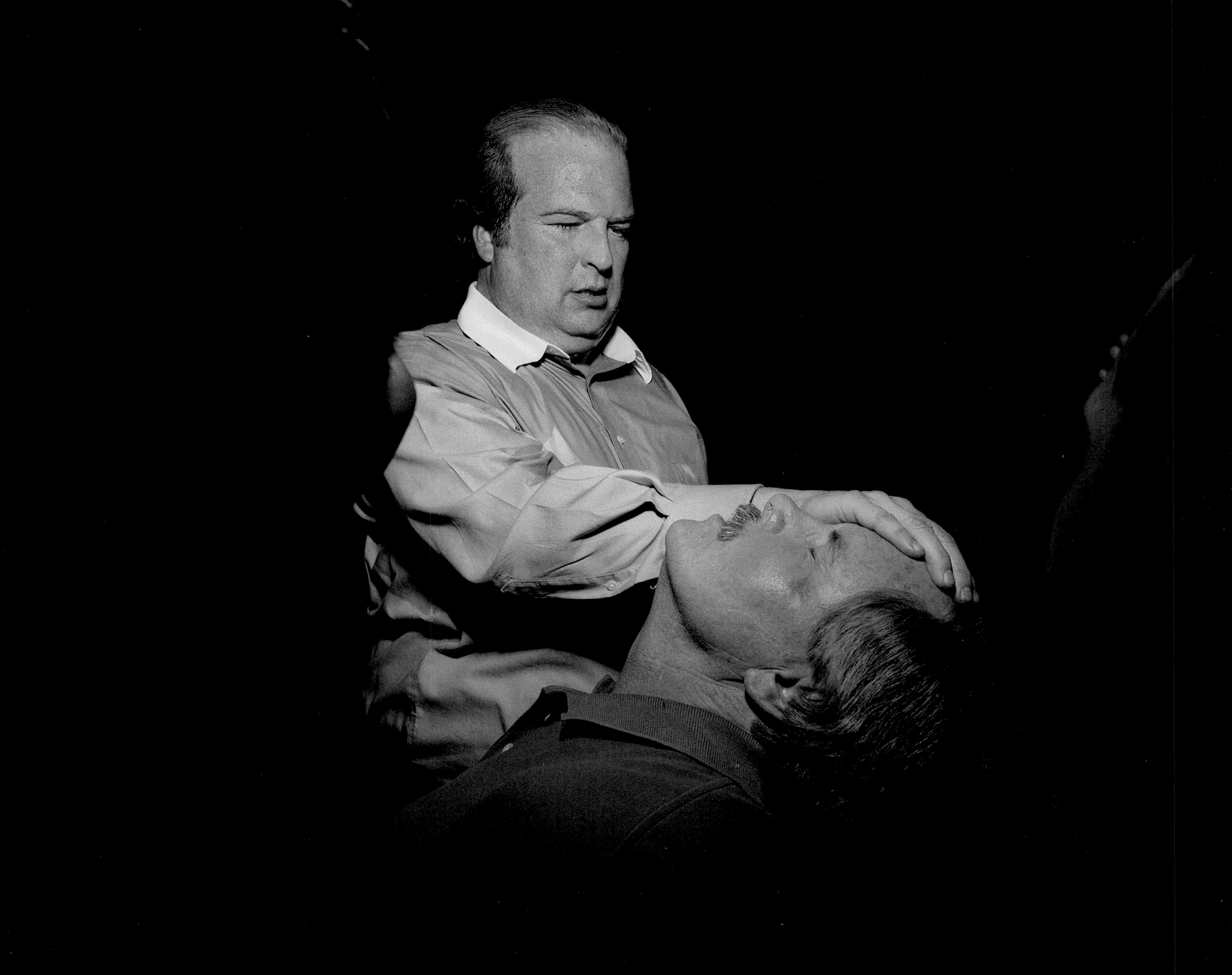

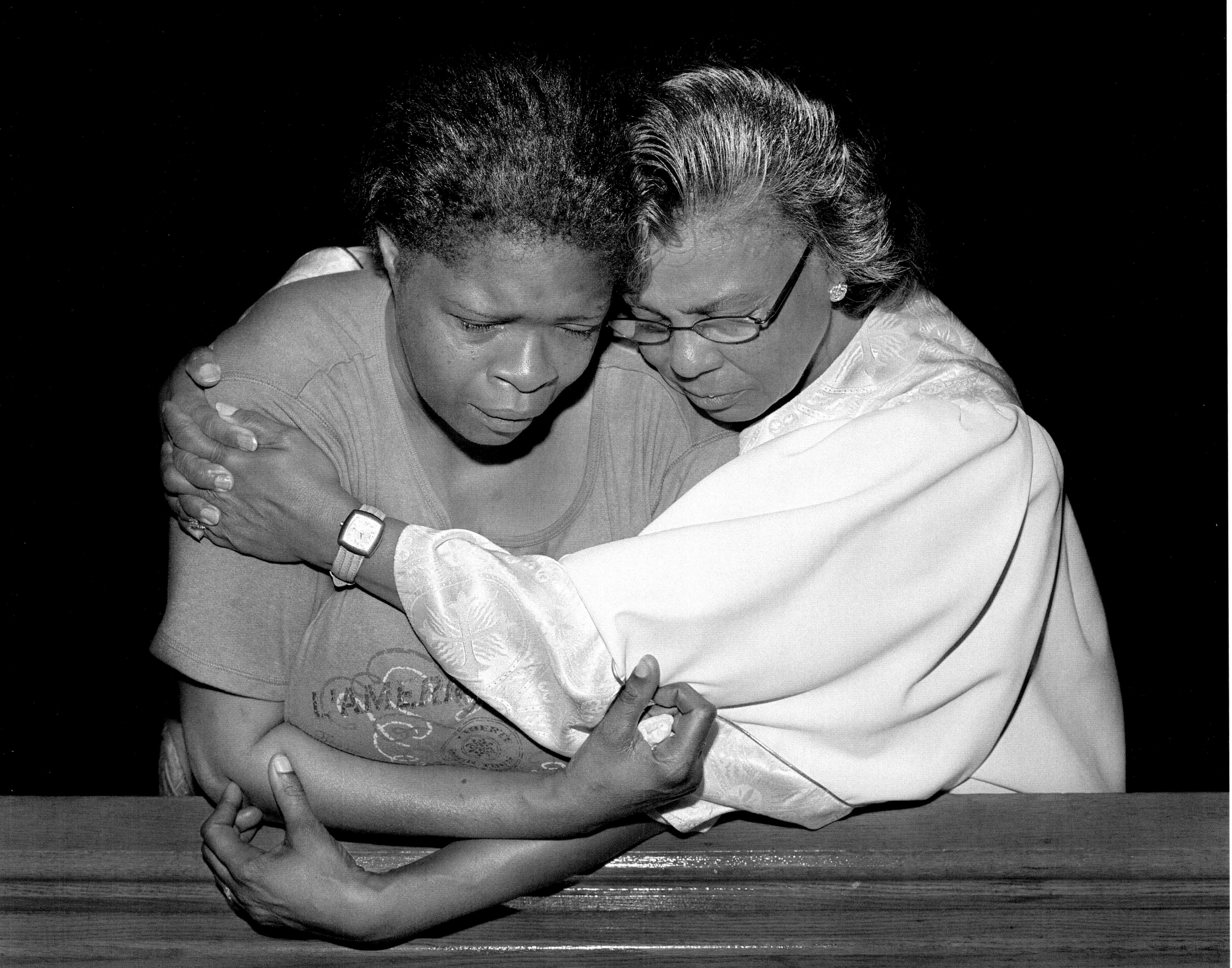

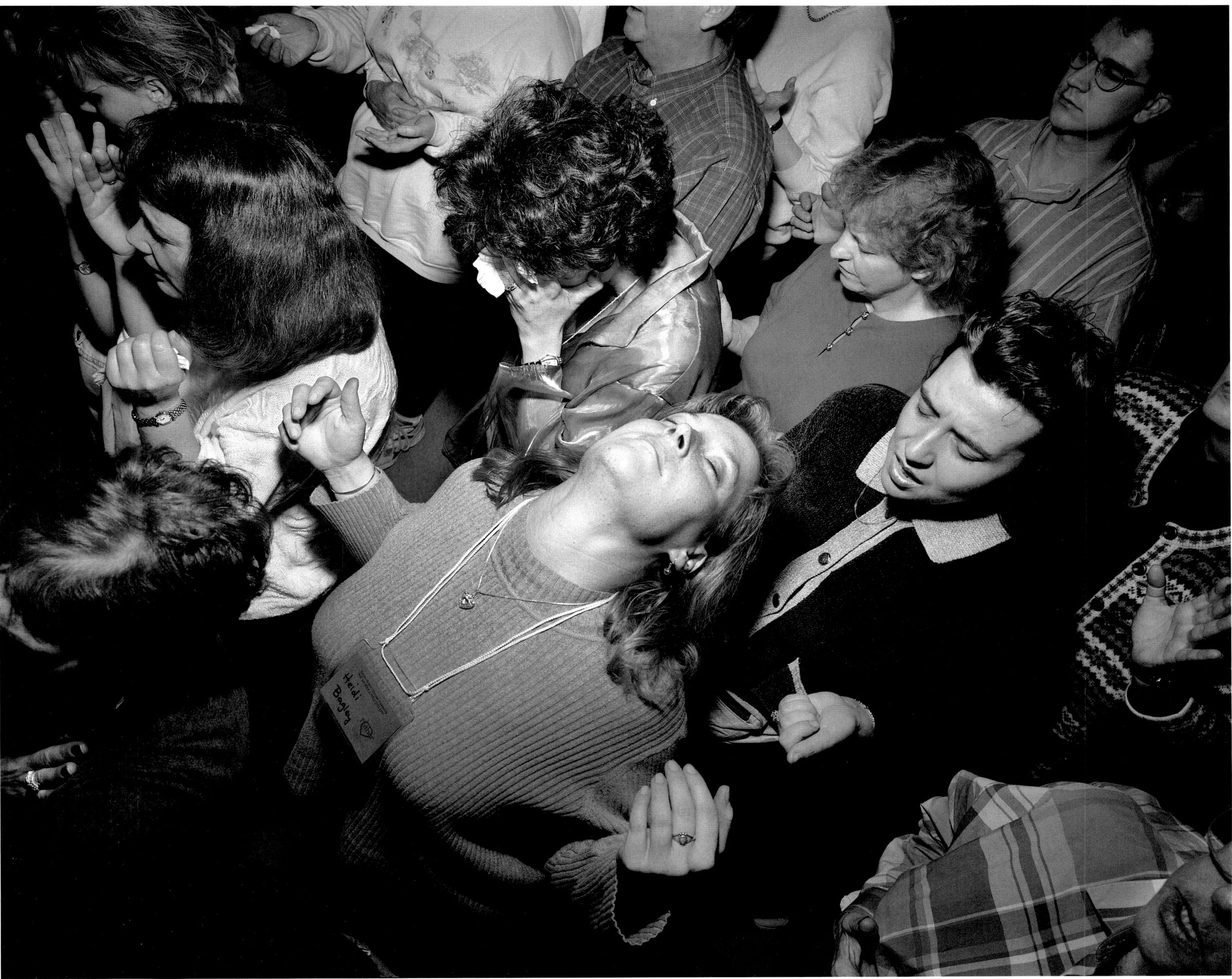
Heidi
Bagley

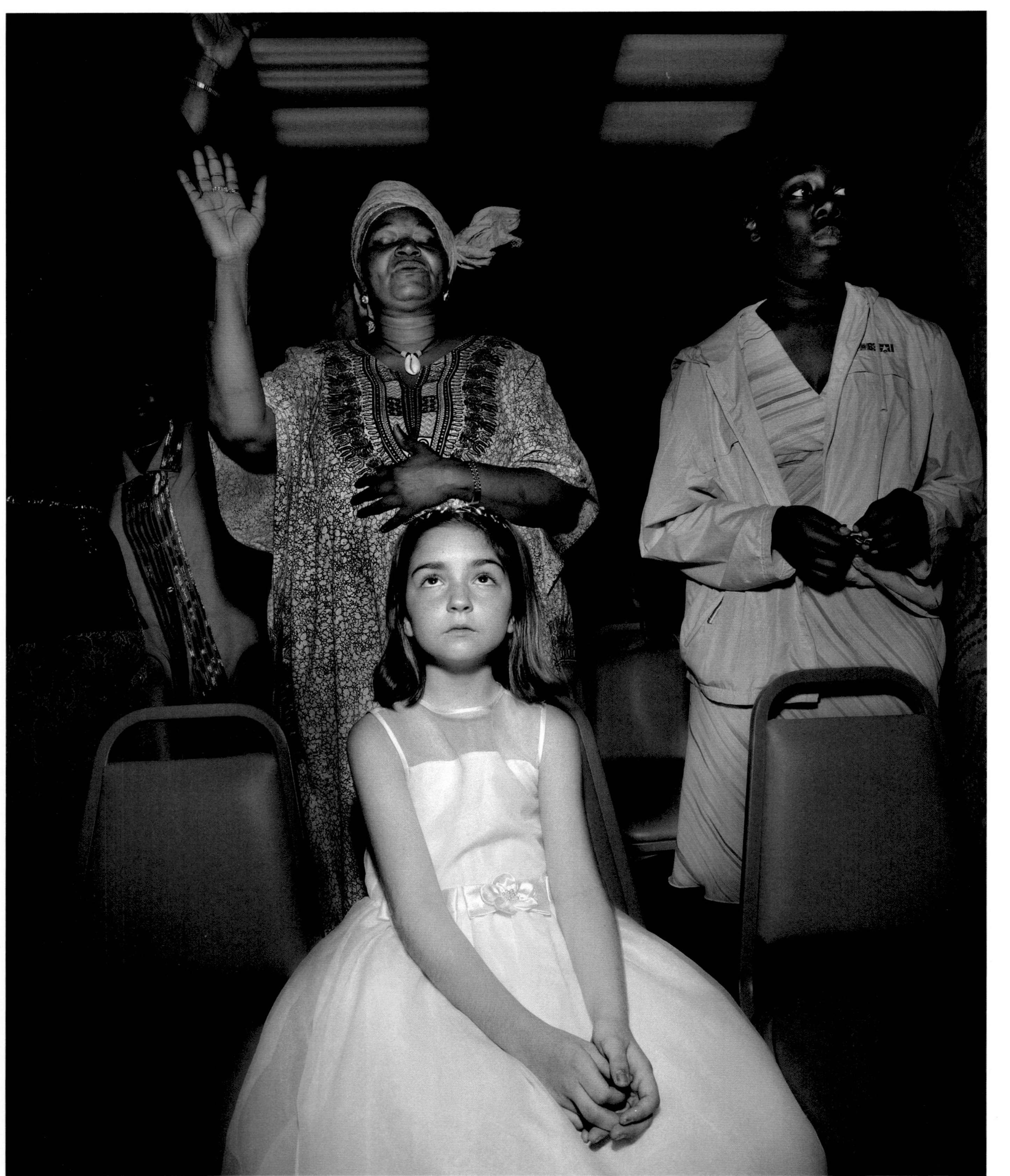

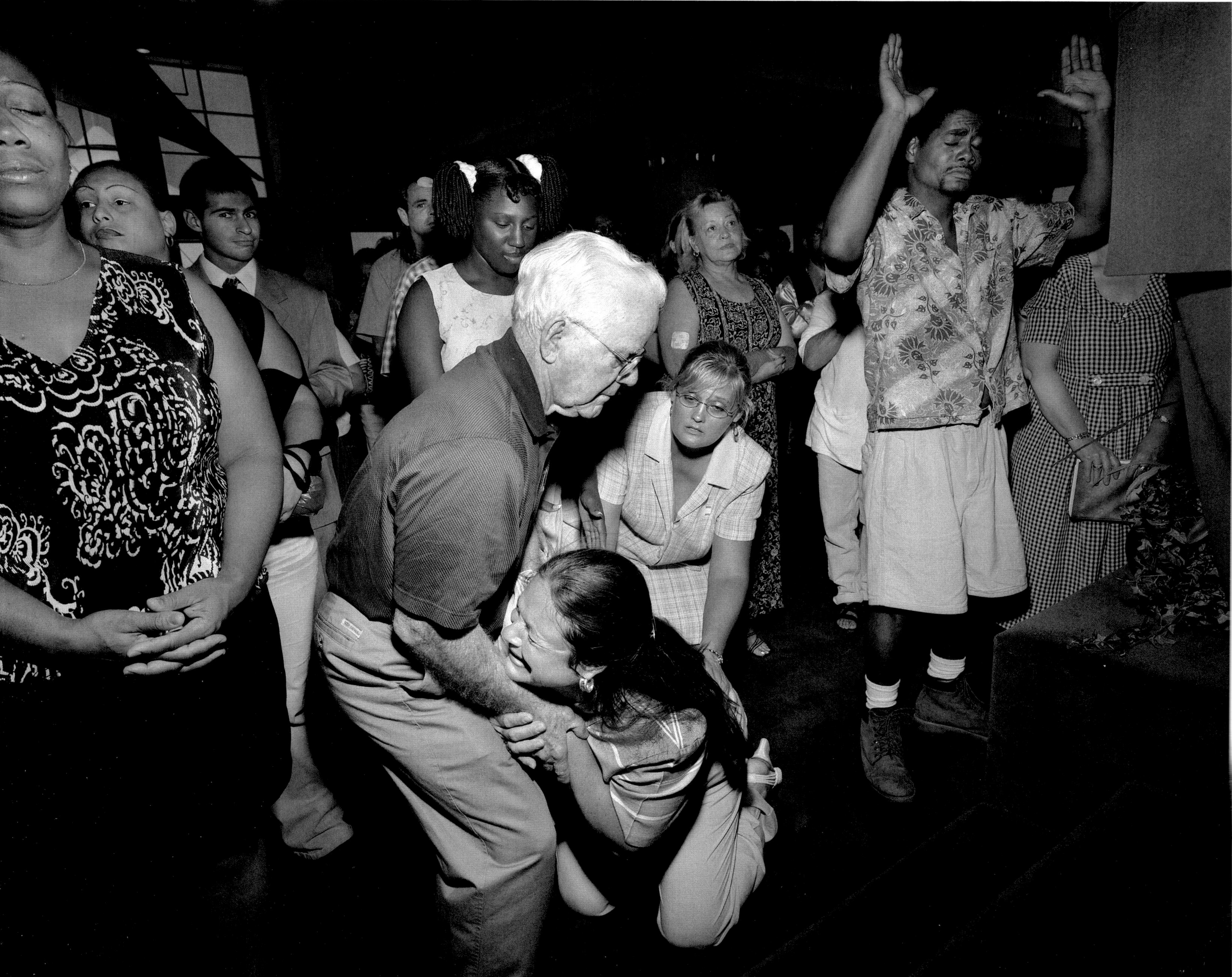

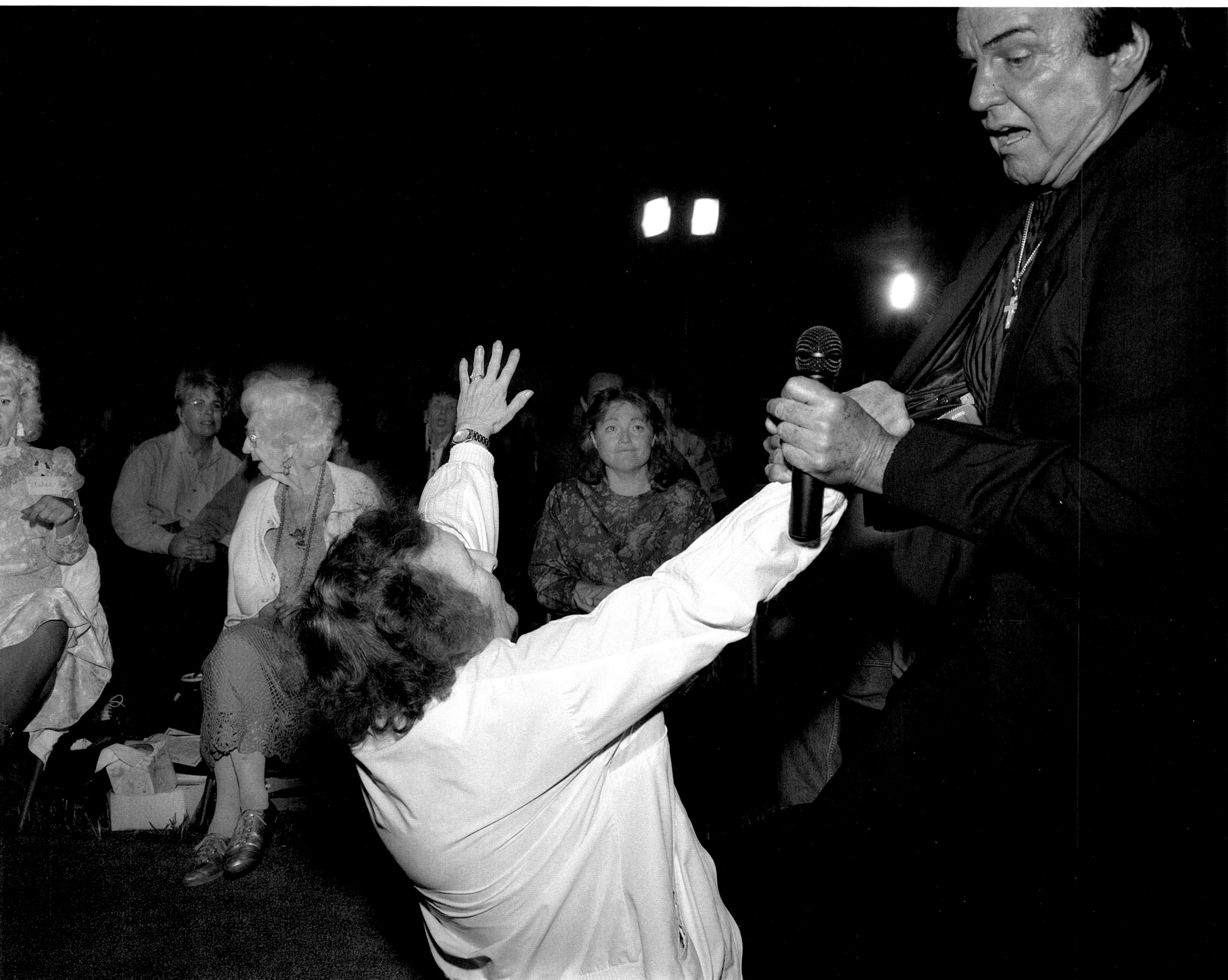

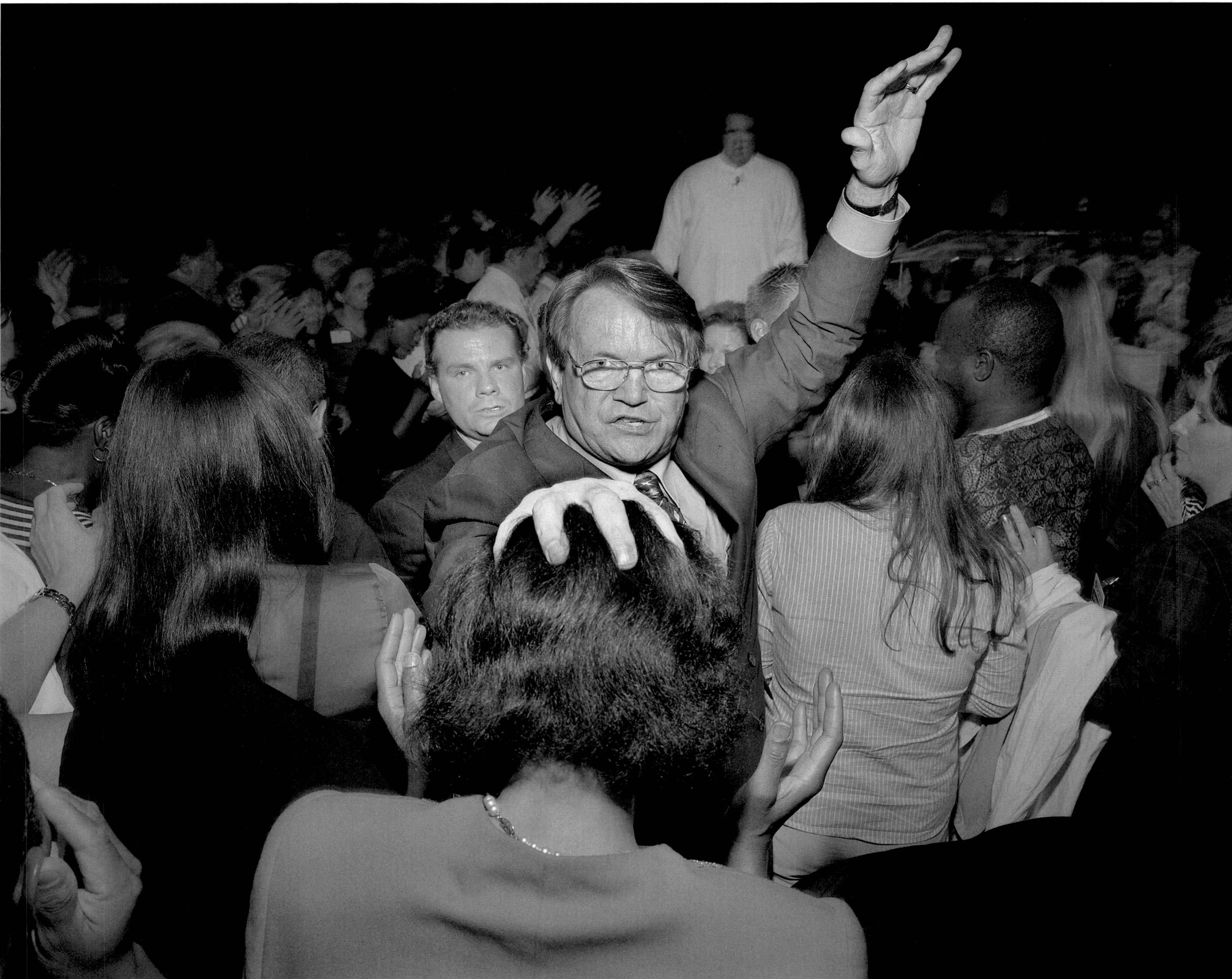

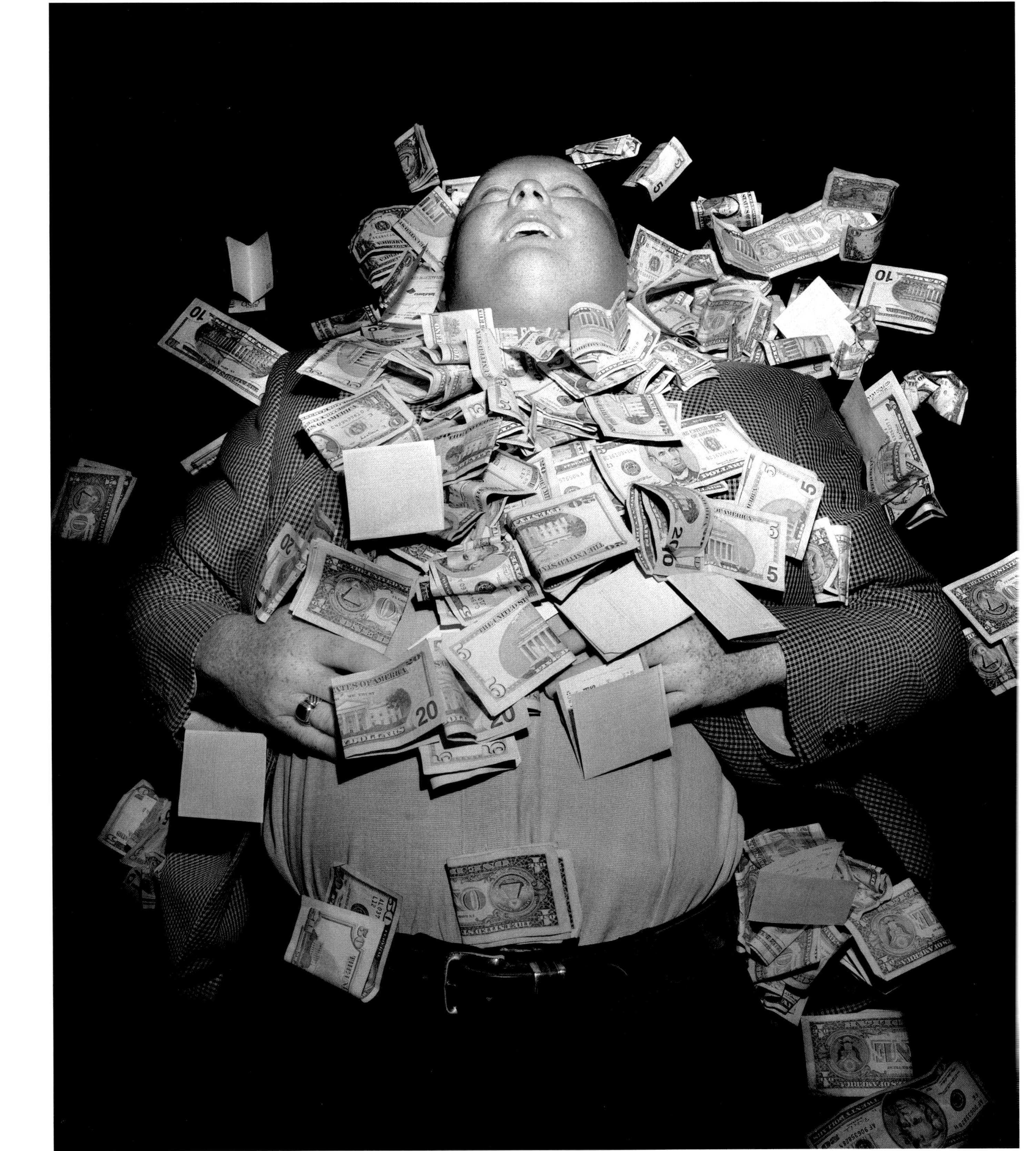

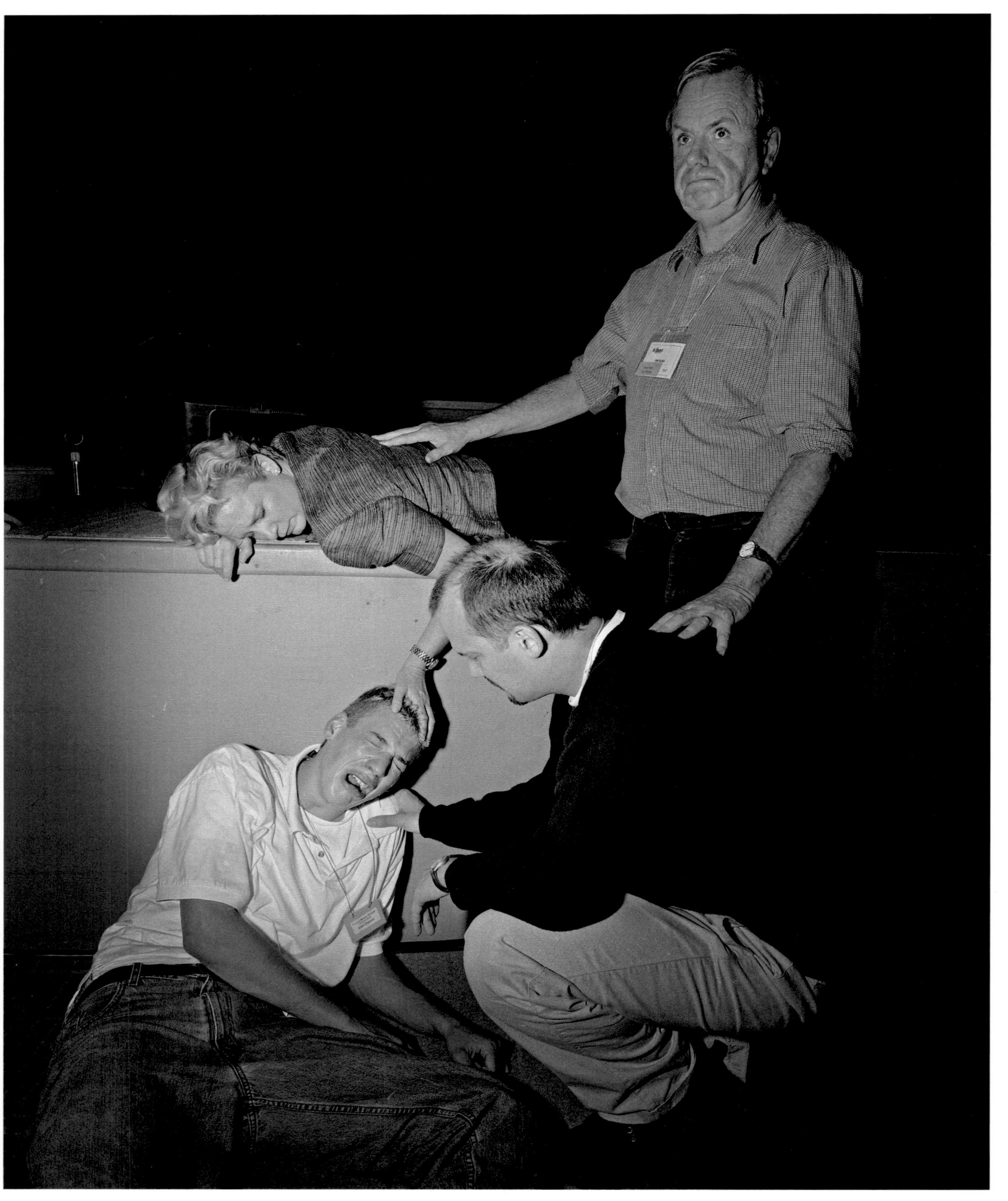

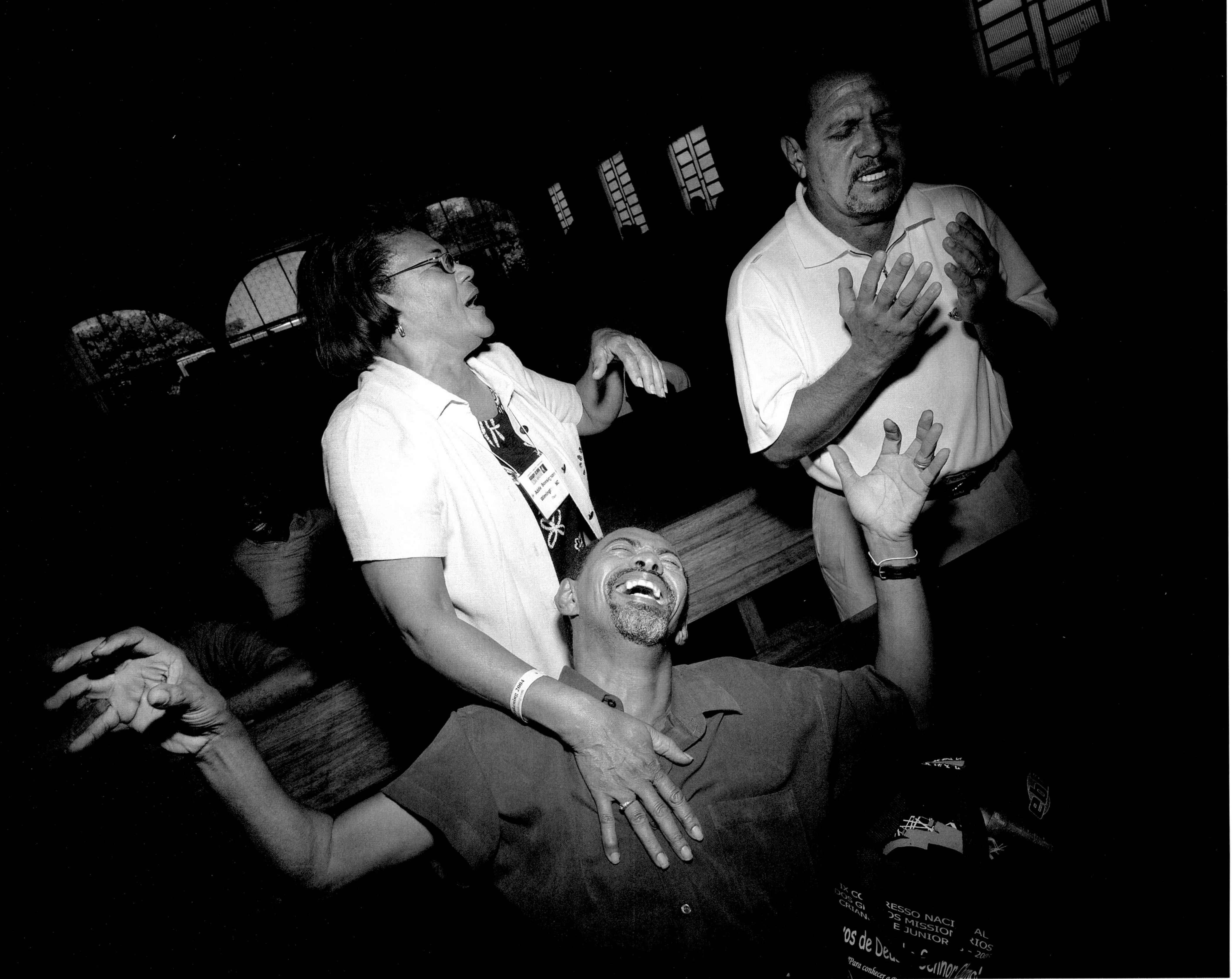

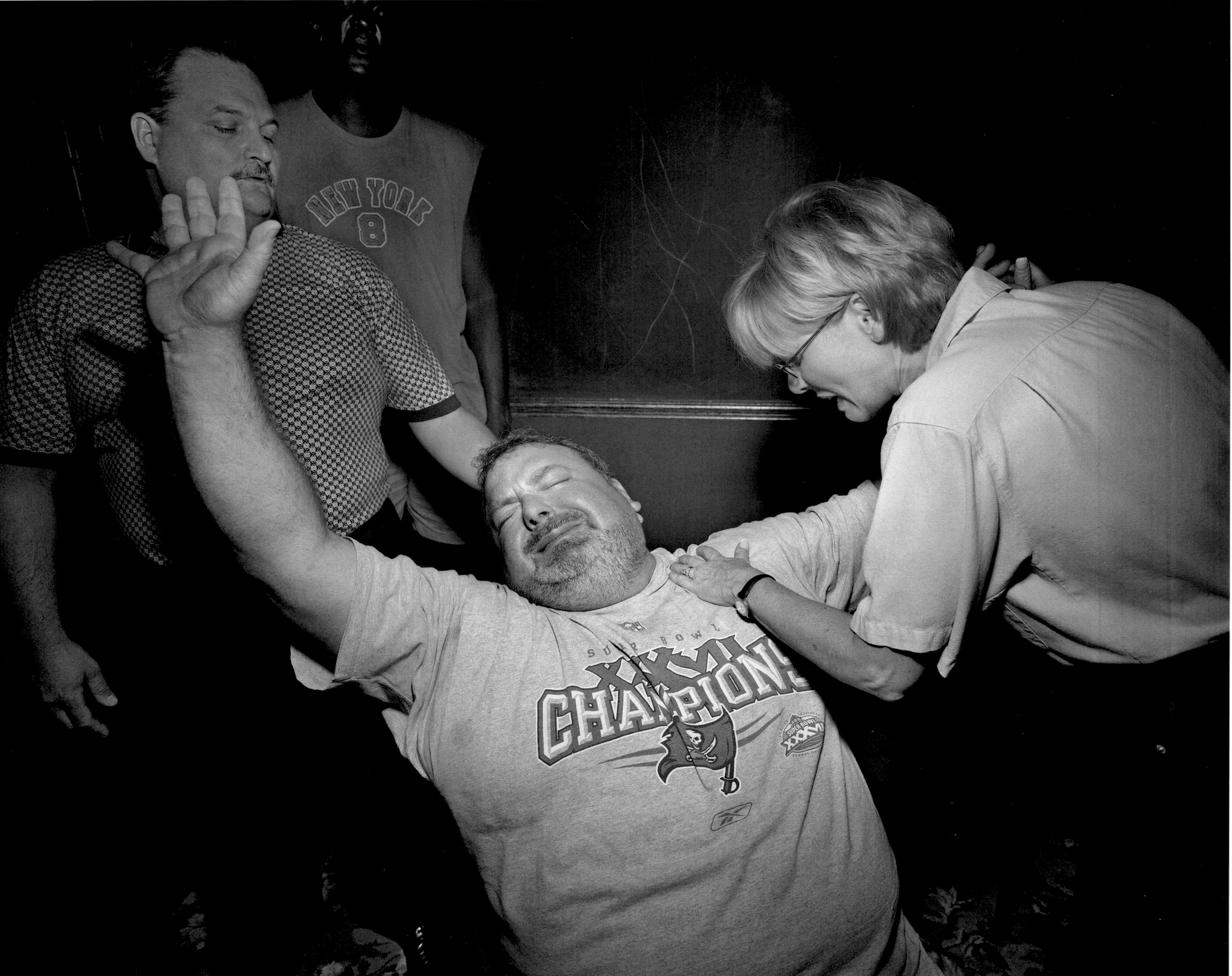
NEW YORK
8
CHAMPIONS

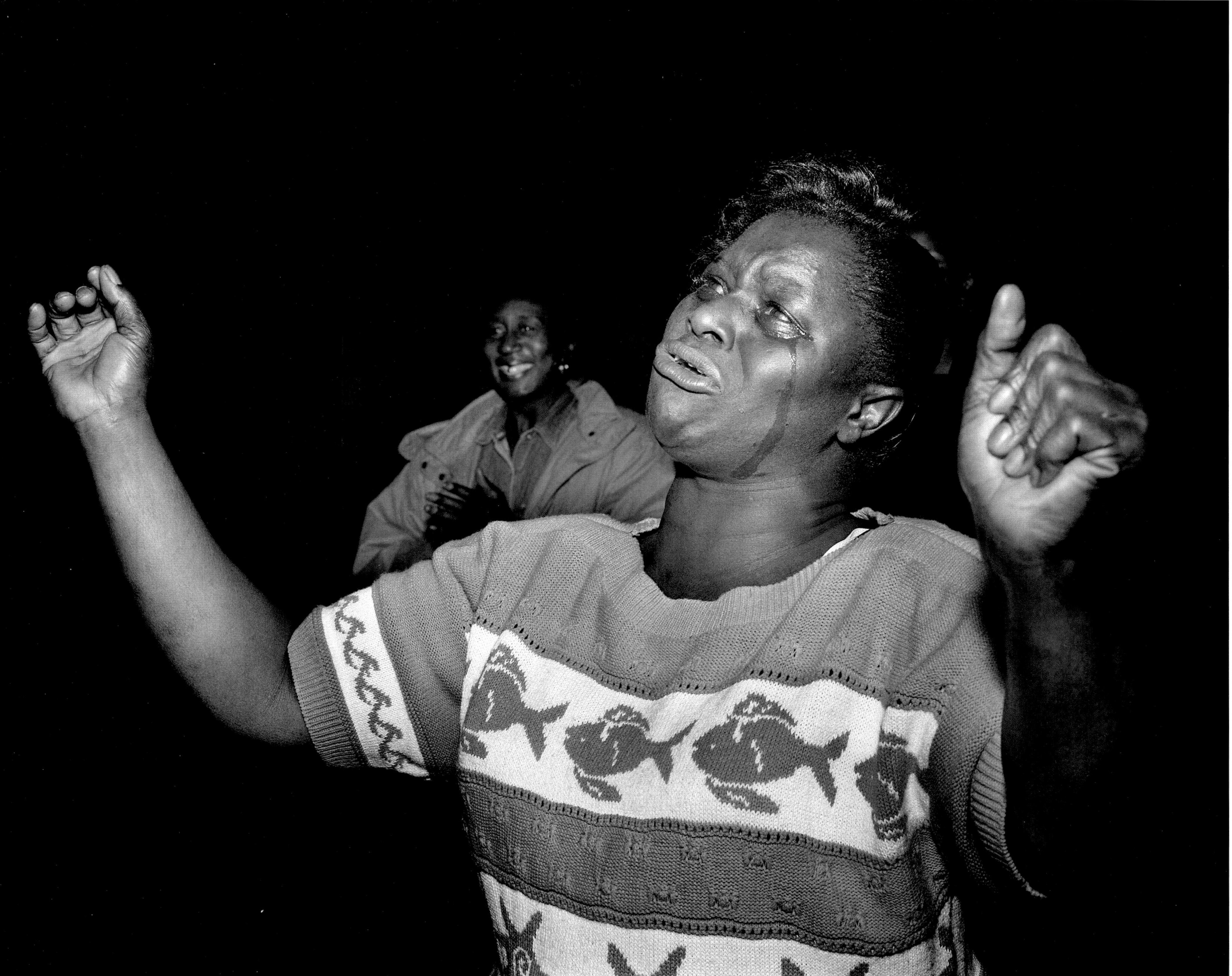

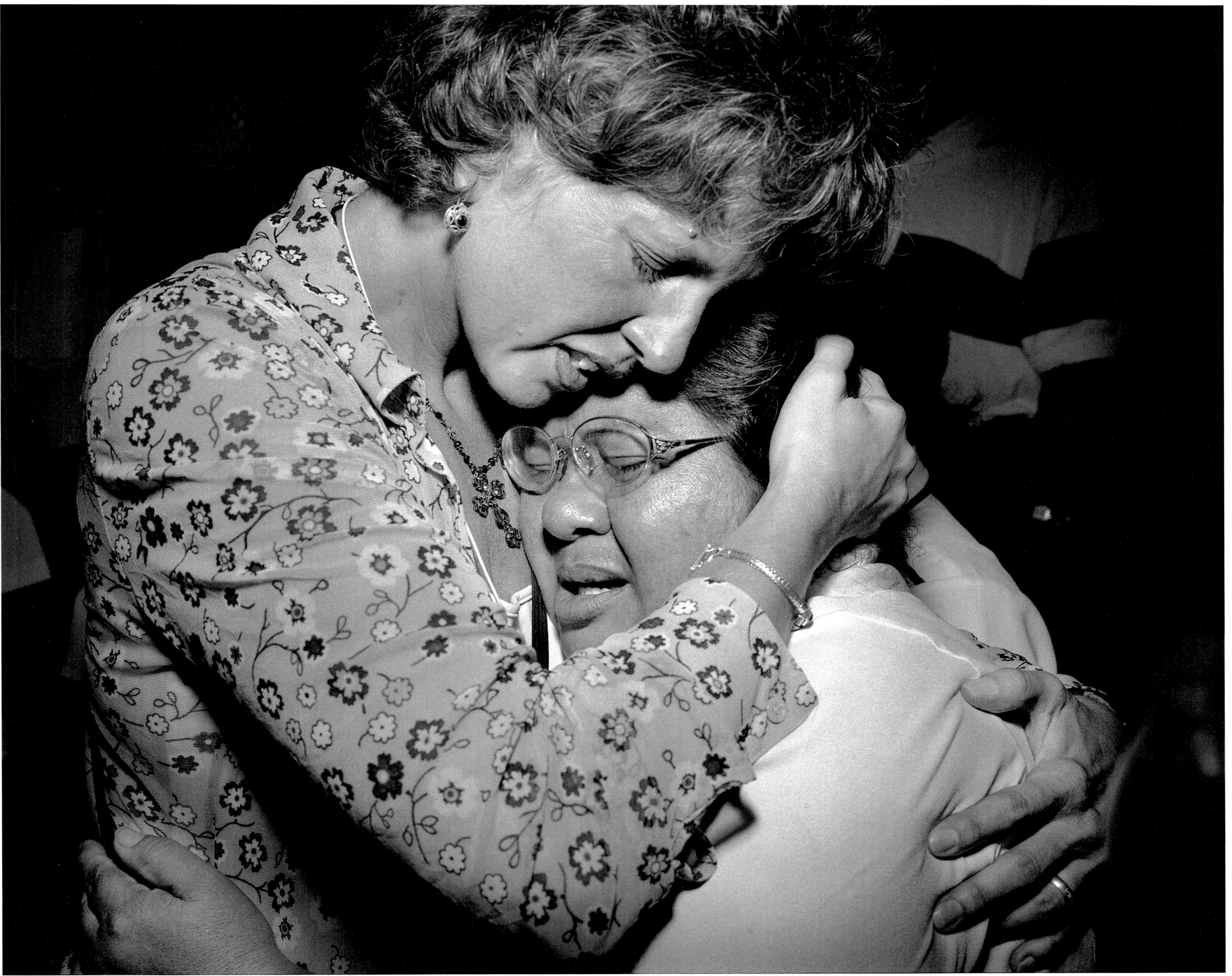

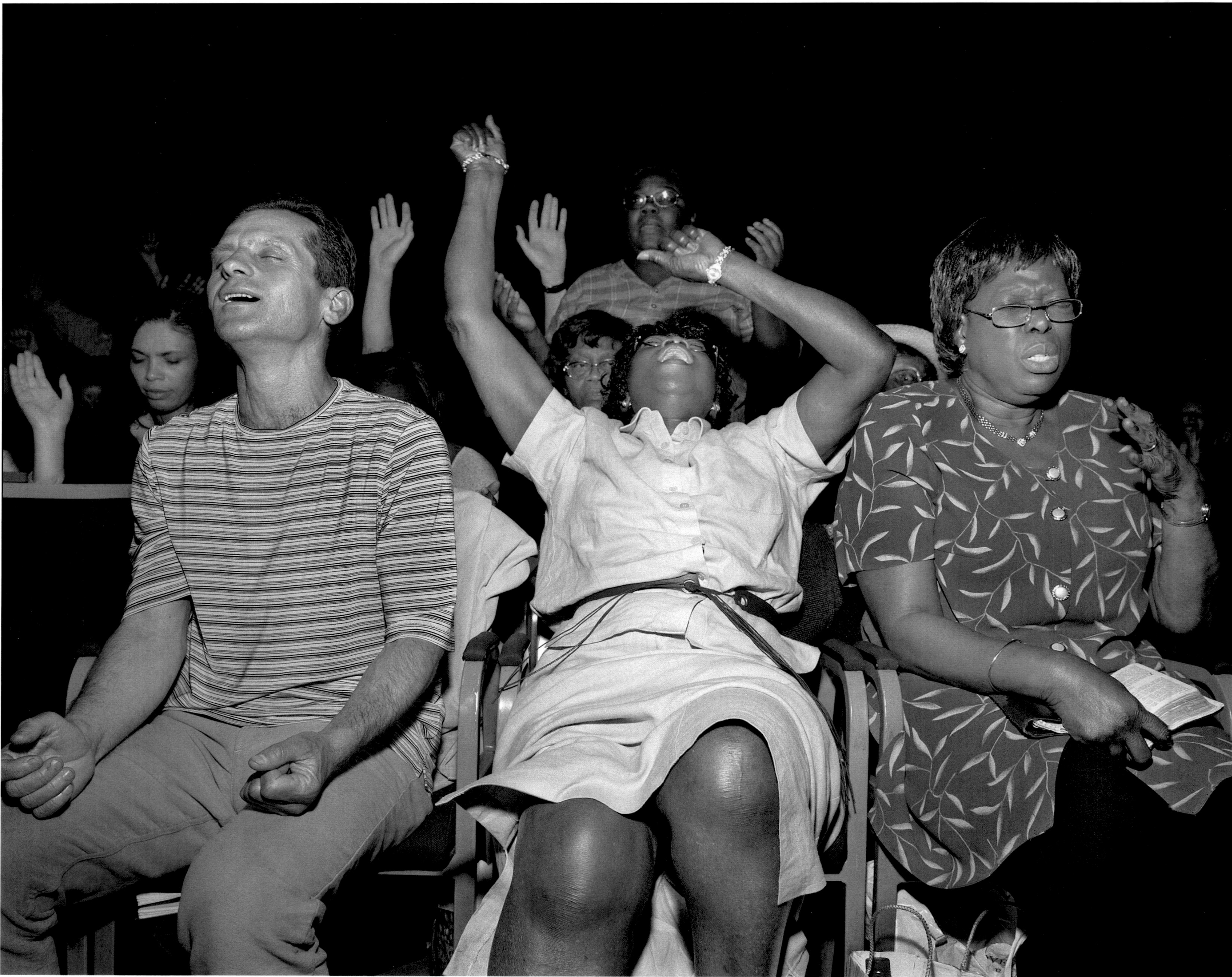

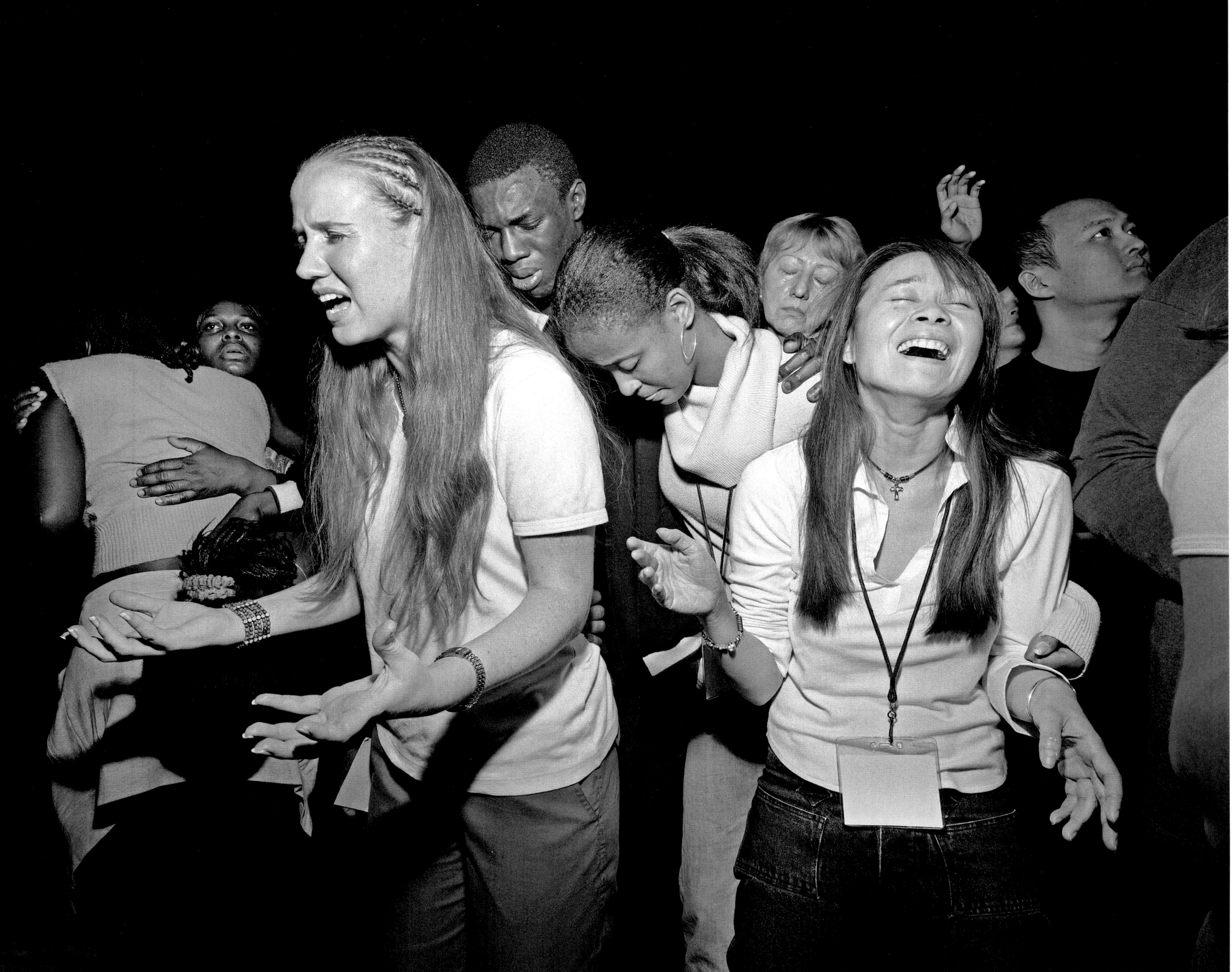

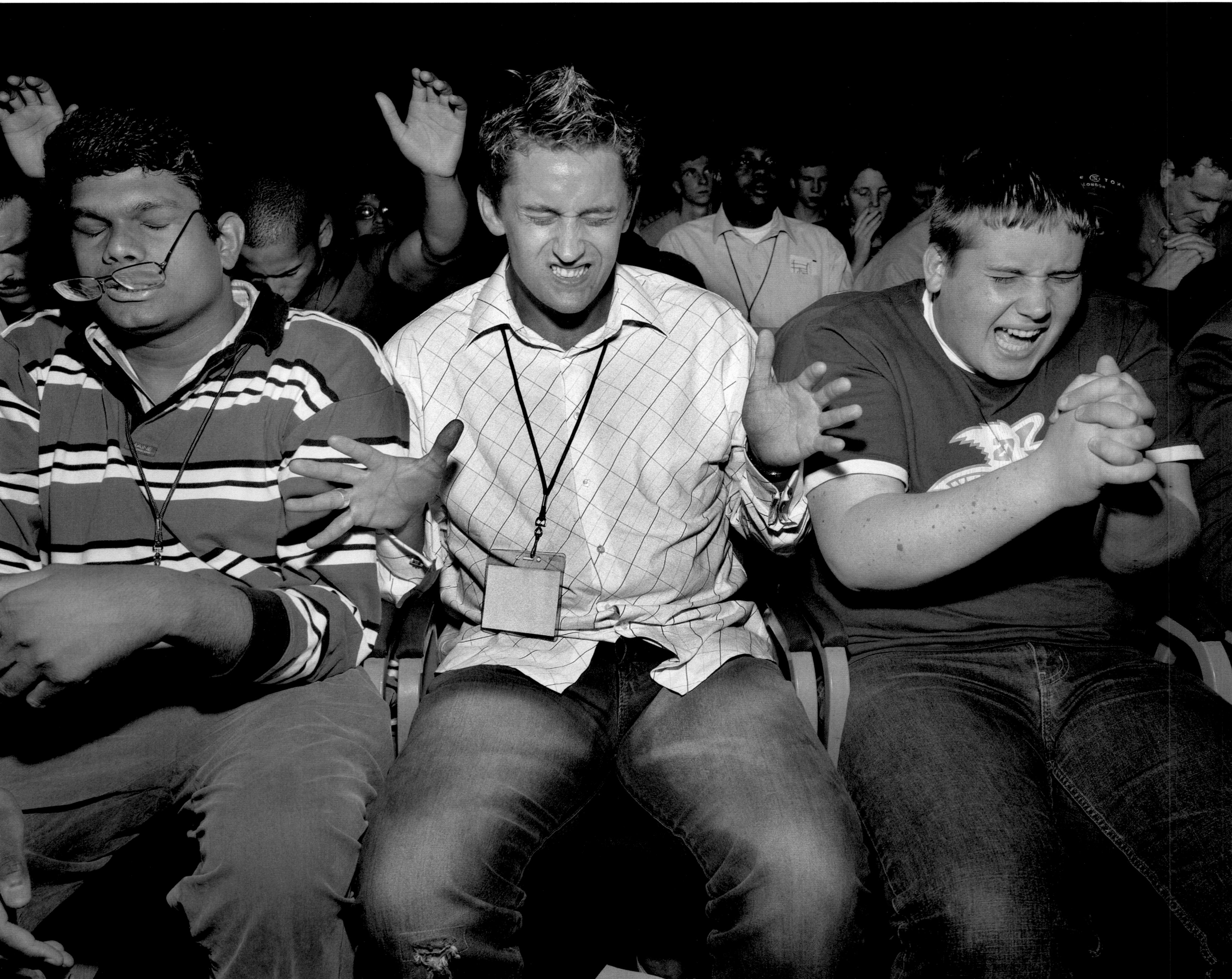

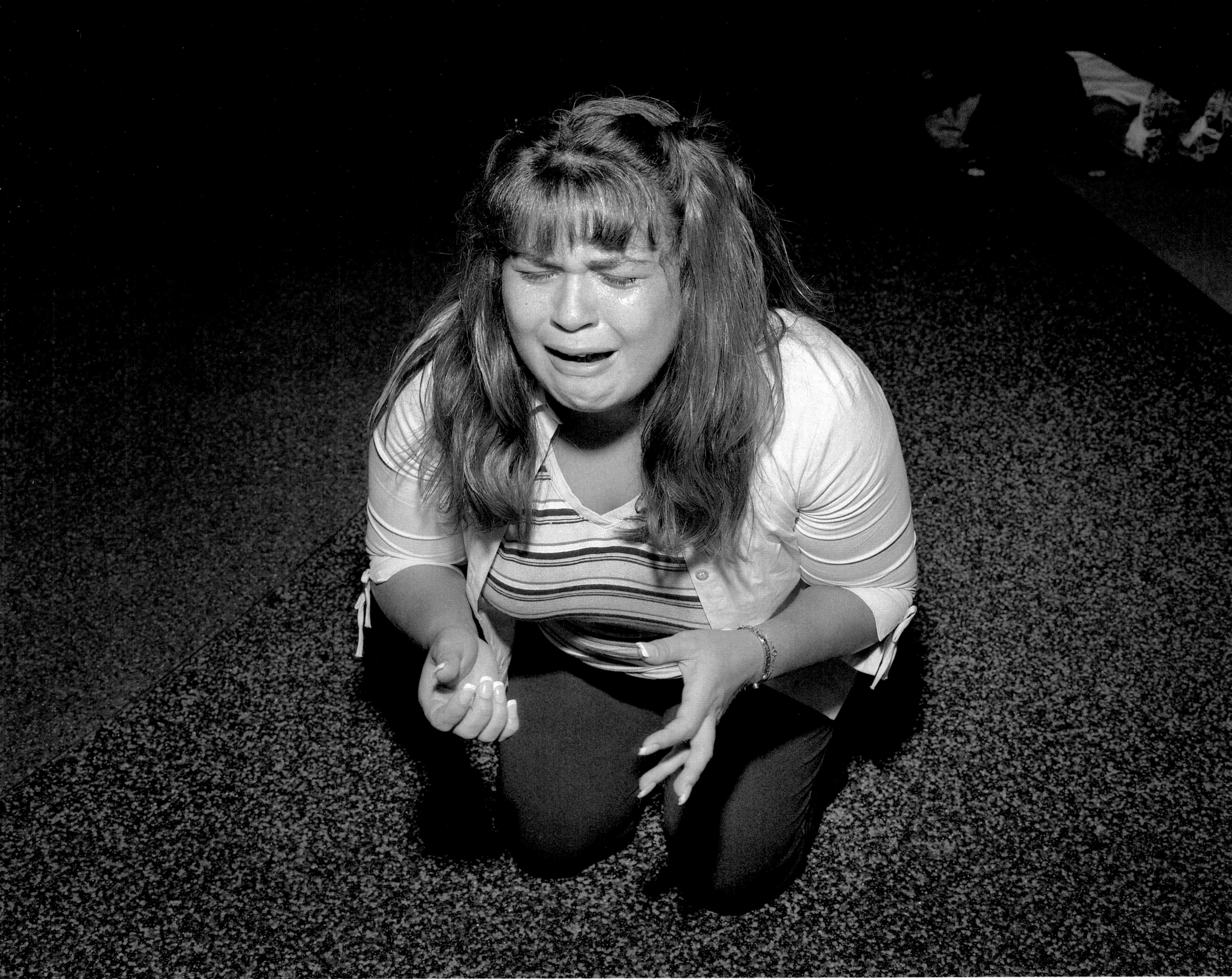

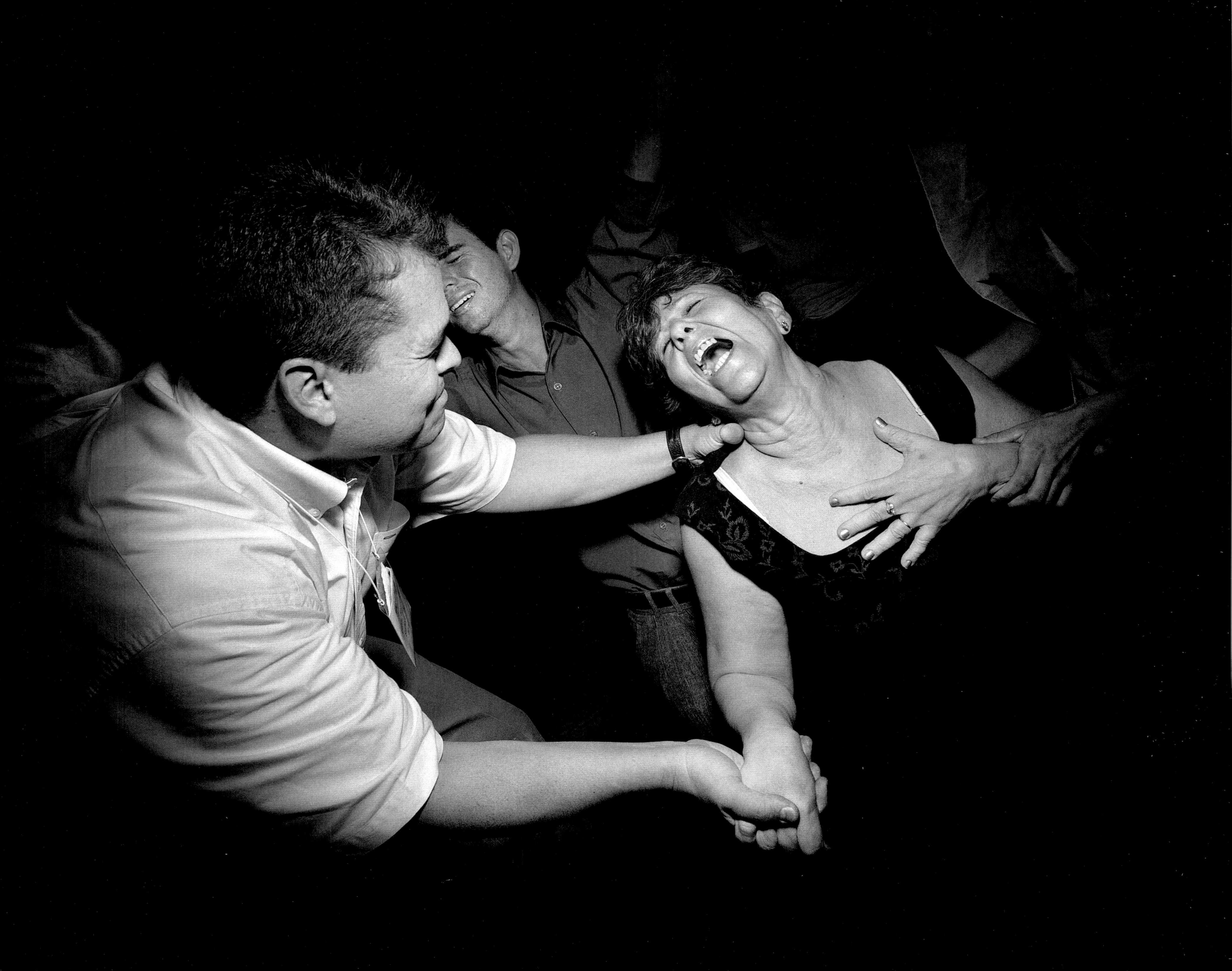

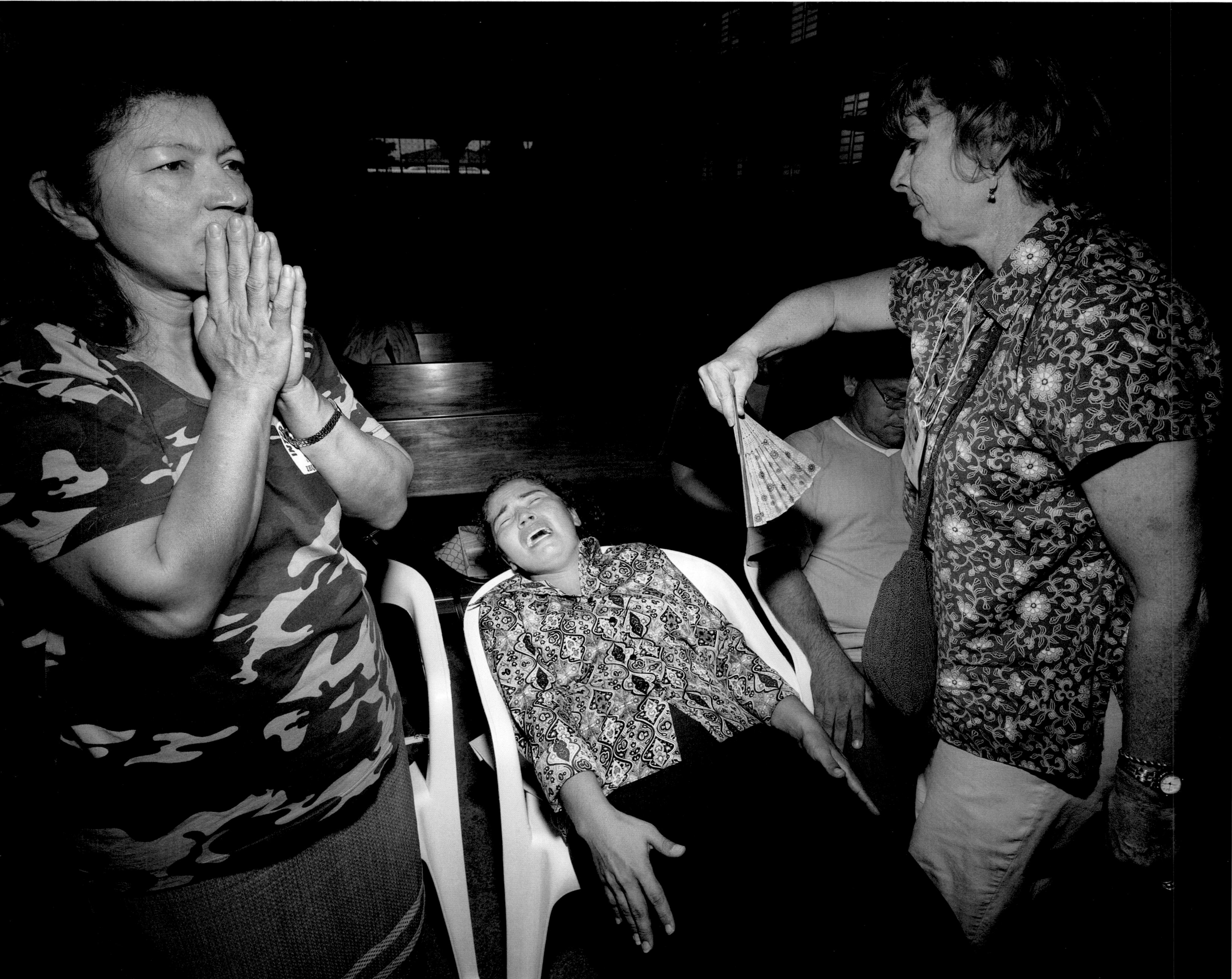

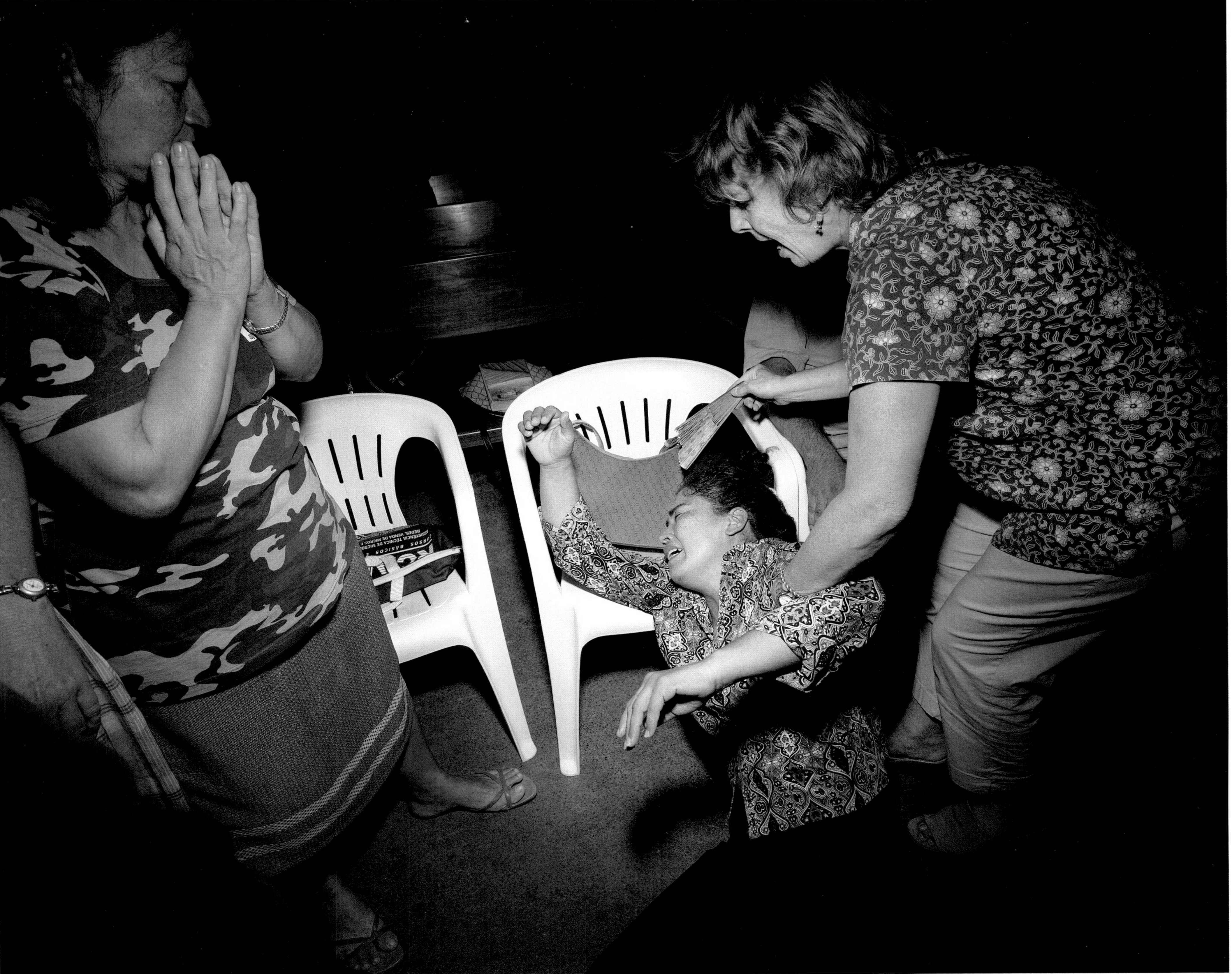

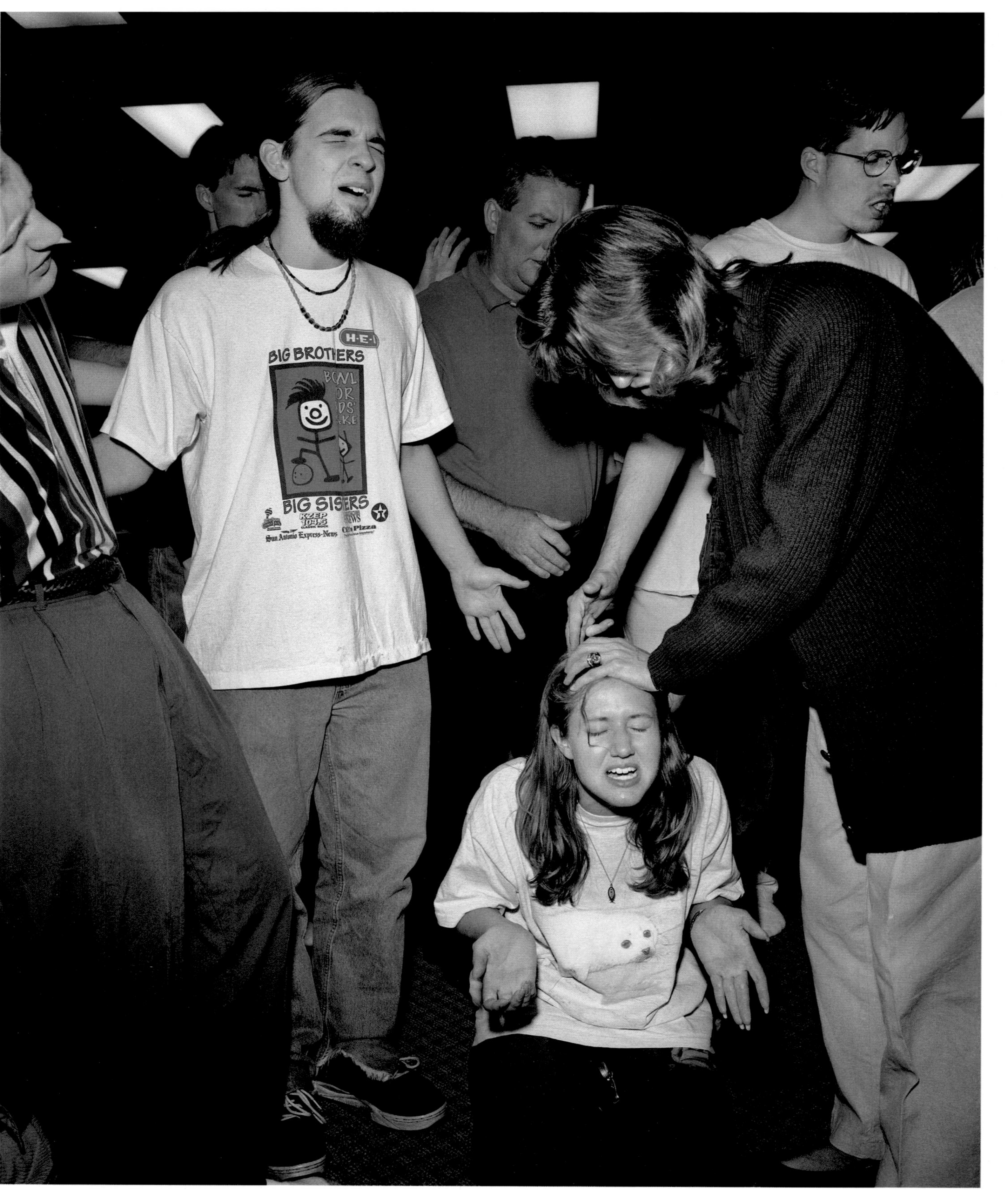
BIG BROTHERS
BIG SISTERS
KZEP
104.5
CLASSIC ROCK
San Antonio Express-News

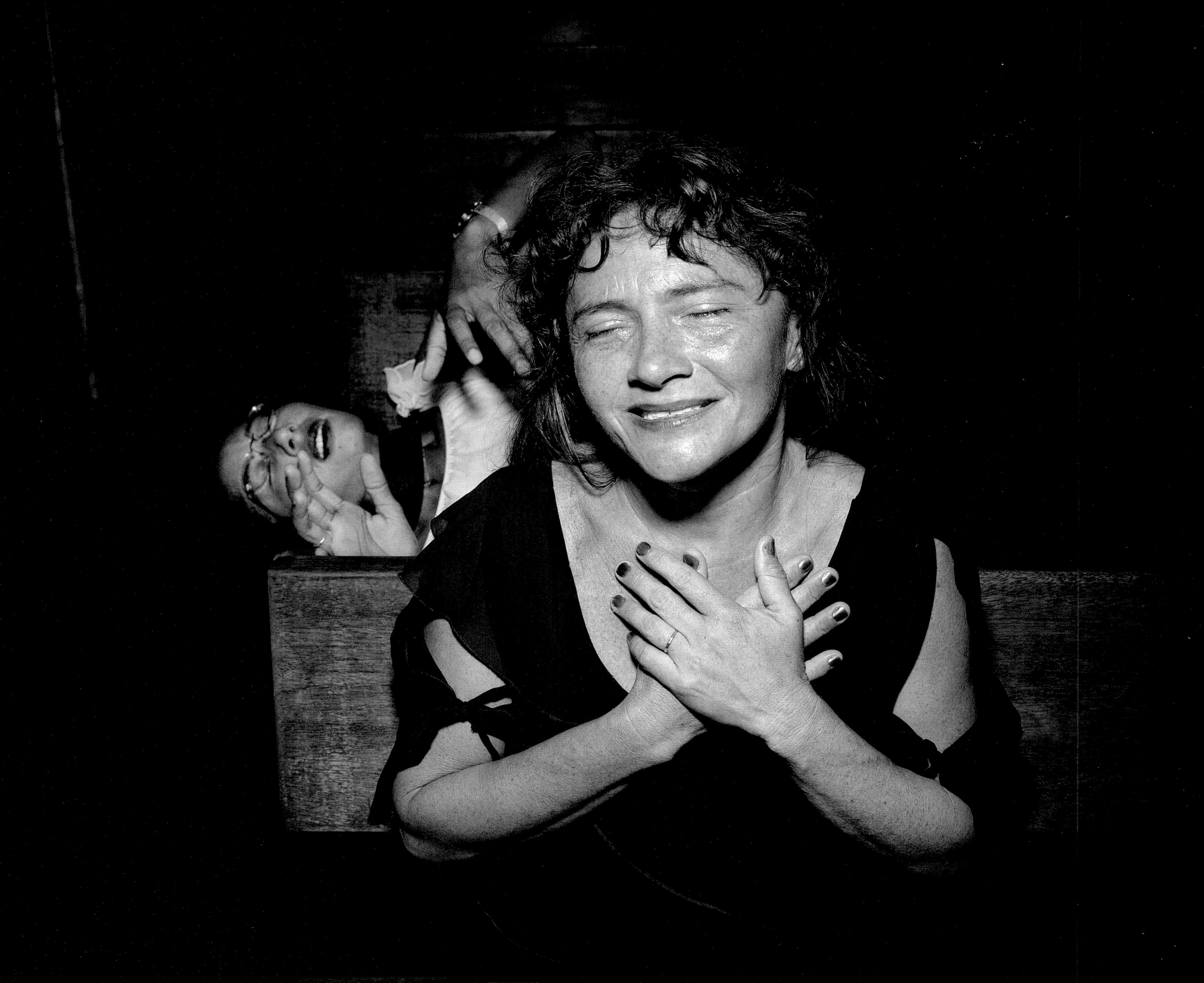

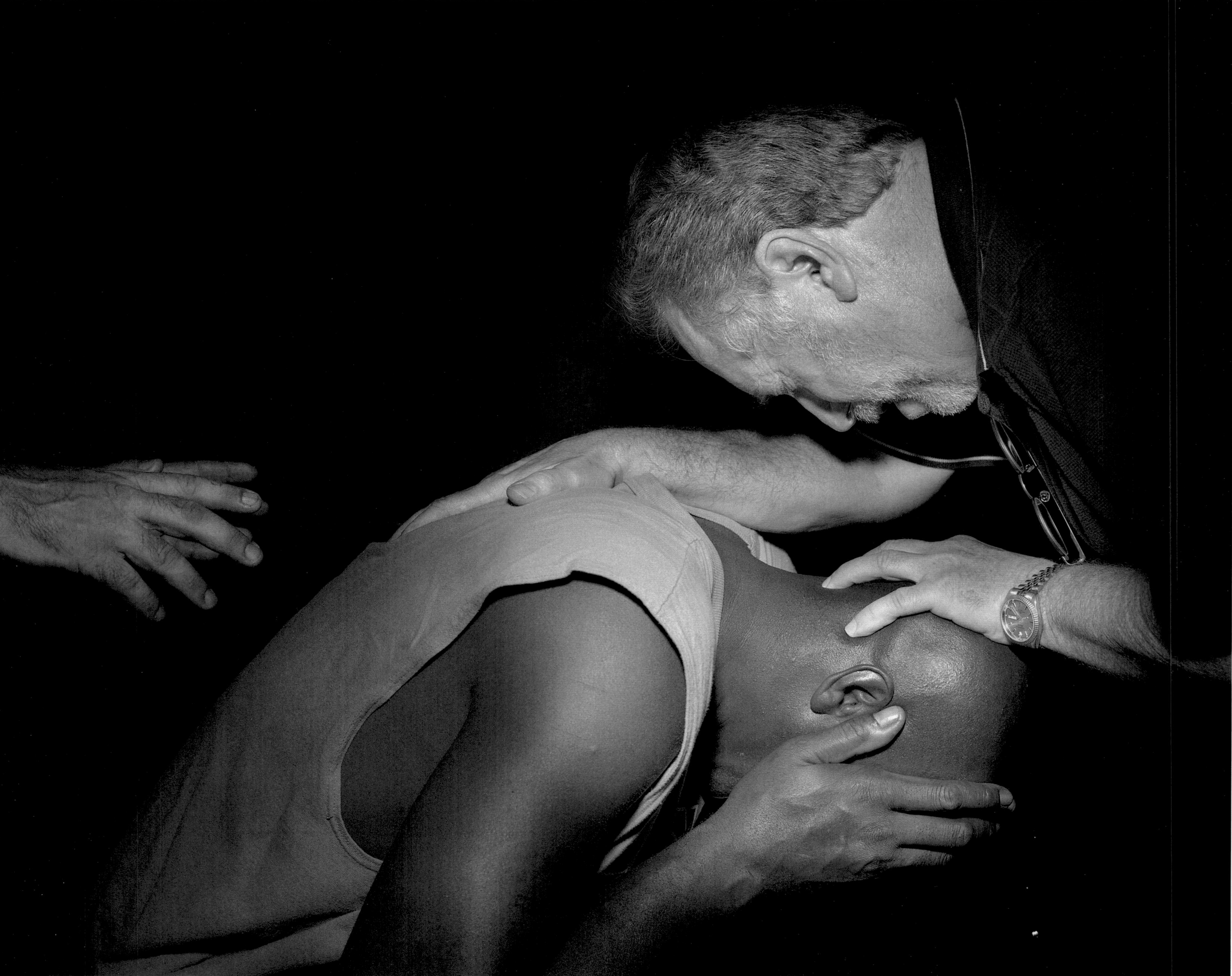

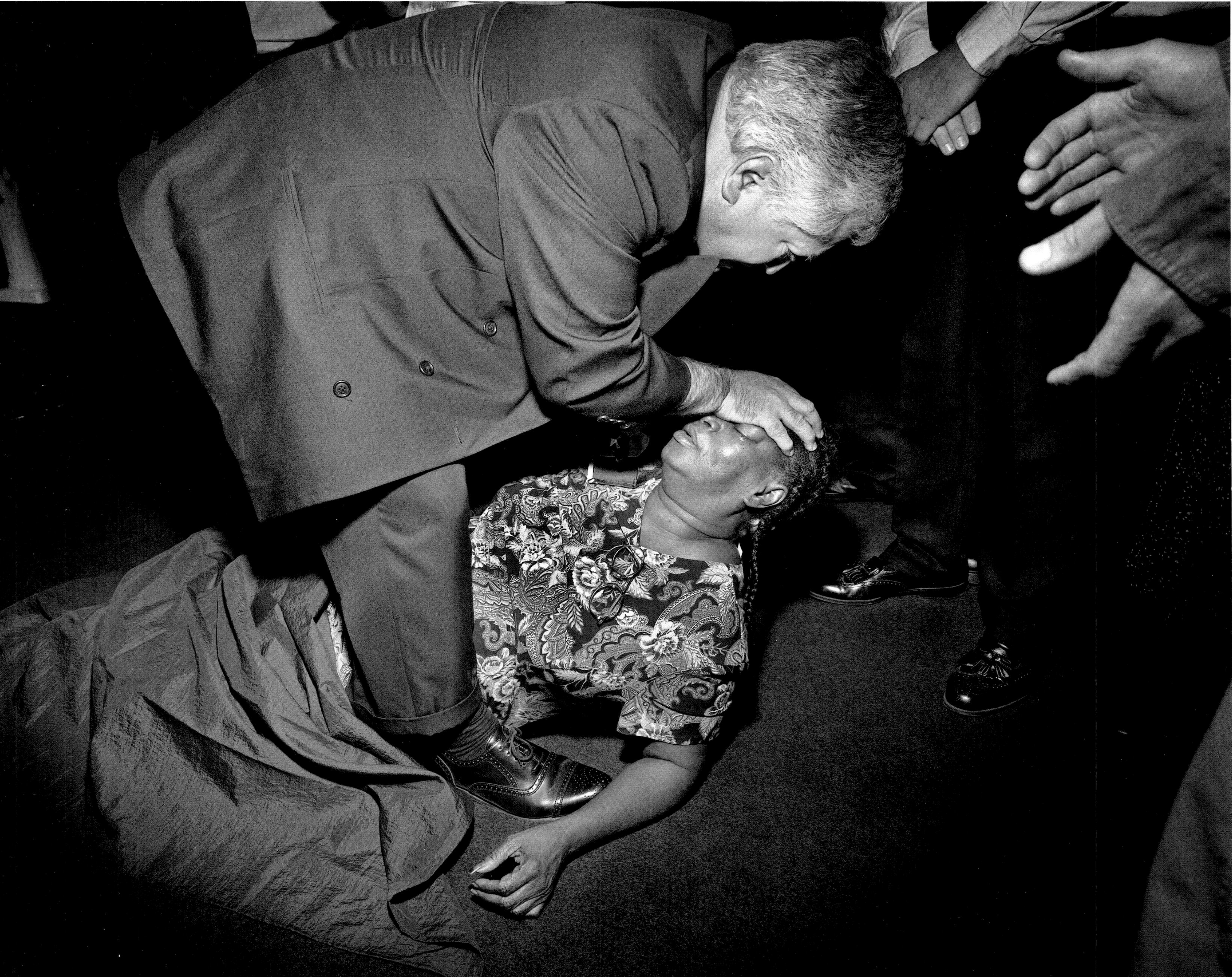

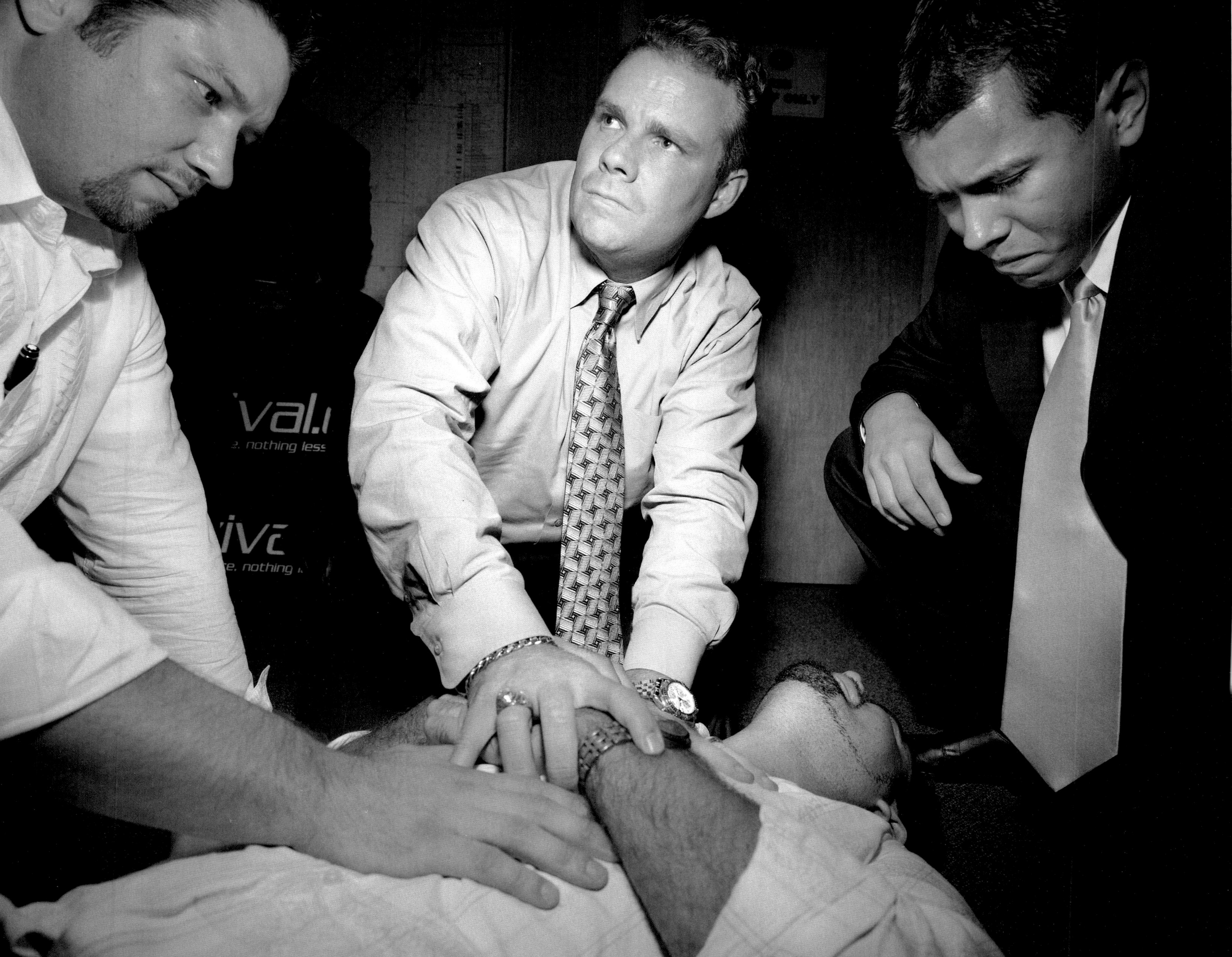
nothing less
nothing

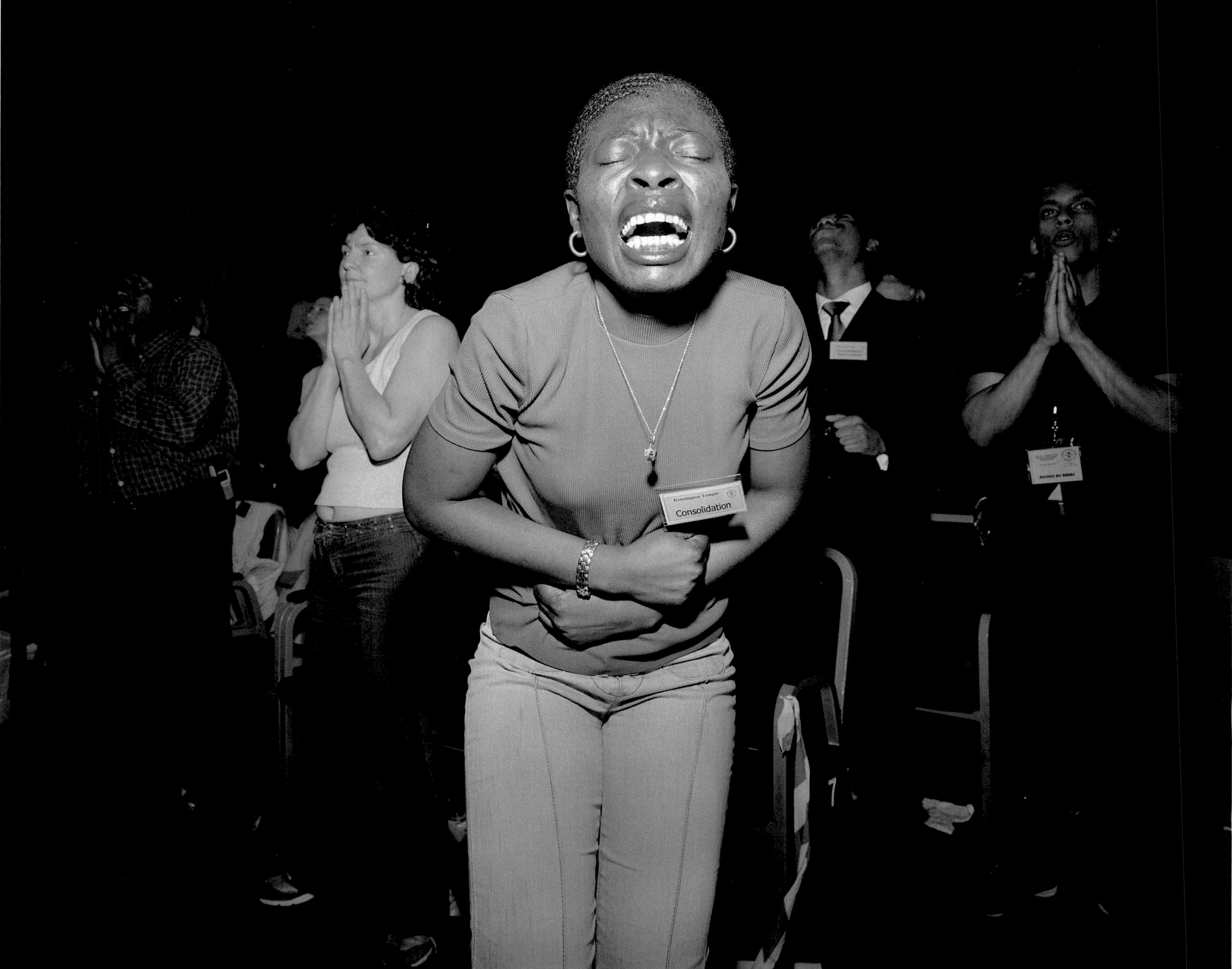
Kensington Temple
Consolidation

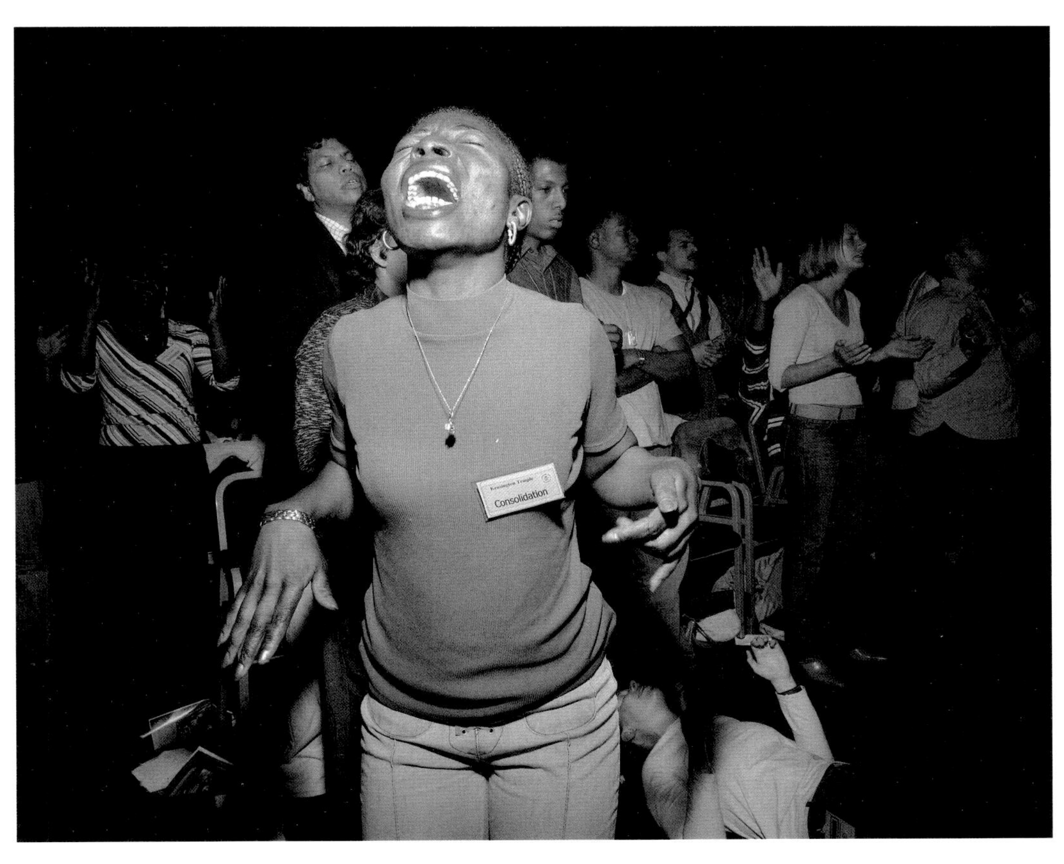
Consolidation

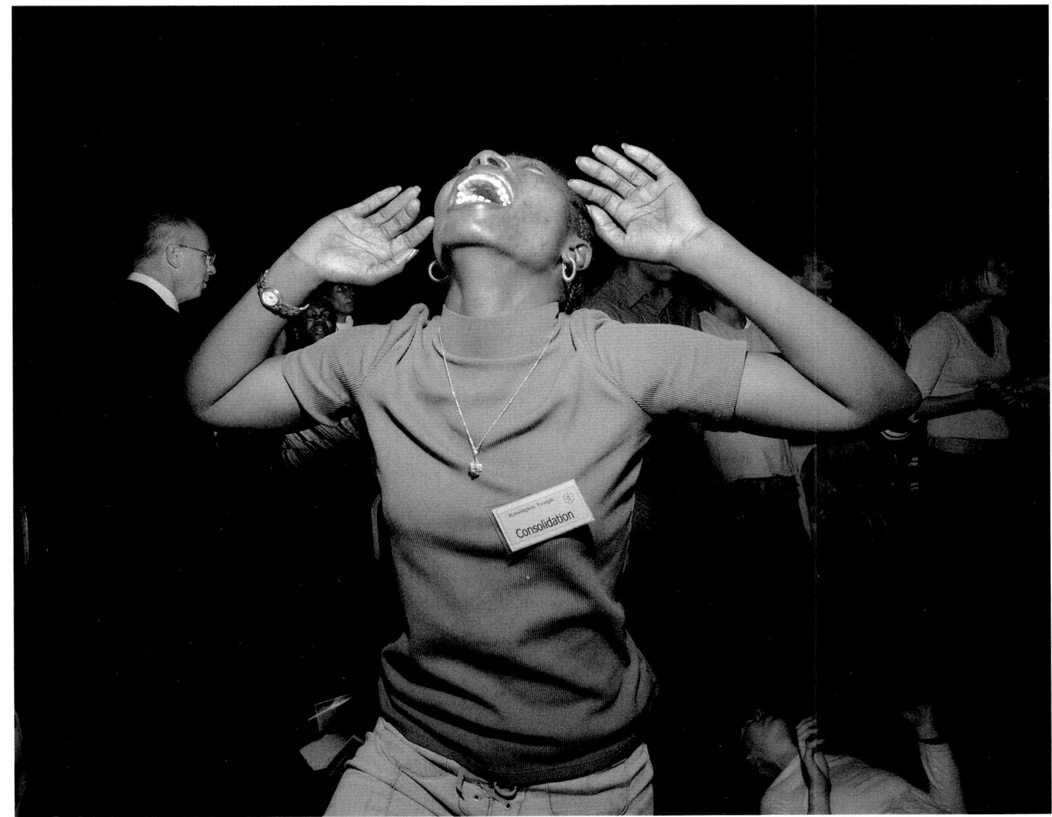
Consolidation

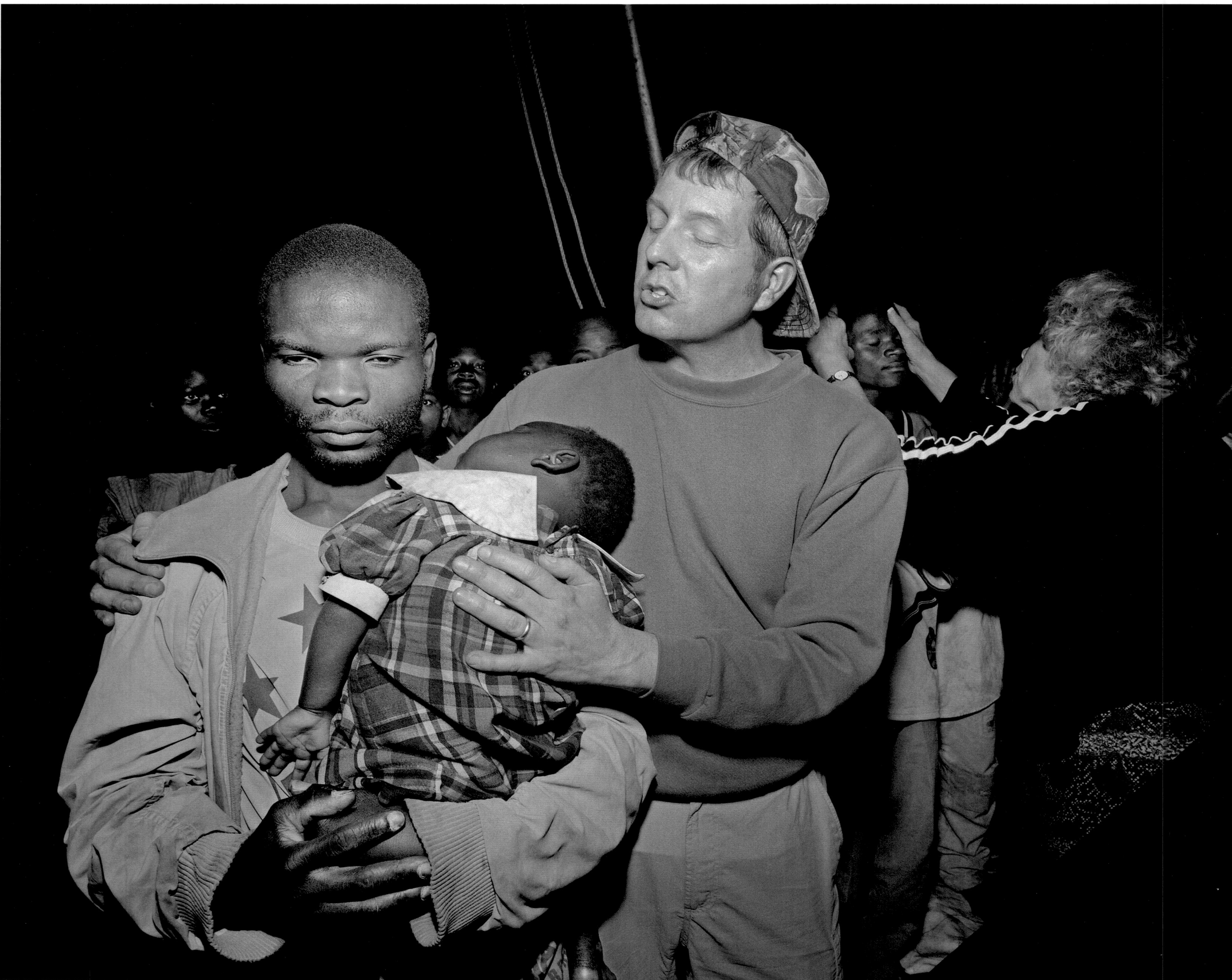

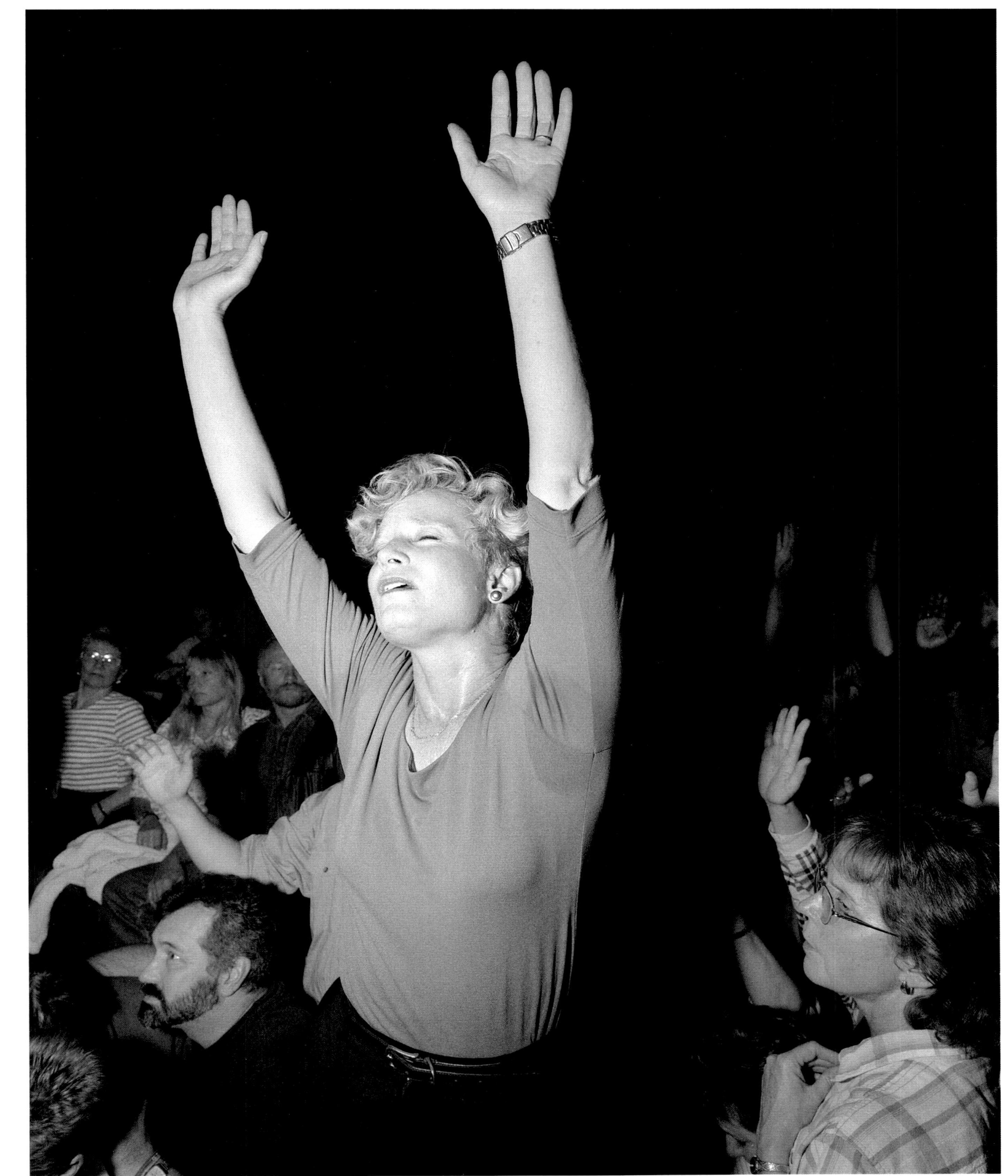

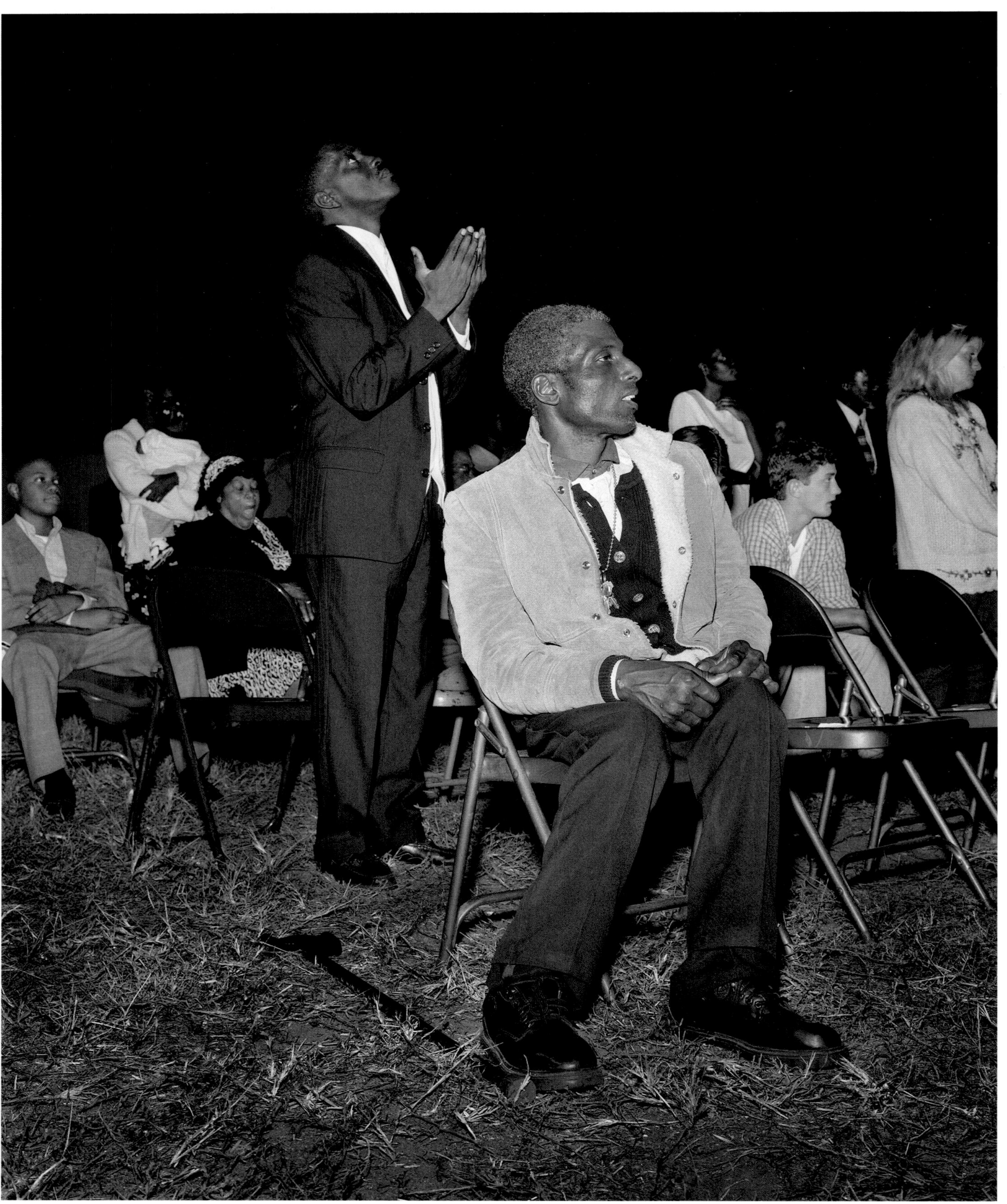

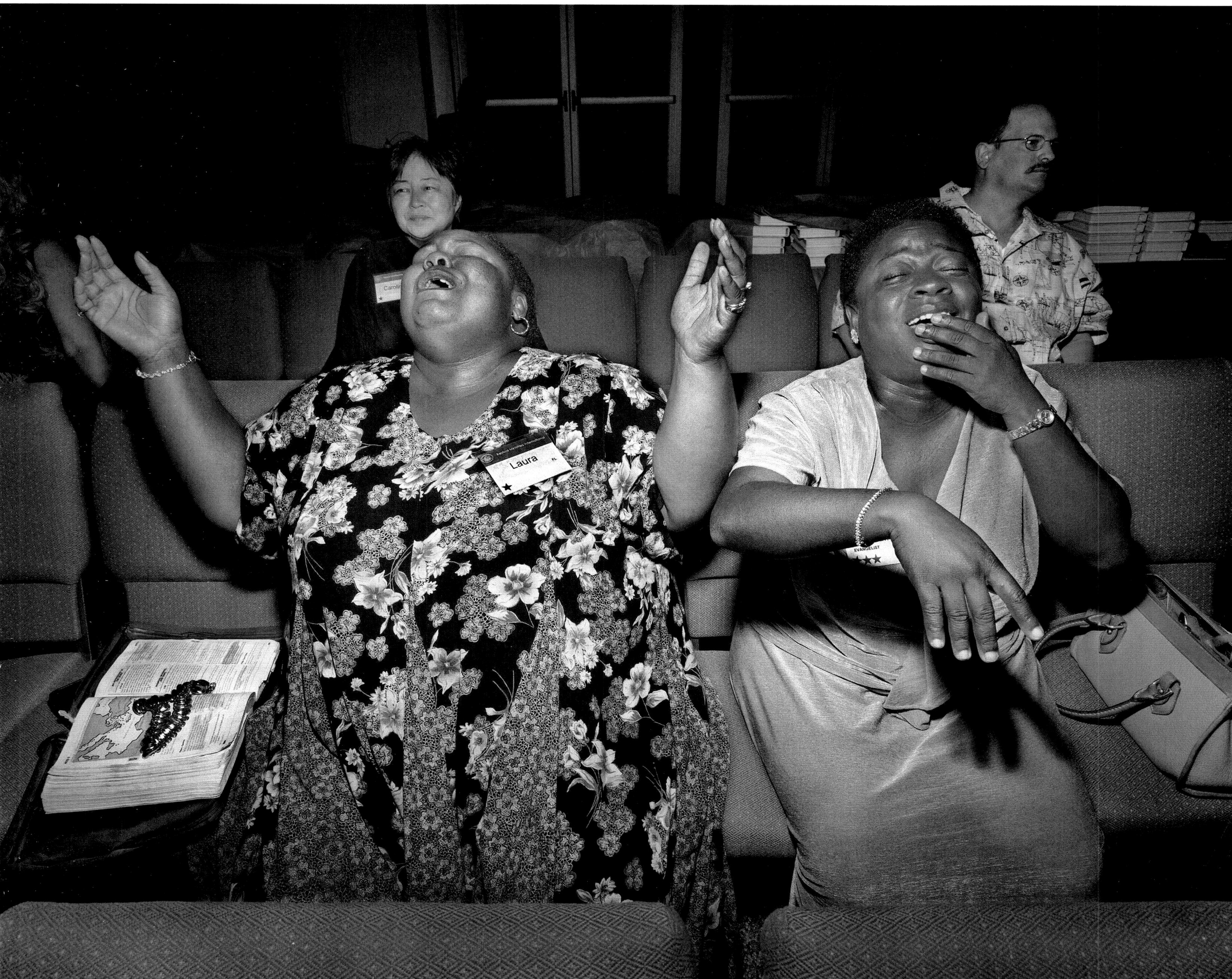
Laura
EVANGELIST

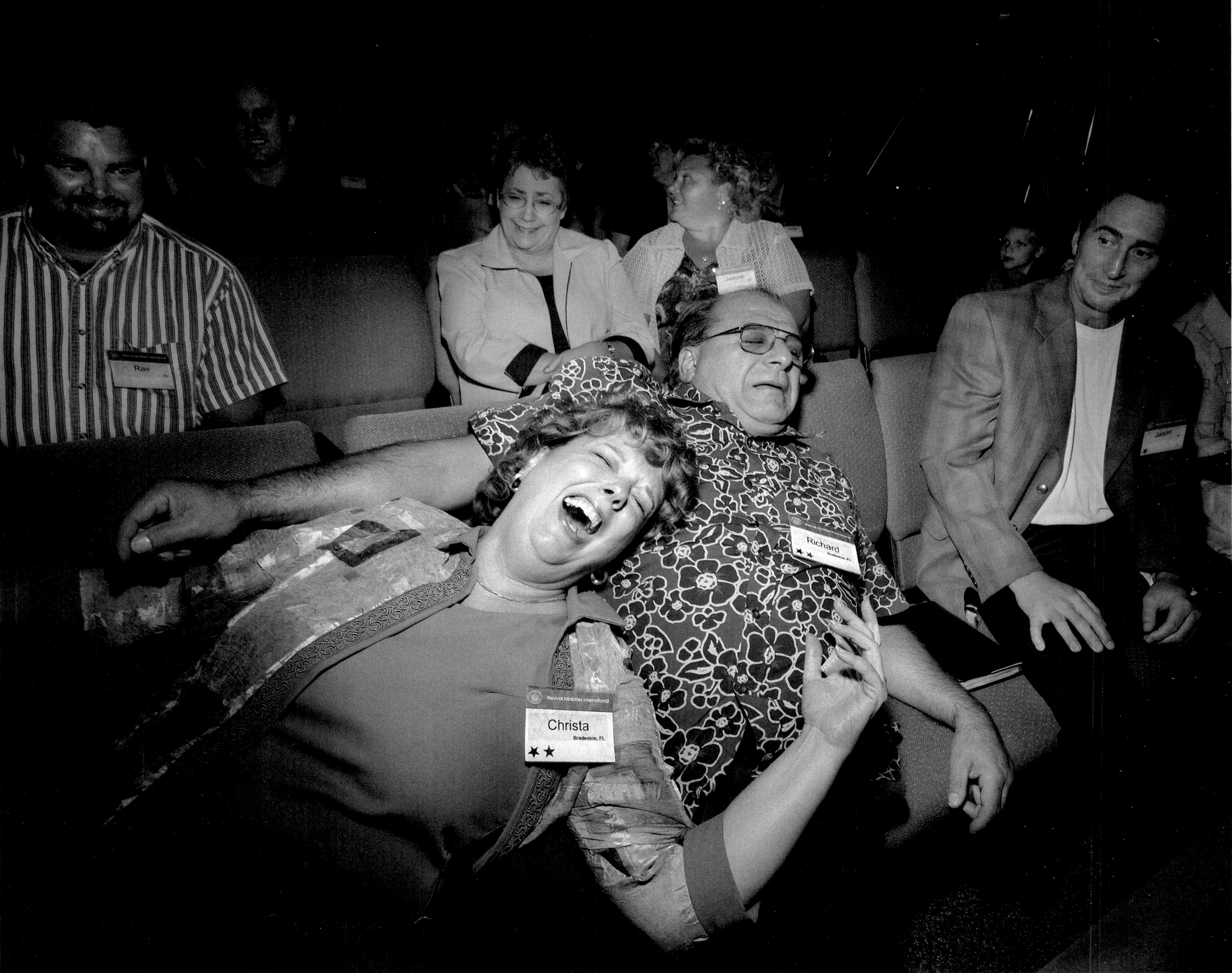

Ray
Revival Ministries International
Christa
Bradenton, FL
Richard
Jason

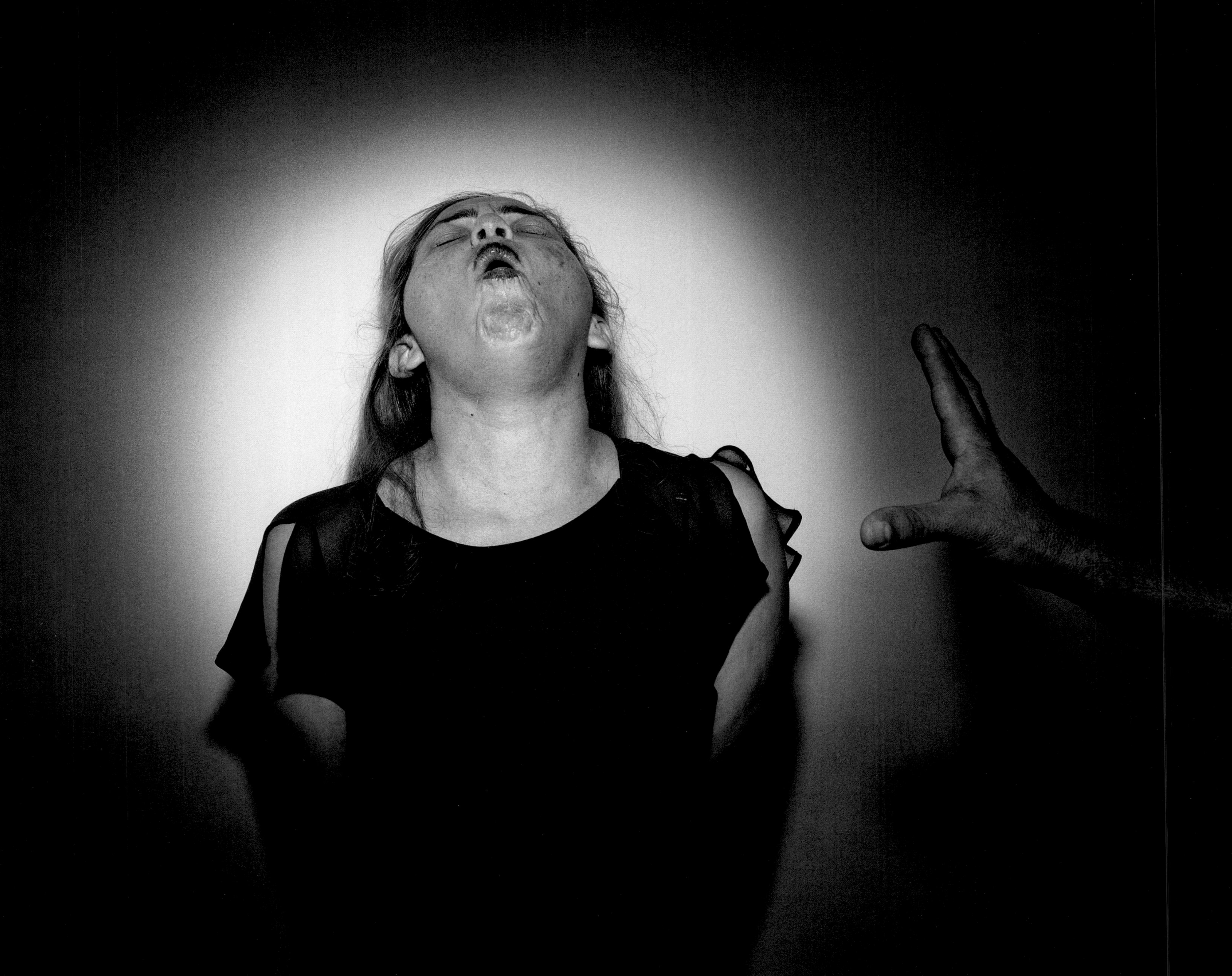

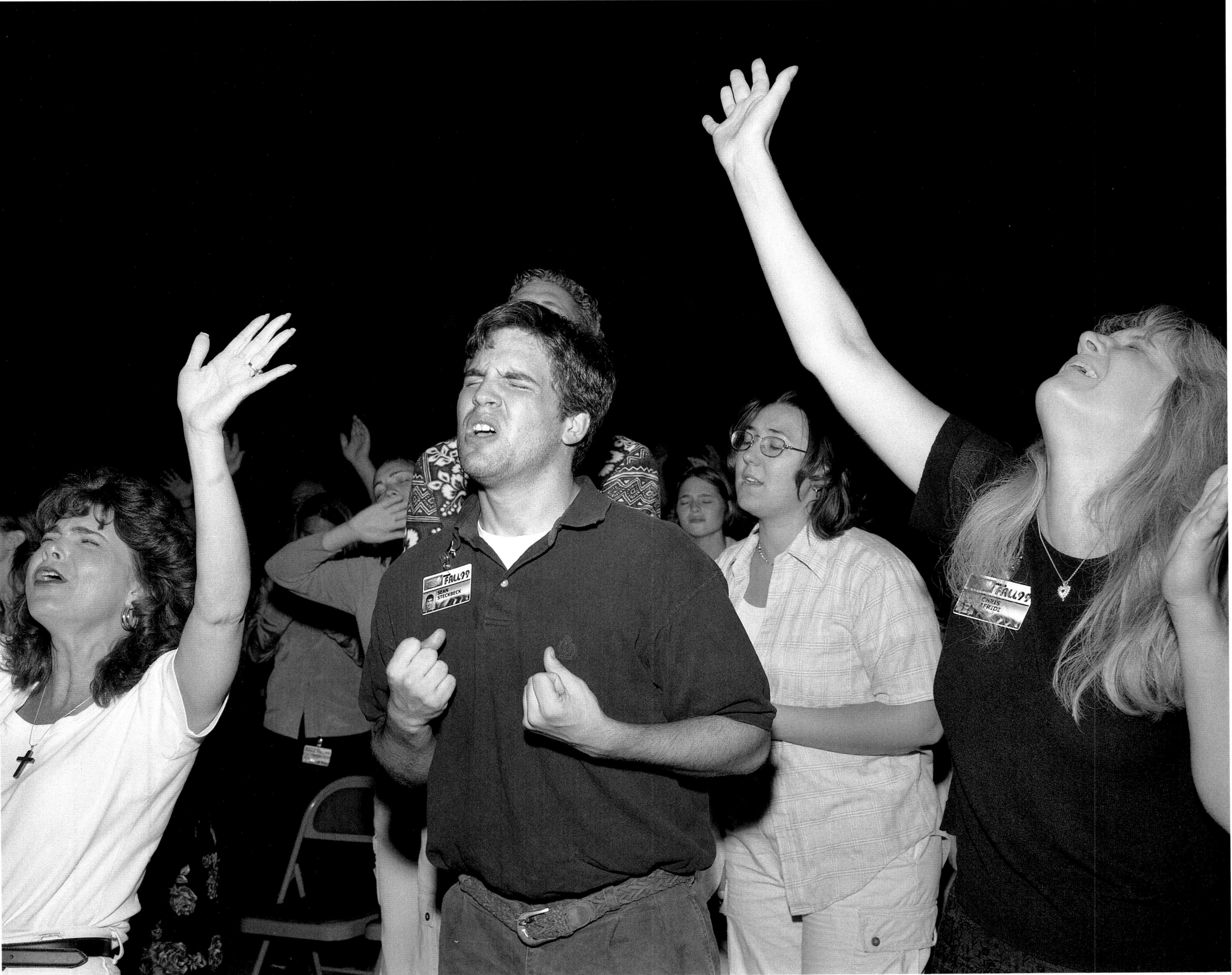
FALL99
SEAN
STECKBECK
FALL99
CHRIS
AFRIDI

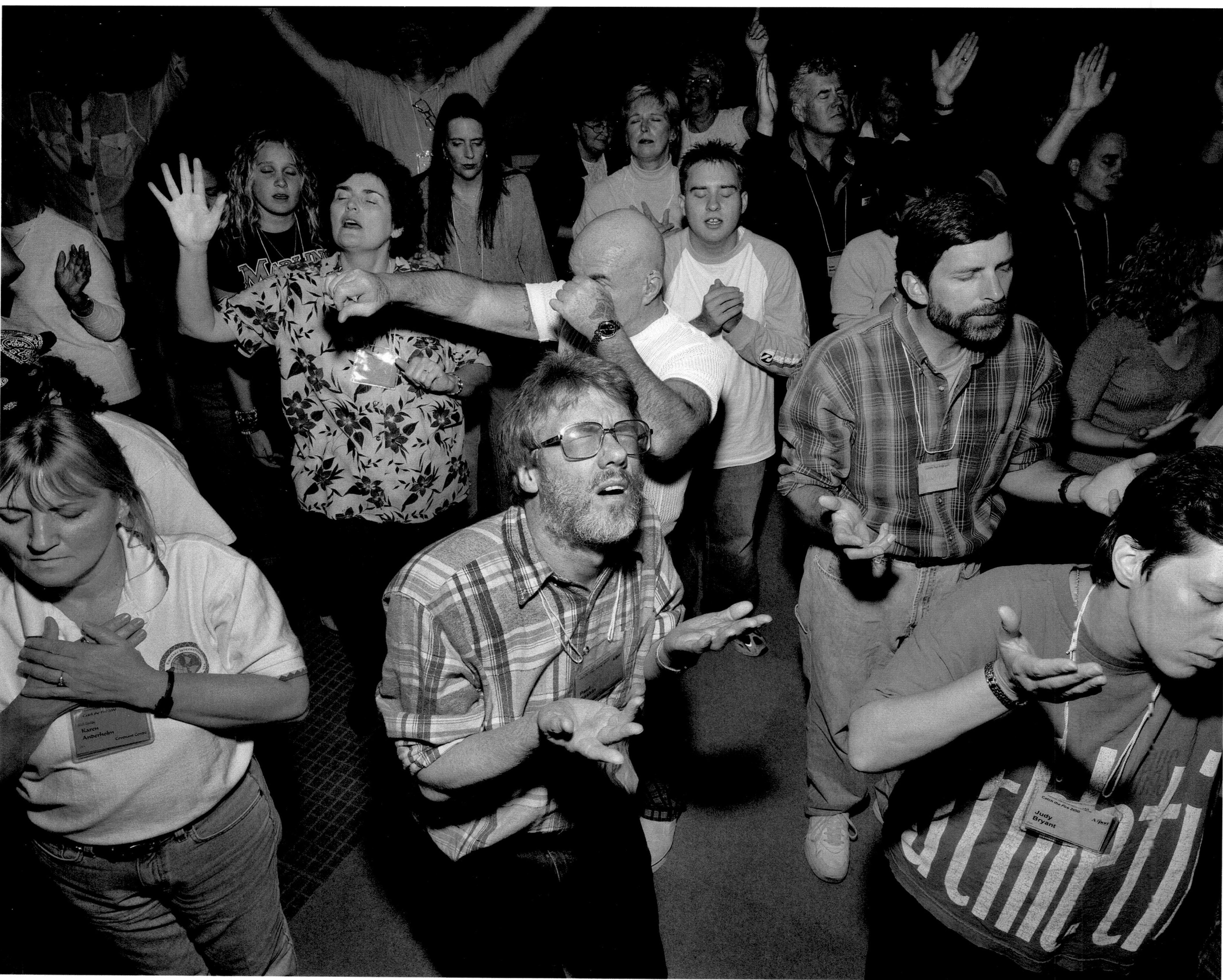
Karen
Anderholm
Covenant Centre
Catch the Fire 2000
Judy
Bryant

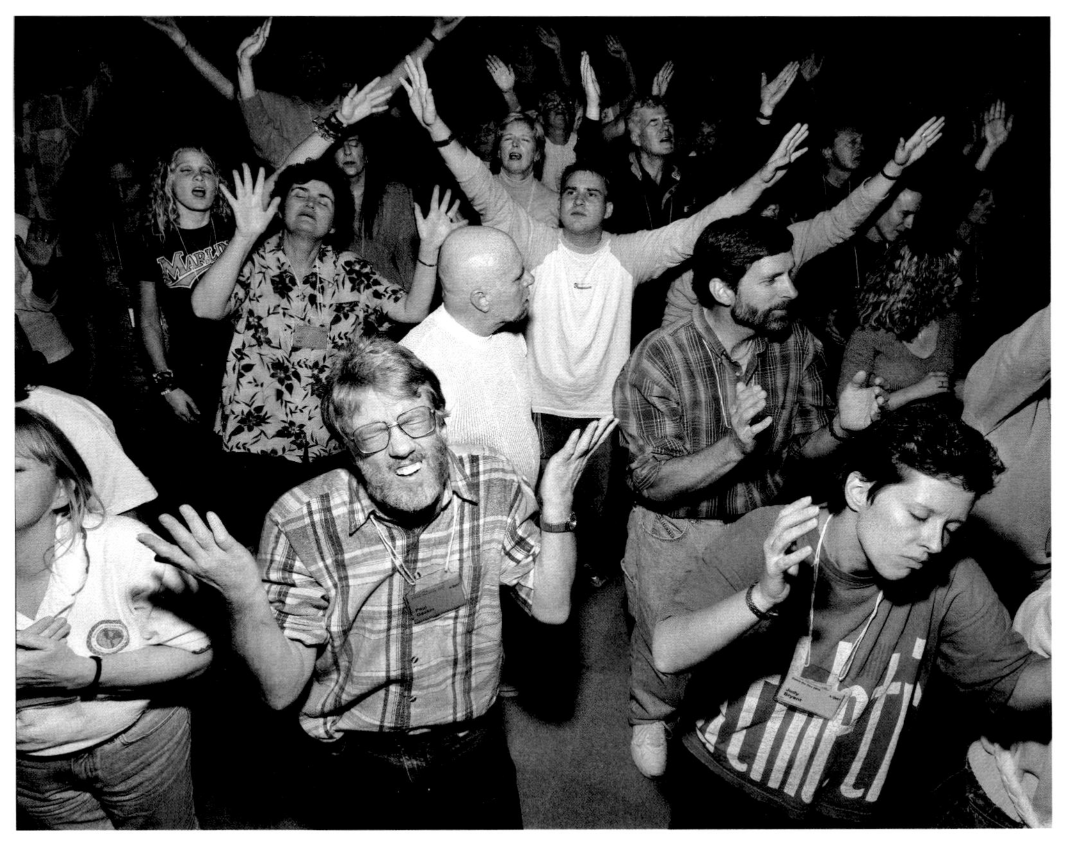

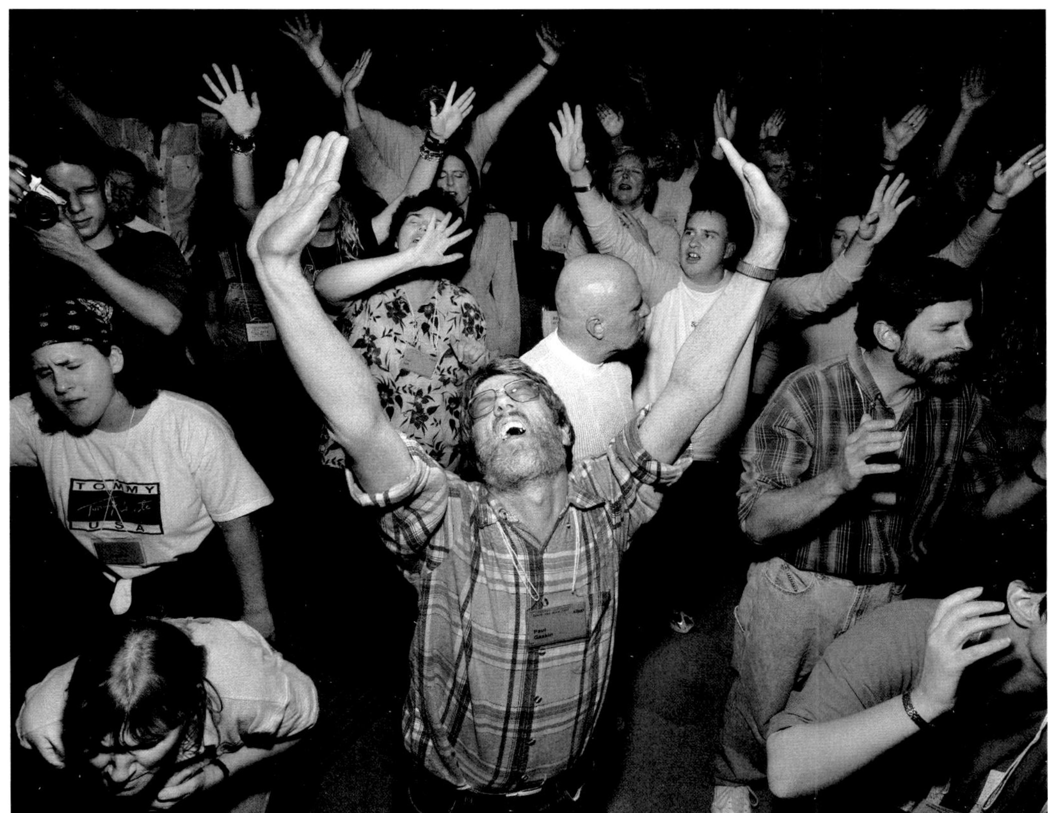
TOMMY
USA

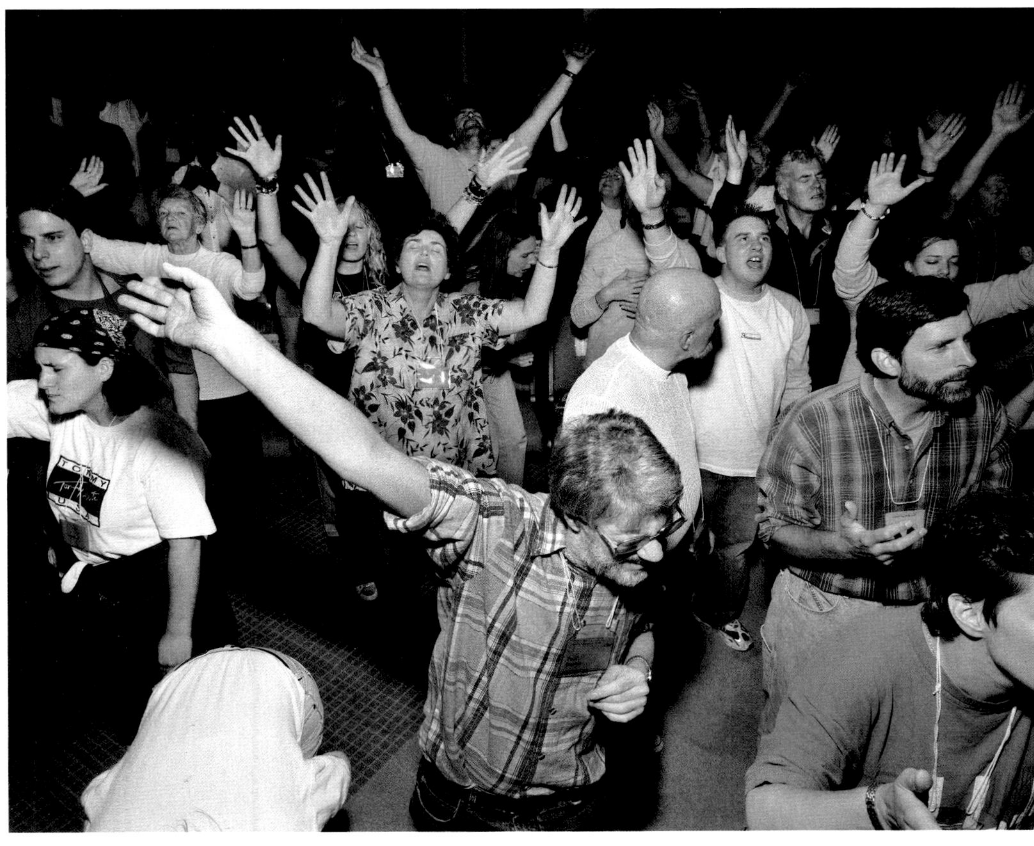
TOMMY

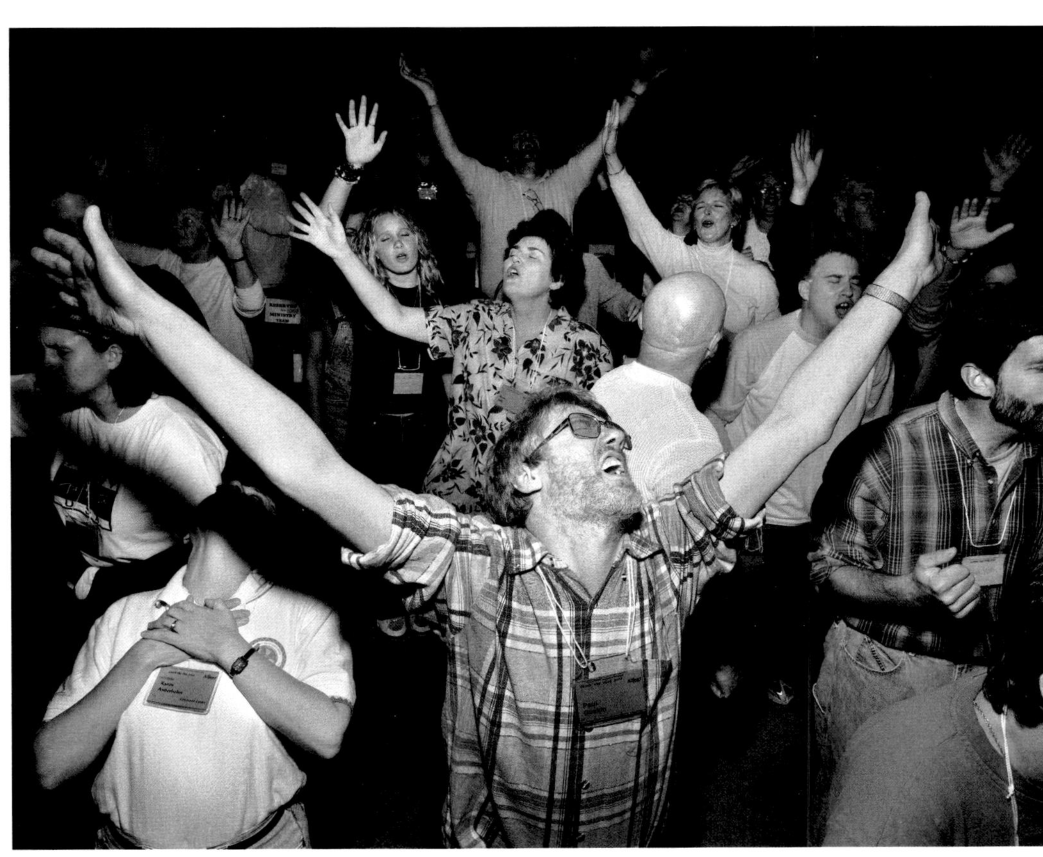

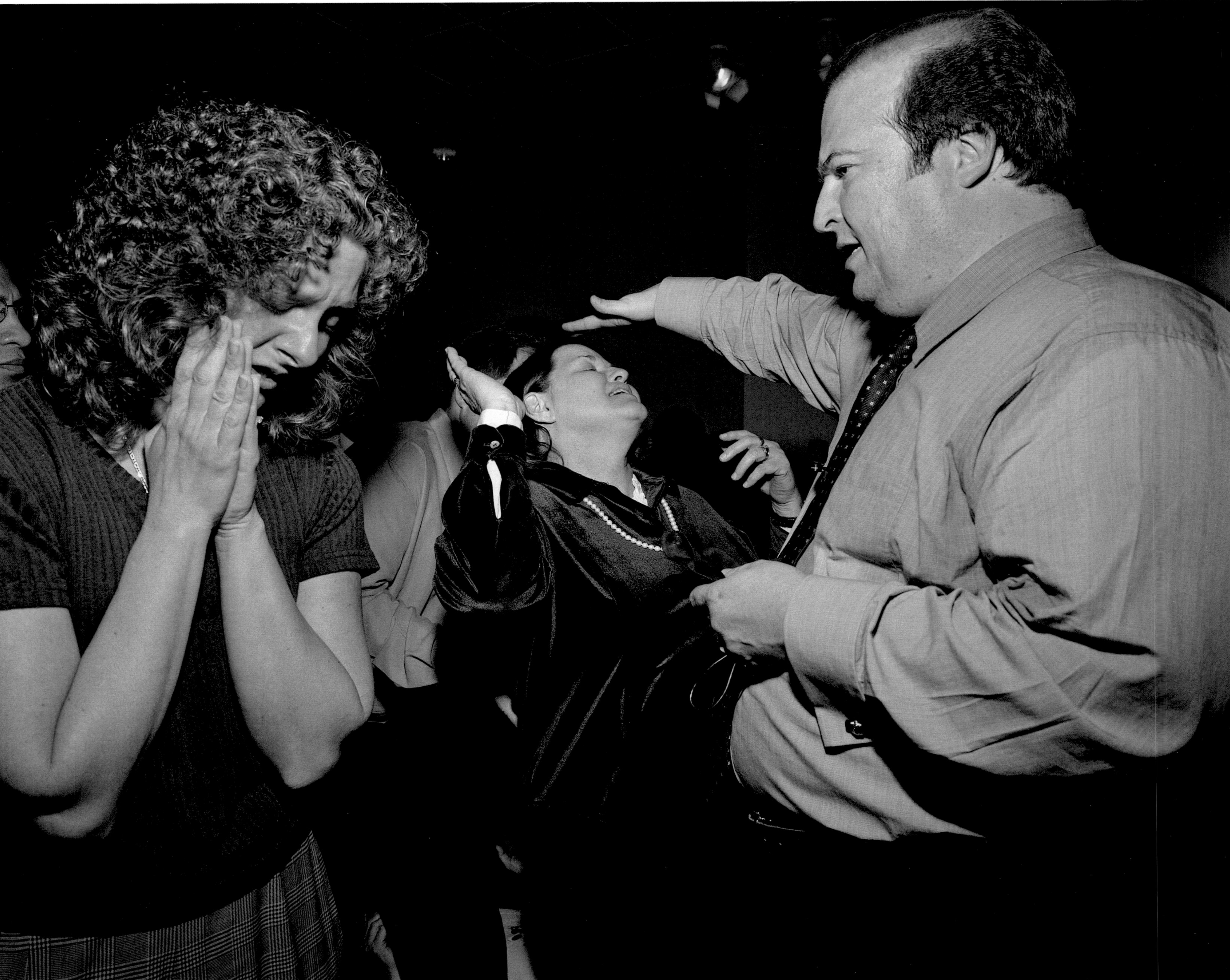

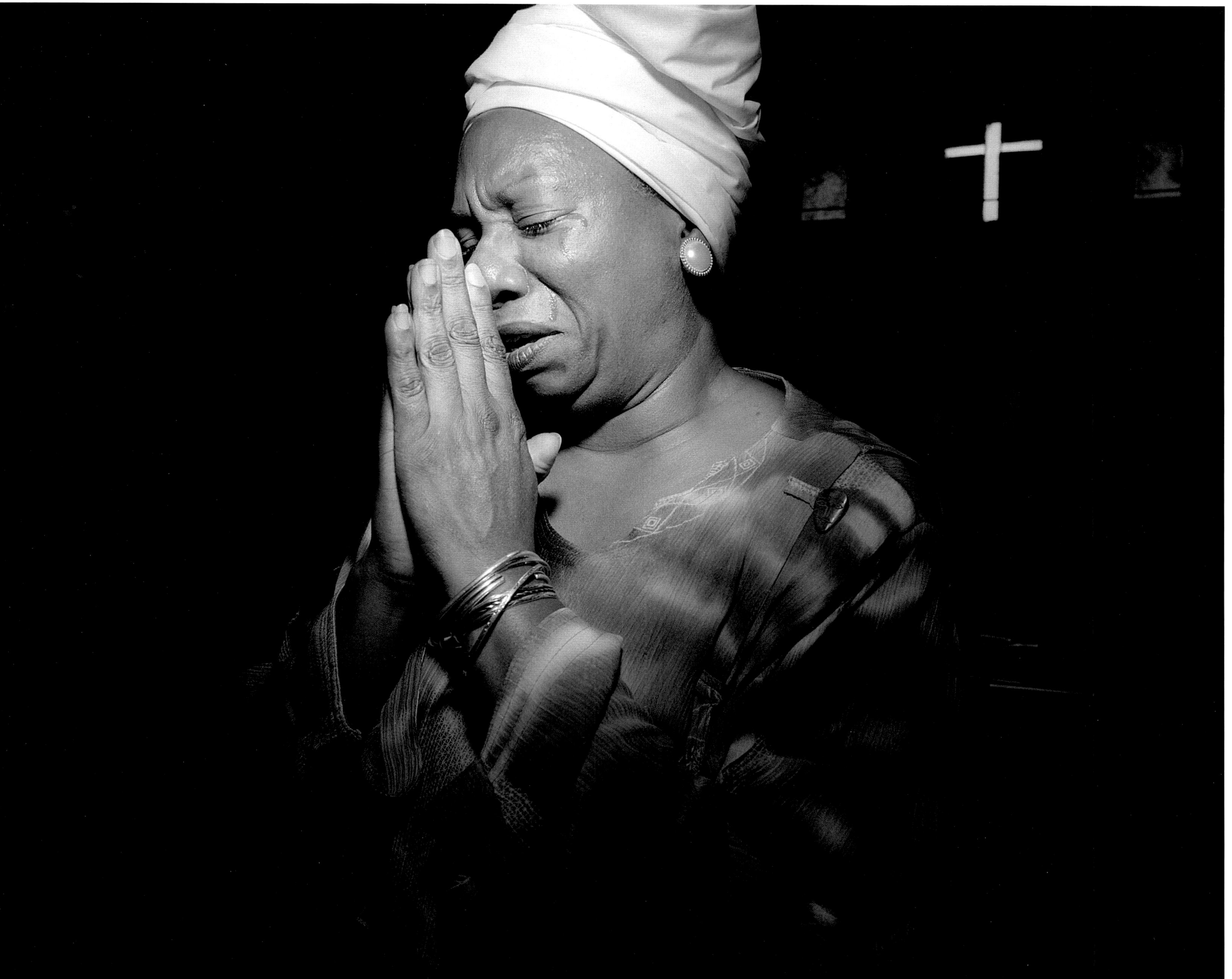

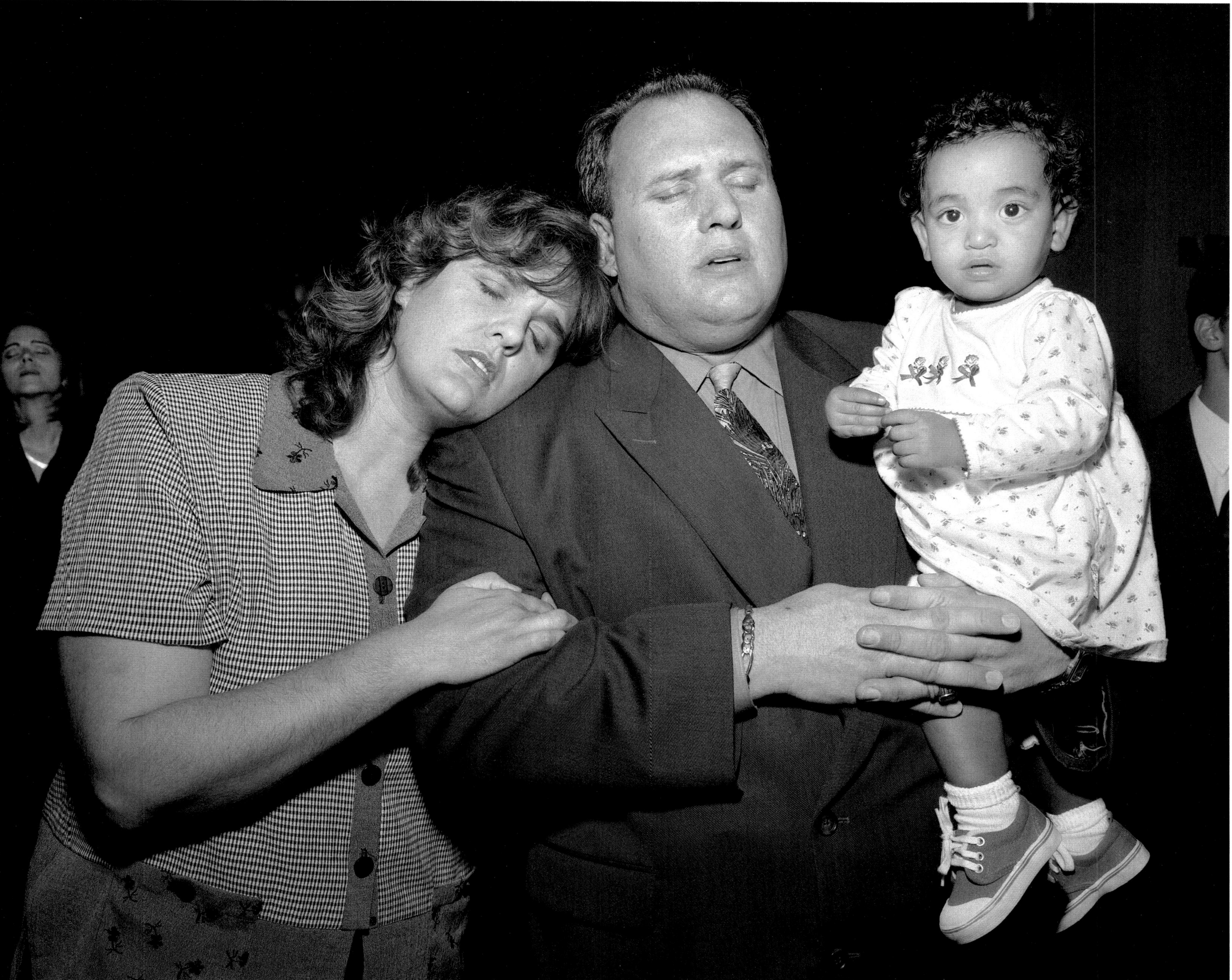

EVOLUTION OF THE MOMENT
A TESTIMONY BY STEVEN KATZMAN

"Come to the Miracle Tent. Come witness the blind see, the crippled walk, the deaf hear, the prostitute and drug addict be cured. Come to the Miracle Tent." I wasn't looking for salvation (I believed I already knew all of the answers to life's questions) nor did I need a pair of religious crutches from the Salvation Army. I was simply looking for subject matter to shoot for my next project, and the newspaper advertisement in the Sarasota *Herald-Tribune* in 1999 had all the criteria necessary for an interesting photo essay. Mankind in conflict; with himself, his world, and his God. "Place your hand on the TV screen and be healed."

It was a cold, brisk Sunday when I arrived at the Miracle Tent, pitched in a deserted parking lot across the street from the winter headquarters of the Chicago White Sox. "Greetings brother." This isn't the salutation of shabbat shalom I have experienced at the synagogue and the greeting made me uneasy. On the other hand, it had been years since I'd been to temple other than the obligatory Bar Mitzvah for my nephews. I had stopped attending the High Holy Days of Rosh Hashanah and Yom Kippur. Sometimes I would get the feeling that I should go to at least one of the holidays, just in case He does exist. But that would always pass. Why should I be judgmental of these decisions if I don't believe in God?

I felt immediately uncomfortable, not because I had twenty pounds of camera equipment tethered around my body, but because I had absolutely nothing in common with these people. I had more in common with the poor souls burning in the crematorium, which I had just finished documenting, than with these Christians looking for redemption. Religion has driven a wedge between mankind throughout the centuries, and tonight wasn't looking to be any different. I wasn't going to be someone's final solution, nor their ticket to salvation.

My presence didn't go unnoticed. I crouched down in the aisle with a press badge hanging around my neck, anticipating confrontation between myself, the congregation, and their minister. Suddenly the evangelist Leroy Jenkins pointed directly to me and exclaimed, "Faith has no religion! Do I hear an Amen? Do I hear an Amen?" The crowd returned with an, "Amen, hallelujah, praise the Lord."

And the word amen fell from my mouth.

That first service opened my eyes to a world that I was completely unaware of; an environment of pathetic people, poor dental work, and a driving search for unobtainable answers. At the same time I admired my subjects as I observed their passion through my lens, their commitment through prayer. Was life so difficult for these people that they could no longer come to any resolve other than to ask their God for forgiveness and redemption?

I felt strange intruding upon this private moment. Was I trespassing, violating a personal sanctuary, preventing these lost souls from communing with God? As I continued to document the Miracle Tent, I began to develop a relationship with my subjects—where disdain once walked, I now felt a sense of compassion for my fellow man.

The only comparable behavior I had ever witnessed was at a funeral. But inside the Miracle Tent people weren't dying, they were going through a primal scream. Tainted by the temptations of the flesh, the latest reality TV shows, and supermarket tabloids, they were trying to cast away their sins. This was God's emergency room, and I was drawn to it the same way I had been drawn to the crematorium like a moth flying to the light, getting too close to the heat. I was alive in the here and now, capturing such torment on film only reaffirmed my stability among the throng of lost souls being blinded by His light.

It was impossible to keep my mind away from the tent meetings, witnessing behavior that seemed almost pathological. I continued to document Leroy Jenkins' revival until the last Sunday in January brought the conclusion of the service, and the end of his camp meetings in Florida. The air-conditioned tent was taken down, its sides slowly deflating in the late afternoon sun, and scores of metal chairs were stacked into the semitrailer. The calm after the storm finally gave me an opportunity to really talk to some of the congregation. "What are you taking pictures for?" "I'm documenting personal faith, spiritual revival." "Have you ever been to Brownsville?" This was the third time I had been asked this question. Not wanting to appear ignorant of revival's epicenter, I always replied, "It's too far away. I can't afford to travel to Texas." This time I was immediately corrected: "Brownsville's in Pensacola." The following Monday I started to make arrangements for my trip to the Brownsville Assembly of God.

After making further inquiry I was told that I could photograph the service, providing that I only shoot during praise and worship, along the outer aisles of the church, and without a strobe. Upset and discouraged, I decided to cancel the trip. How would I be able to continue this project under those constrained conditions? But after further encouragement from my wife, Sharon, I committed to the eight-hour drive. Along with my strobe (just in case), medium format camera system, a borrowed 35mm, and high expectations, I was ready to confront whatever Brownsville had to offer.

When I arrived on Thursday afternoon and checked into the local Days Inn, I was surprised to see that they had a map in the lobby with directions to Brownsville. Surrounded by a depressed African-American neighborhood catered to by various Baptist churches, Brownsville Assembly of God is an oasis within this urban blight. I first saw its black metal fence, which seemed to be saying "Keep Out." Then I noticed the pristine, manicured lawns and a line of people stretching around the main chapel, baking in Florida's heat, sheltered by an occasional beach umbrella. It could have been for a rock concert or the World Series but, no, it was for a church service promising salvation and redemption through Jesus Christ.

Prior to Thursday's evening service I had a meeting with Dr. Michael Brown, director of the Brownsville Revival School of Ministry. I had shown Dr. Brown some of my previous work on caregivers, which depicted children's advocates, physicians, and children at risk. I was still uncomfortable showing the images I had shot at the Miracle Tent, but this was more of a reflection of my personal discomfort and the questions that had started to rise up inside of me then, only to be quickly dispelled and replaced with denial. Was I turning my back on my spiritual inheritance from the God of Abraham and ignoring the persecution of my ancestors at the hands of the very people I was documenting?

I could see that my work moved Dr. Brown, and we started to discuss the feelings I had encountered in the Miracle Tent. He then gave me his personal testimony—he was a Jew from an upper-middle-class family, his father was a senior lawyer in the New York Supreme Court, and his parents still lived happily married in Long Island. As a young man, ready to commit suicide with an overdose of thirty hits of mescaline, he went from LSD to PhD—he found Christ.

As we left his office, Michael assured me that he would be there for me in whatever capacity he could, photographically and spiritually. I mentioned the photographic restraints that the church had imposed. "You can shoot our student services Friday night after the main service." "I use flash." "No problem, the church and the school are separate. I'll tell the minister to expect you." I thanked him with an embrace of respect and admiration, and left his office feeling equally enlightened and confused. Am I the next poster boy? The visual voice for the next crusade?

As I walked down the hall, Dr. Brown's assistant, Scott Volk, mentioned that it is impossible to see Michael. "Pastors with congregations of ten to fifteen thousand members can't get an appointment and yet you are able to walk right in. You call from Sarasota, some photographer doing a series on revival and he doesn't say, 'Take a message.' He says, 'I'll talk to him now.' God bless you brother."

Upon arriving at the church, I was greeted by Kathy Woods, their staff photographer and my chaperon for this Thursday night's service. In her care, I felt immediately at ease. Without hesitation, I placed all of my trust with this perfect stranger. As the service began, Wendell Cooley, Brownsville's musical director, led a phenomenal ensemble. I was outside the velvet rope, in the required attire against the walls, shooting at the religious mosh pit in front of me. I had never witnessed such mass pandemonium. I quickly became frustrated because I knew that, limited by the church's restrictions, these decisive moments would only become memories. As I finished the first roll of film I realized that A, there wasn't a rewind lever on the camera, and B, my glasses were in the car. Unable to see the fine print—"PHD," push here dummy—I couldn't rewind the film on the unfamiliar camera. I became discouraged, impatient, and angry, questioning why I bothered coming up to Pensacola.

Since I couldn't remove the film, I had no other choice than to listen to the service. Being Jewish, I was unaccustomed to church services, especially a service that lasts over four hours! Since I was with Kathy we were in the "best" seats. Yes, I was in the best seat in the house without a camera. Then an opportunity presented itself when we were on the balcony. I suddenly heard shouts and screams from men and women. Were these the same people who stood in line all day waiting to be prayed for? Not being able to locate the source, I leaned over the balcony railing to witness the killing fields—slain bodies, lying on top of each other, some keeping still in a blissful slumber while others jerked and twitched in epilepticlike seizures. Another missed photo-op. Kathy Woods saw the utter amazement on my face and, over the sounds that filled the sanctuary, turned to me and asked, "Would you like to go down into that?" Without hesitation, I replied, "Yes."

A whirlwind of energy surrounded Stephen Hill, Brownsville's evangelist—he was laying hands. Hill was the eye of the hurricane as people shoved against each other in a six foot deep mob, demanding to be prayed for. These were the same people that stood in the sun earlier in the day, patiently waiting to be seated in the main sanctuary for the evening service. With great trepidation, I found myself standing in the foyer. The doors opened and slammed against the walls. The tidal surge pressed against me. There were bodies dropping, screams, laughter. I am held, I am touched, I am prayed for, in His name. I feel my blood, warmed by prayer, racing down from my head, shoulders, arms, legs, and knees. I am out. I am down, I am crying, twitching, and embarrassed. I am frightened. I am a Jew!

When I opened my eyes the storm had passed; bodies lay strewn in its wake. Sobbing, I got up to seek refuge in a corner. "Steven, you're supposed to stay down so the Lord can have more time to work on you." "For Christ sake, I've been circumcised, I've been bar mitzvahed. I'm not supposed to be on the ground so the Lord can work on me!"

The service over, I drove back to the motel, knowing that my life would never be the same again.

The following morning I called my wife. Before I could get the words out of my mouth, she said, "You did it didn't you." "How did you know?" "Because you get totally involved with everything you do." "I know, but this is different. I can't explain it...losing all sense of self-control. It's a feeling, a sensation that I've never experienced before. The heat, the fire inside. It's like a chemical rush without the withdrawal, without all of the negative symptoms, without all of the toxins that I've violated my body with. They call it the Holy Spirit. This is crazy, but I want more." "Be careful." "I love you." "I love you too."

That Friday night the service started as usual—music, praise, and worship. I figured out how to use the camera this time and shot a few rolls from the sidelines, still outside the velvet rope. This time my chaperon was Kathy Woods' best friend, Sharon. Again, I put my trust in the hands of a total stranger.

Sharon had just introduced me to a few members of the prayer team when another group came rushing past, carrying a young woman who was struggling to free herself from her captors' grip. Seeking refuge in a small room, they slammed the door shut behind them and demonic sounds began emanating from behind the closed door. "The Devil," Sharon explained. I was too dumbfounded to utter a reply. I had never heard such evil sounds other than at the movies. The noises defied human description and, at that moment, I vowed that I would never let an opportunity like that escape me again.

During Stephen Hill's sermon, "Die Right," I began to reflect upon my personal life. I hadn't believed in God in such a long time, perhaps because of what Rabbi Kripke once told me: "God will only exist in a man's heart once he becomes totally mature and at peace with himself." Hence no need for any dogmatic belief system, external or internal. I am very aware that it was possible to have misunderstood the rabbi. After all, I was an impressionable eighteen-year-old going through a personal hell with my family, fathering a child I still don't know to this day.

I survived two broken marriages, and then met Sharon, my third wife of sixteen years. I felt deeply fulfilled and enriched in our relationship. I was at peace with my parents. I felt that I could leave this world without regretting that I never said "I love you." I would have liked to think that I had learned something from falling down and getting back up along the way. But what about the other people in my life? I wasn't ready or prepared to meet my maker, let alone believe in one. Nor was I ready to forgive and ask them for forgiveness.

As the sermon continued, I was overcome with emotion, grief, and pain. Deep anguish burned in my gut, poison ran through my veins—I was being pulled down from the weight of all my crap, gasping for air only to be sucked down again into my personal undertow. My screams of despair became one with the congregation. I was the lost soul in my photographs.

And then there was an altar call. A young man saw my torment and came up to me. "Would you like to kneel with me before Christ?" I could barely see him through my swollen eyes. Mucus pouring from my nose, tears splattering off my camera, I looked up and shook my head, declining his offer. Sharon asked if I would like her to accompany me to the bloodline, a strip of red tape on the sanctuary floor, symbolizing Calvary. I muttered, "Yes."

Up until then I had been unable to forgive those that hurt me the most. Kneeling at the bloodline, I raised my hands above my head, as if to surrender. Suddenly Tracy, my first wife and the mother of my son, comes through me. I am forced face down into the carpet, the concrete floor preventing my forehead from going through it. Who slammed me to the floor with such force? Where did she come from? I can't lift myself upright. This isn't about staying on the floor so "God can work on you." Helpless and paralyzed, I can't raise myself up. Tracy leaves my gut, and as suddenly as I was thrown down on the floor I am back up on my knees. All is safe. I forgive. NO! I am thrown down to the carpet again with greater force, greater screams. Oh God help me, forgive me. Now my sister is laying in my gut. Where did she come from? I thought she was buried deep inside my mind. No need for her then, no need for her now. I can't hear the screams of those around me, only my own, I am drowning out the congregation of two thousand people. I am one voice for so many. I am the face for all of those in the parking lot. I find myself back up, looking towards the dais, my swollen eyes making contact with Michael Brown. "Please help me."

Our eyes meet and without warning I am back on the floor, forehead stuck to the carpet. Another primal scream. Who is next, who must I forgive in order to be free of this torment? Justin, my son who I raised until I kicked him out of my house at age sixteen. Justin, who carries my birthright, and those of my ancestors Abraham, Isaac, and Jacob. More tears, the carpet in front of me is soaked with my fluids. I am the new poster child of spiritual death and rebirth. Waiting for another wave of despair and torment, I slowly rise, expecting more screams and tears of anguish. Nothing. I wait. Nothing.

I suddenly realized that an immense weight had been lifted from my shoulders. Three times I found my forehead pinned to the carpet, asking for forgiveness by three people who have deeply impacted my life. The cleansing had an immediate impact on me, physically and mentally, and through this healing process I realized that my journey was now far different from the one I had originally embarked on.

The church had given me a digital camera to shoot the service for their website. I was now inside the velvet rope, but I was still under no condition to photograph during the altar call or shoot any faces. This strict policy was posted at the doors prior to entering the main sanctuary as well as announced at the start of every service. After my personal burden was lifted, a photo-op presented itself to me on the bloodline. I rose to my knees, lifted up the digital camera, took aim, and fired—once, twice, a third time. Unknown to me, five ushers rushed to stop me but were immediately waved off by Pastor Kilpatrick from the pulpit. From that time on I was permitted to photograph at the Brownsville Assembly of God with my medium format camera and strobe, during the altar call.

I returned to my preferred seating along with Sharon, crying a different song. I felt alive, wanting to share my experience. I had prayed to God for His forgiveness, a God that I had buried alongside a dead bird in Omaha, Nebraska when I was five years old.

After the altar call, I was prayed for by Michael Brown. Unlike the previous night, I had gone through some radical spiritual surgery. Evidently I hadn't gotten everything out on the bloodline. Again I'm down, clutching my sides in a fetal position, afraid that my organs will explode. I hold myself even tighter, rocking back and forth as if I'm trying to do that last sit-up for the President's Challenge Physical Fitness Award.

I finally make it to my feet, walking down the aisles where I sense a greater presence of His spirit. Pastor Kilpatrick sees this lost lamb and prays for me. I go down suddenly, hitting my head on the corner of a wall. Concern arises, evidently from the force of the blow. I don't feel anything; I am out, letting God do his work on me. I awake, there are just a few of us who remain from a congregation of two thousand. Elvis has left the building.

It is now 1 A.M. Saturday morning and I am drunk on the Holy Spirit.

I forced myself to sober up in order to get to a photo shoot at the School of Ministry. Once I reached the campus, I was met by a young ministry student whose responsibility was to ensure that my work was not interrupted or impeded by any misconceptions from the other students. Late every Friday night, the students would gather in the lecture hall to have their own special service after they returned from ministering on the mean streets of Pensacola. The service was very unstructured: music, praying, and more praying. When I arrived, students were still drifting in one at a time, worshiping in their own personal way, smiling, laughing, crying—faces distorted in pain, trying to get closer to God, closer to His face.

When enough students had arrived, a minister asked them to come up to the "river" and pray for those going into the mission fields. He asked the students to tell of their illnesses. Responses varied from a sore throat, muscle ache, and bad knees. All of this time I was thinking that they were missing the point. We were talking illness, not some minor inconvenience. Then a young girl raised her hand. "I have melanoma." There was uncomfortable silence. My personal pain was no longer important, praying for this dying girl was, and the laying of hands began, the fevered pitch of prayer, crying for His strength, for His works, wonders, and miracles.

She filled my viewfinder—"The Lost World: Jehovah's Park" scrawled across her T-shirt. Then more praying, shouting, more photographs. She clutched her throat as if to strangle the cancer within. I could no longer think let alone shoot. As I cried, tears found their way into my viewfinder. I sat down, weak from my own spiritual episode and continued to clean off my viewfinder in vain, trying to catch my breath. Then I started the whole cycle over again—shooting, crying, and praying for this young girl.

During this process, a young man saw my distress and asked if he could pray for me in the midst of all of this spiritual chaos. At that moment I realized that I was no longer a stranger shooting from the outside. I was now inside the velvet rope, on the inside looking out.

I left the student service around 3 A.M. Saturday morning to prepare myself for the long ride back to Sarasota. What would my life be like when I returned home? I had so many unanswered questions. Mentally and physically drained, I was afraid of what lay ahead.

That Sunday evening I received a call from Justin's mother. We had previously communicated only through court-ordered arbitration, but now I listened, and gave her advice and comfort about the difficulties of raising our son. She listened with no animosity, and I was able to quietly go to sleep without anxiety or anger. The following day my sister called after a two-year exile. I told her how excited I was to be a part of the plans for her son's Bar Mitzvah and that I loved her. Tuesday arrived and I met with Justin for the first time in over a year and a half.

Two years later during an exhibit of this work I gave a lecture at a local university. The question would always arise, "Why revival?" I began to explain that I saw an advertisement in the local newspaper, "Come witness the blind see, the crippled walk, the deaf hear. . . ." I have always been interested in the unusual; those people, places, and things that exist on the periphery of society, seemingly non-existent, not conforming to the mainstream. At that moment, I experienced an epiphany in front of the college audience. Recalling the words from the newspaper ad, I suddenly realized that "it was I who had been blind, it was I who had been crippled, it was I who had been deaf."

JANUARY 2005

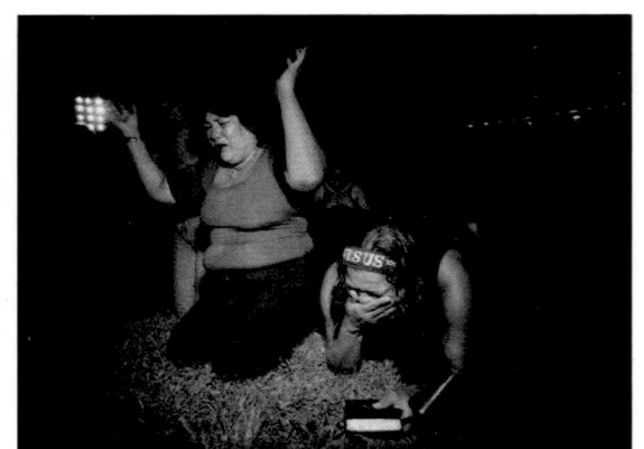

Global Awakening, Belem, Brazil, 2004

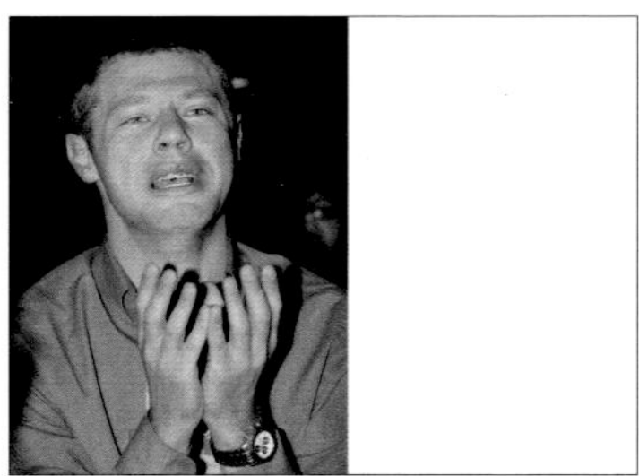

Toronto Airport Christian Fellowship,
Toronto, Canada, 1999

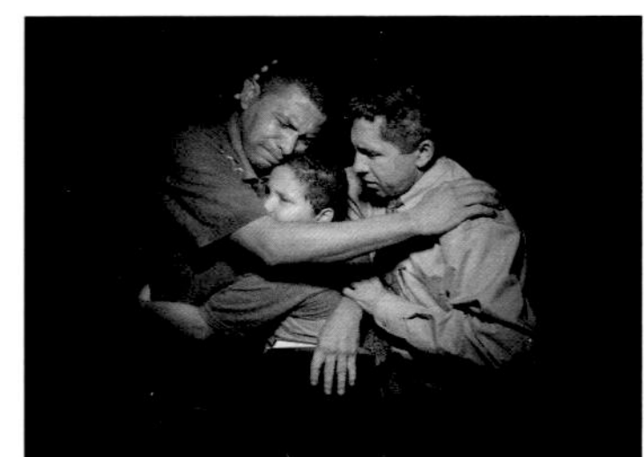

Global Awakening, Fortaleza, Brazil, 2004

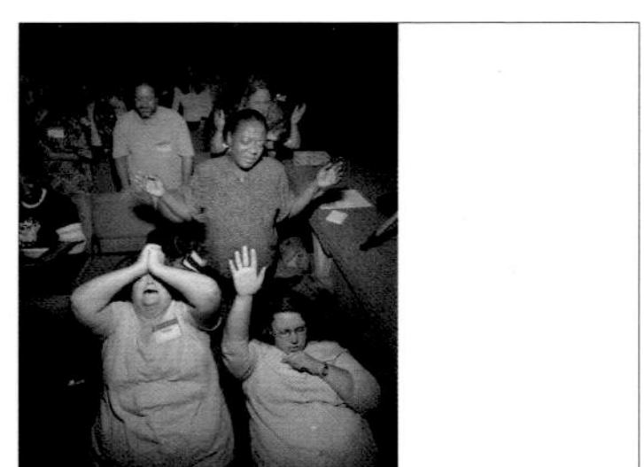

Revival Ministries International, Tampa, FL, 2004

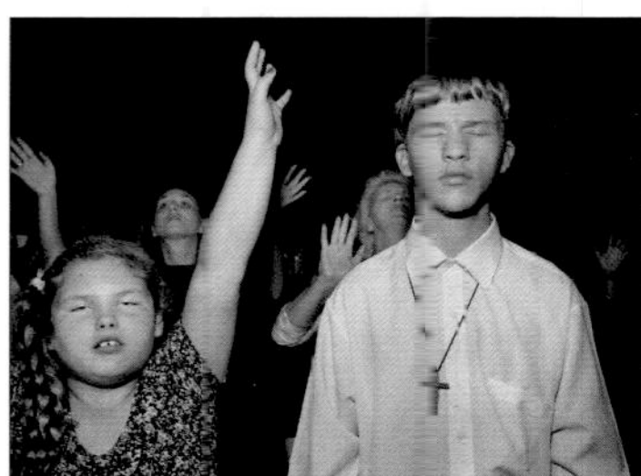

Miracle Tent, Sarasota, FL, 1999

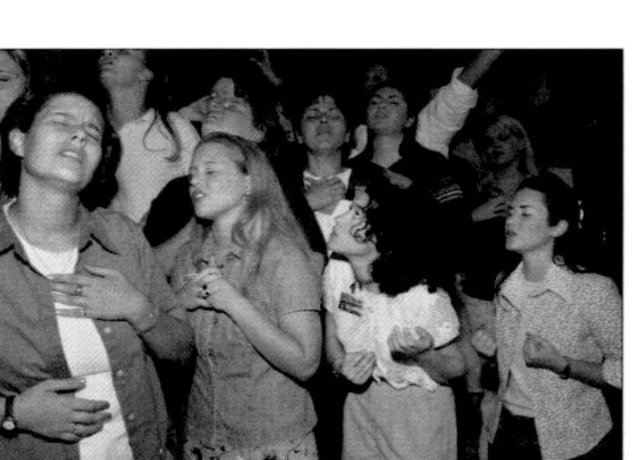

Brownsville Assembly of God, Pensacola, FL, 1999

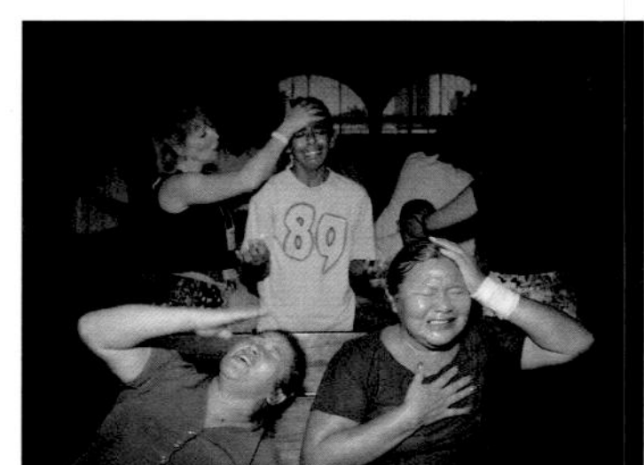

Global Awakening, Belem, Brazil, 2004

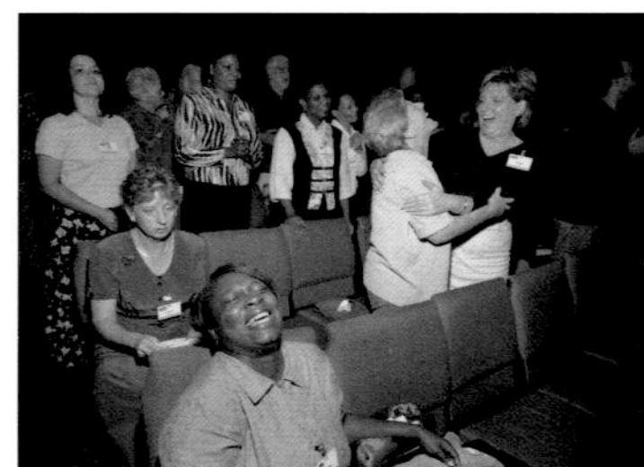

Revival Ministries International, Tampa, FL, 2003

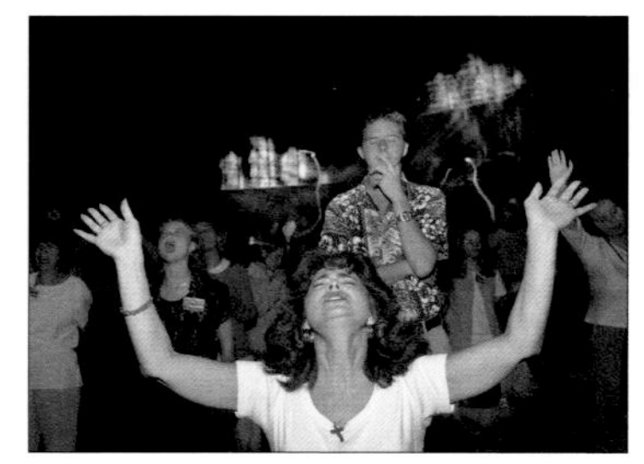

Brownsville Assembly of God, Pensacola, FL, 1999

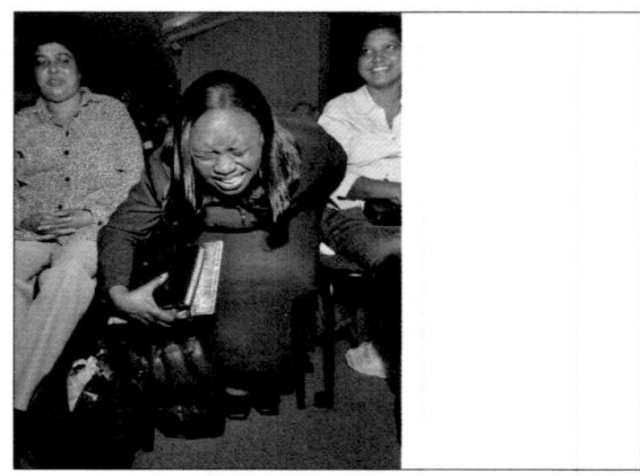

Kensington Temple, London, England, 2003

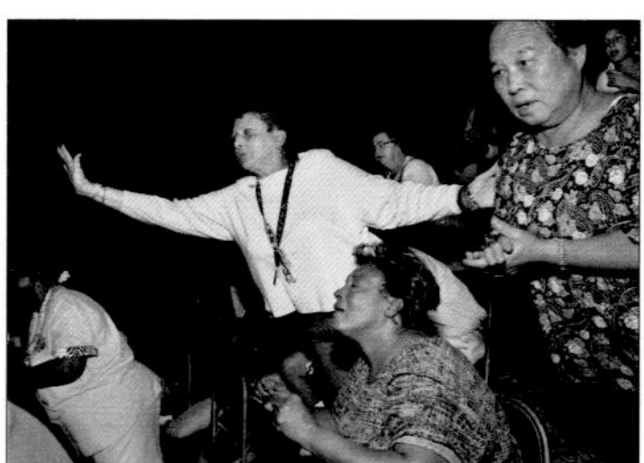

Miracle Tent, Ft. Myers, FL, 1999

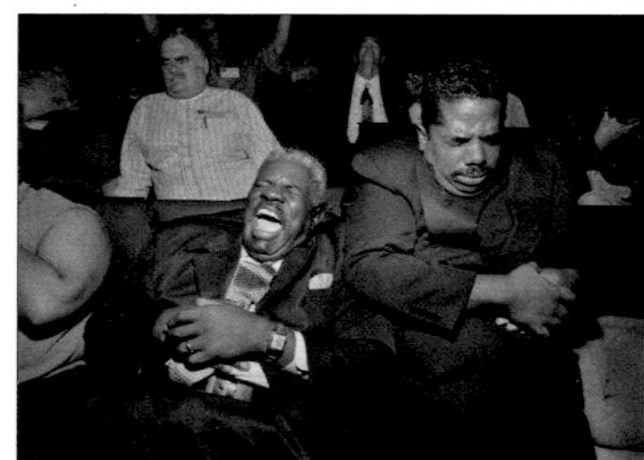

Revival Ministries International, Tampa, FL, 2002

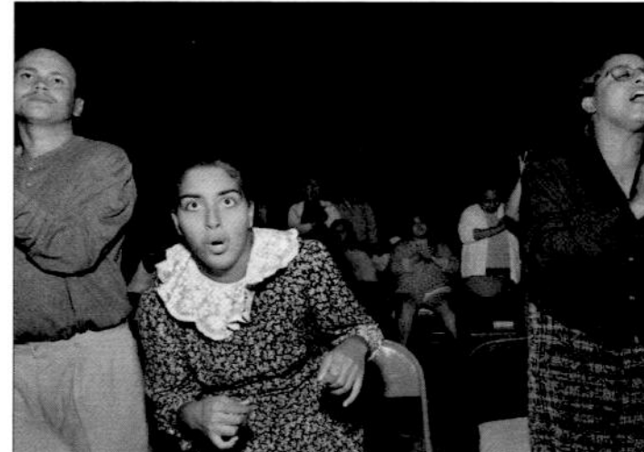

Miracle Tent, Ft. Myers, FL, 1999

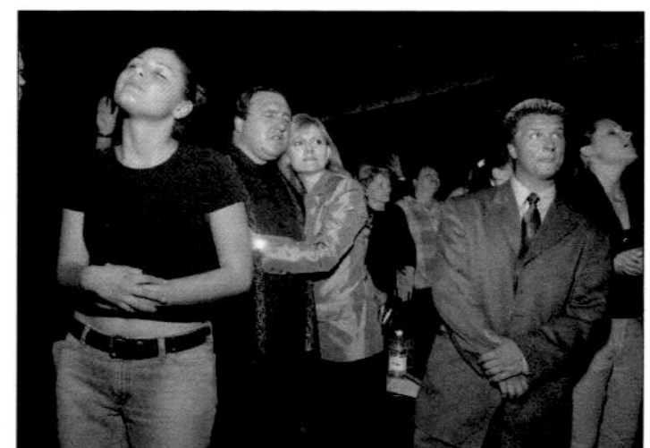

Revival Ministries International, Tampa, FL, 2003

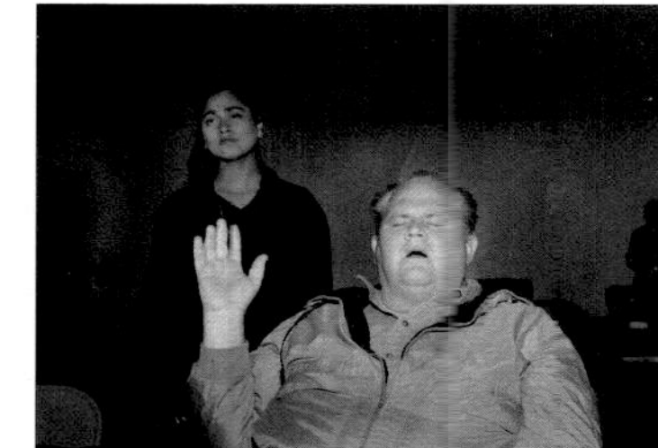

Miracle Tent, Sarasota, FL, 1999

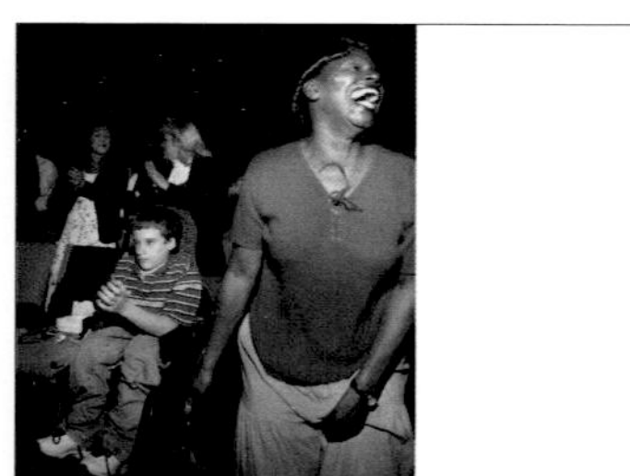

Harvest Tabernacle, Sarasota, FL, 2004

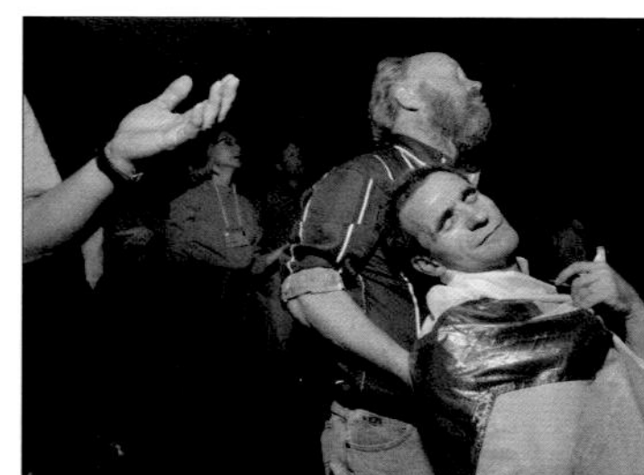

Toronto Airport Christian Fellowship,
Toronto, Canada, 1999

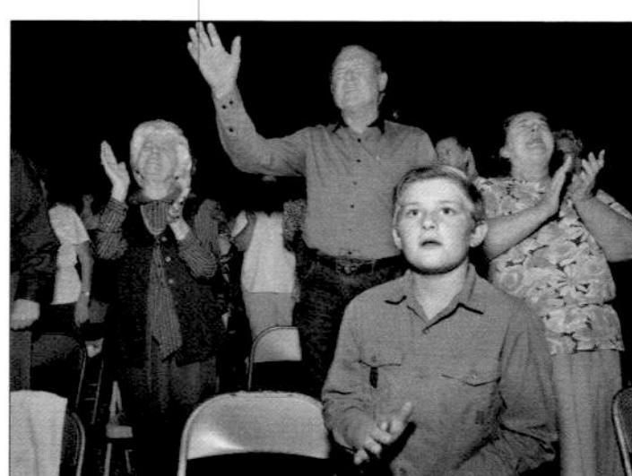

Miracle Tent, Ft. Myers, FL, 1999

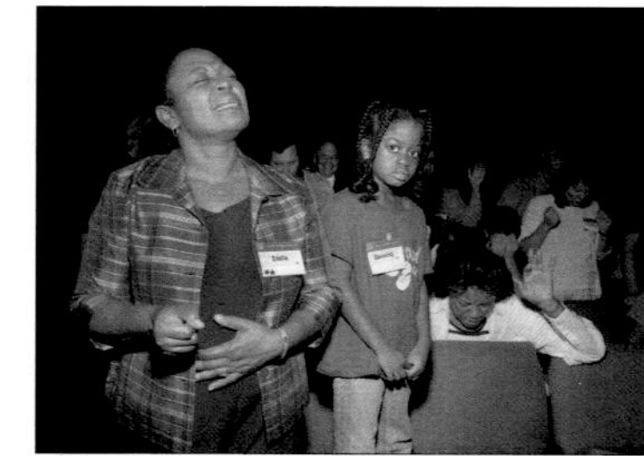

Revival Ministries International, Tampa, FL, 2004

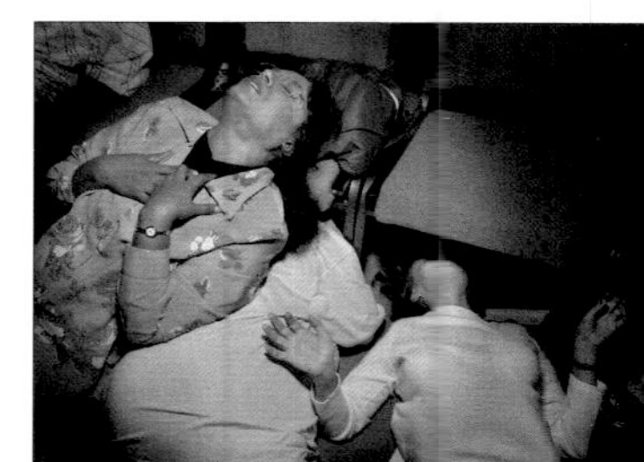

Toronto Airport Christian Fellowship,
Toronto, Canada, 2000

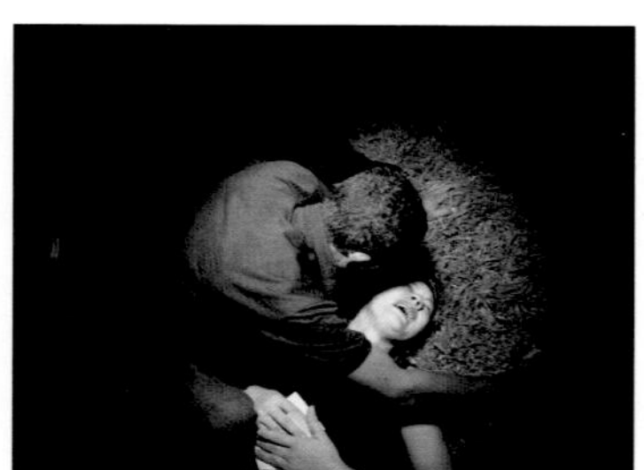

Global Awakening, Belem, Brazil, 2004

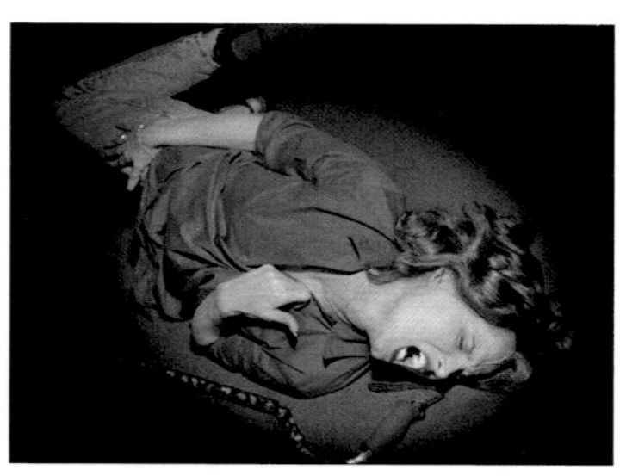

Revival Ministries International, Tampa, FL, 2004

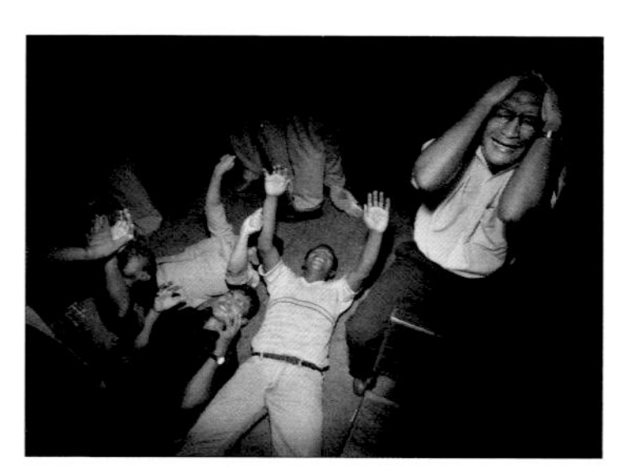

Global Awakening, Belem, Brazil, 2004

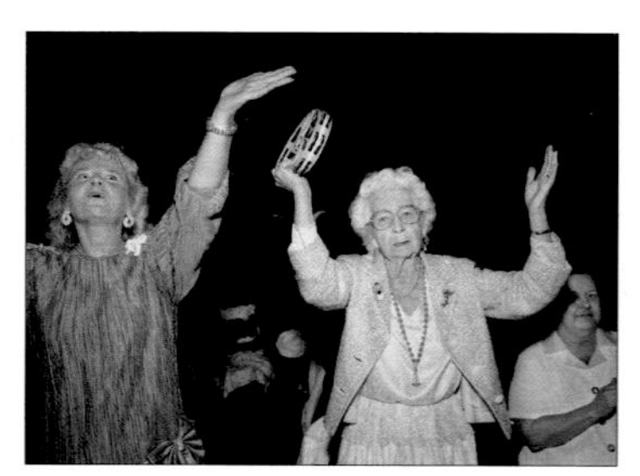

Miracle Tent, Sarasota, FL, 1999

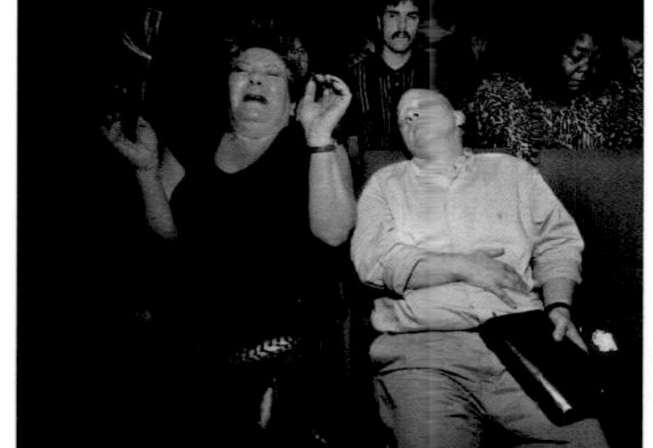

Revival Ministries International, Tampa, FL, 2004

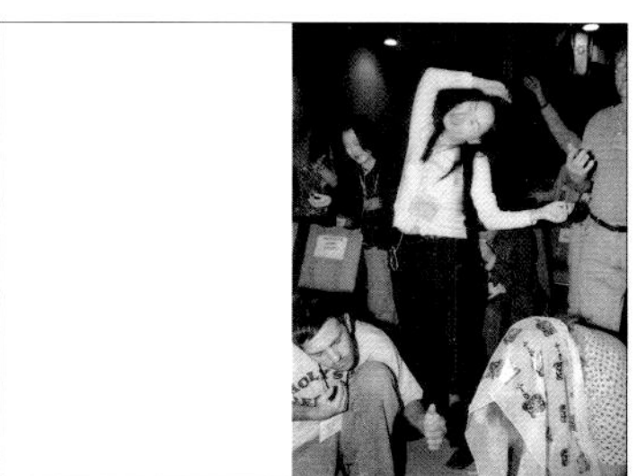

Toronto Airport Christian Fellowship,
Toronto, Canada, 2000

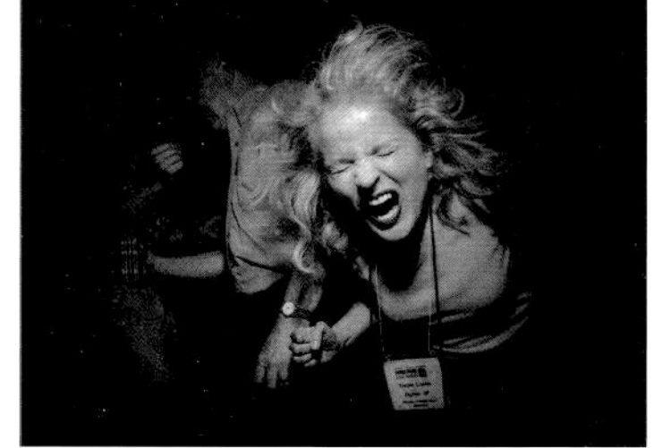

Global Awakening, Belem, Brazil, 2004

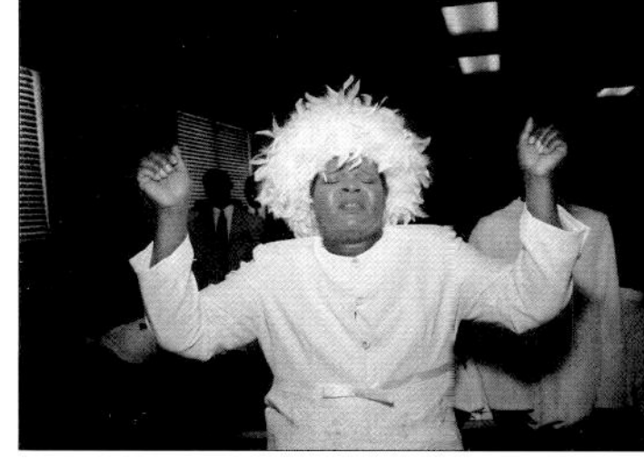

Westcoast Center for Human Development,
Sarasota, FL, 2000

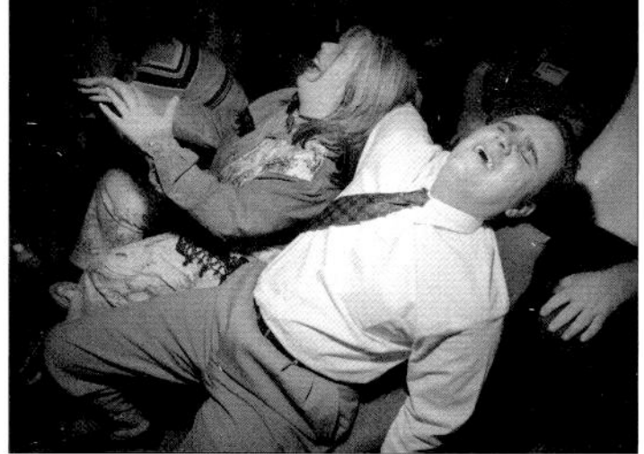

Revival Ministries International, Tampa, FL, 2004

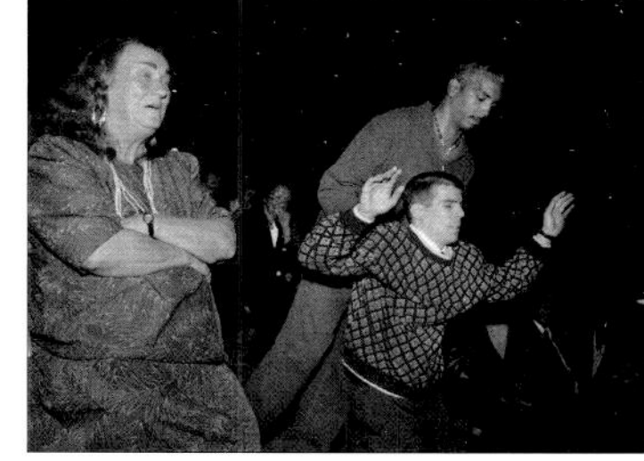

Miracle Tent, Sarasota, FL, 1999

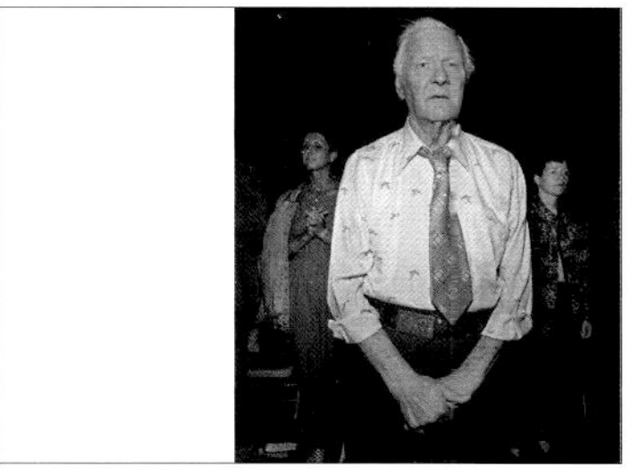

Miracle Tent, Ft. Myers, FL, 1999

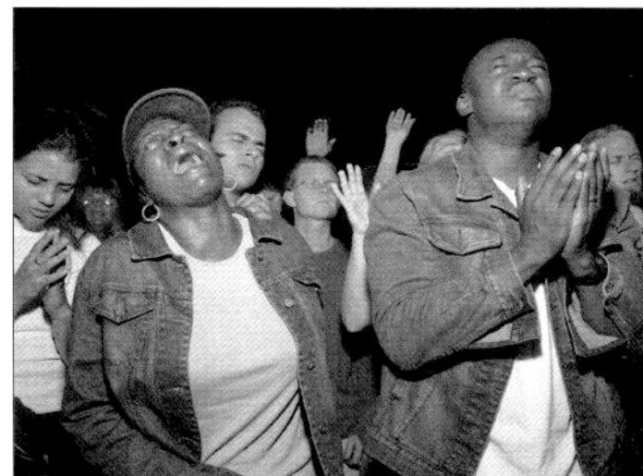

Revival Ministries International, Tampa, FL, 2004

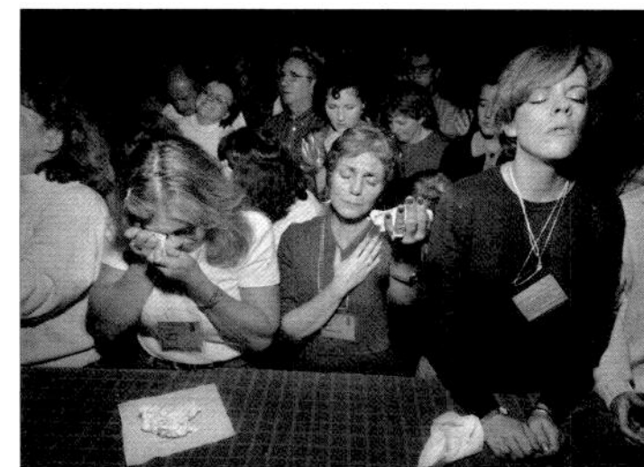

Toronto Airport Christian Fellowship,
Toronto, Canada, 1999

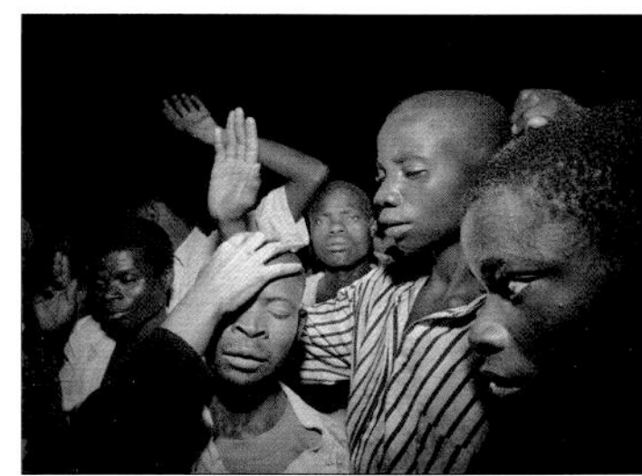

Iris Ministries, Iapala, Mozambique, 2004

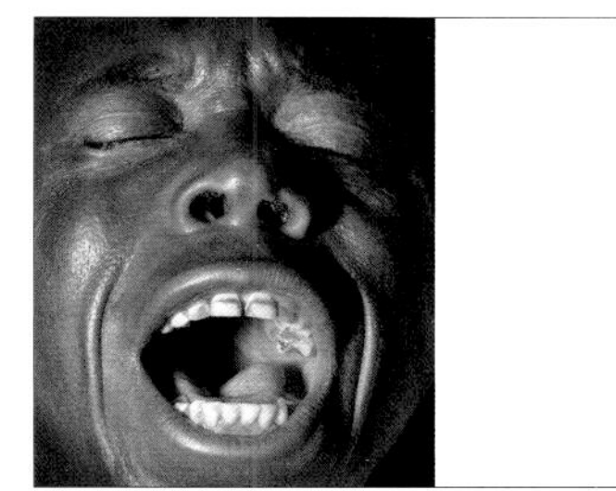

Iris Ministries, Pemba, Mozambique, 2004

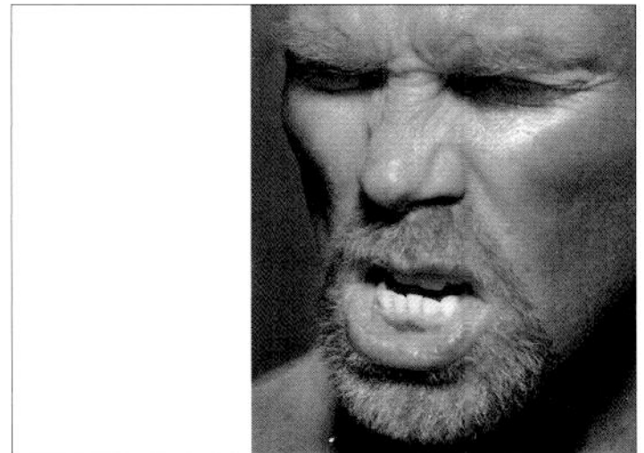

Iris Ministries, Pemba, Mozambique, 2004

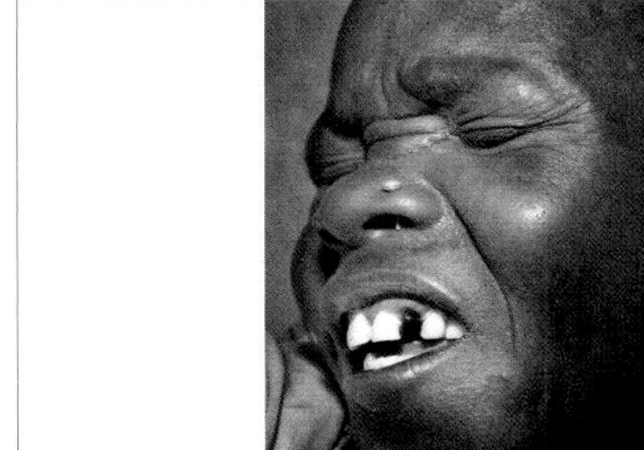

Iris Ministries, Pemba, Mozambique, 2004

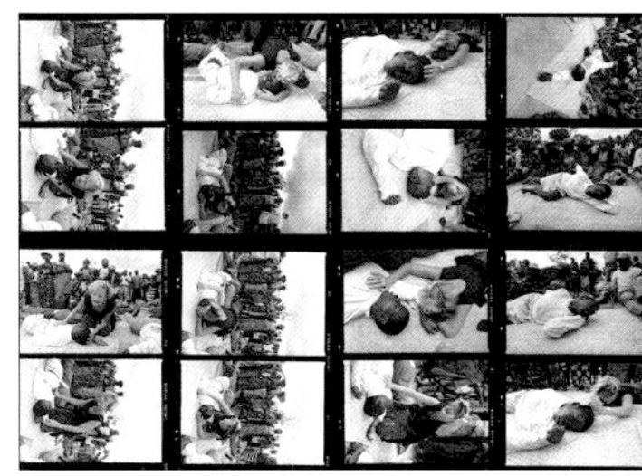

Iris Ministries, Iapala, Mozambique, 2004

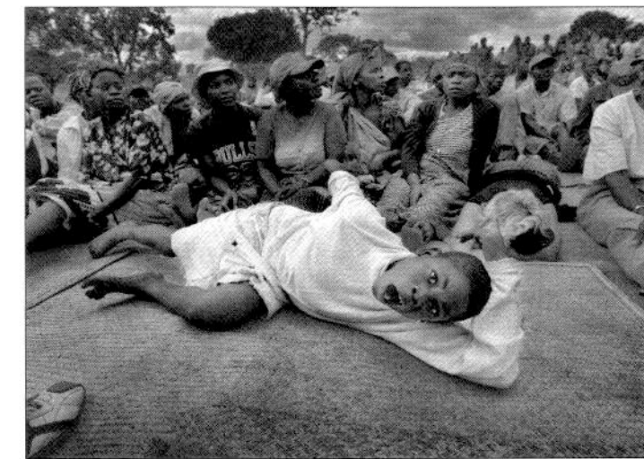

Iris Ministries, Iapala, Mozambique, 2004

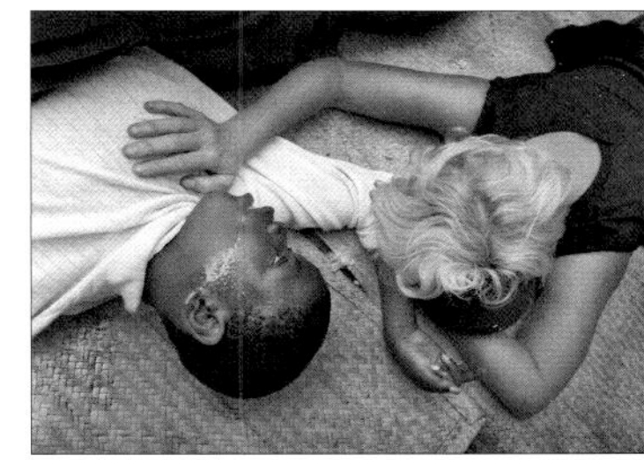

Iris Ministries, Iapala, Mozambique, 2004

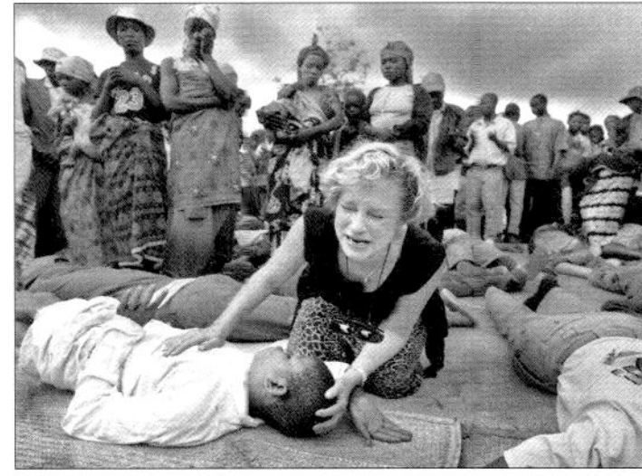

Iris Ministries, Iapala, Mozambique, 2004

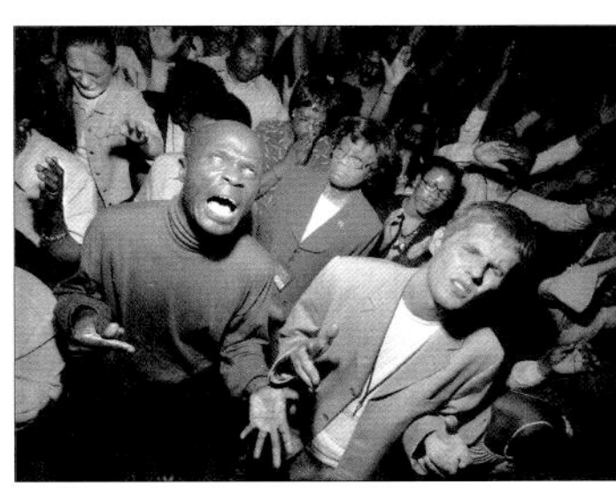

Kensington Temple, London, England, 2003

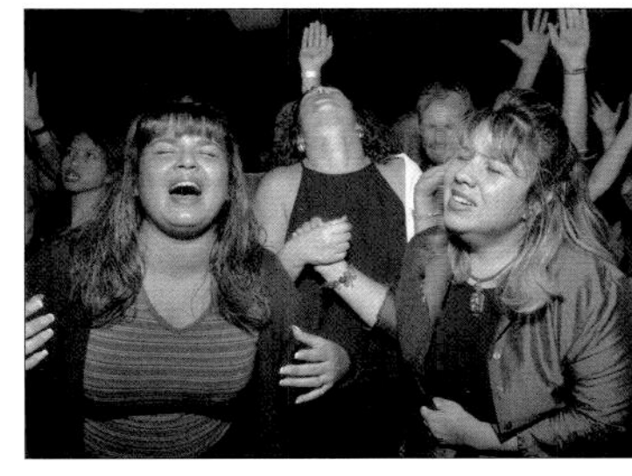

Revival Ministries International, Tampa, FL, 2003

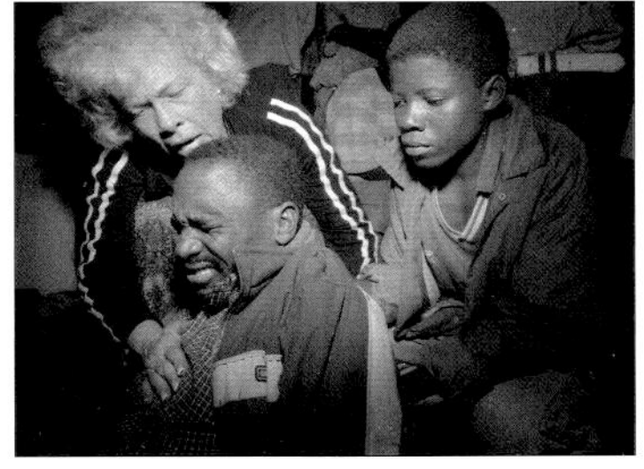

Iris Ministries, Iapala, Mozambique, 2004

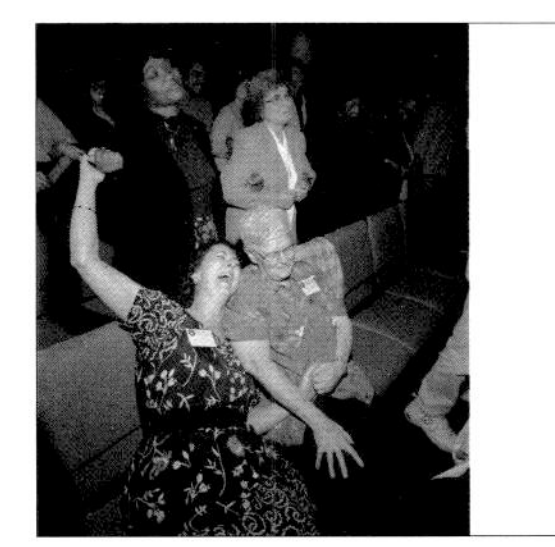

Revival Ministries International, Tampa, FL, 2002

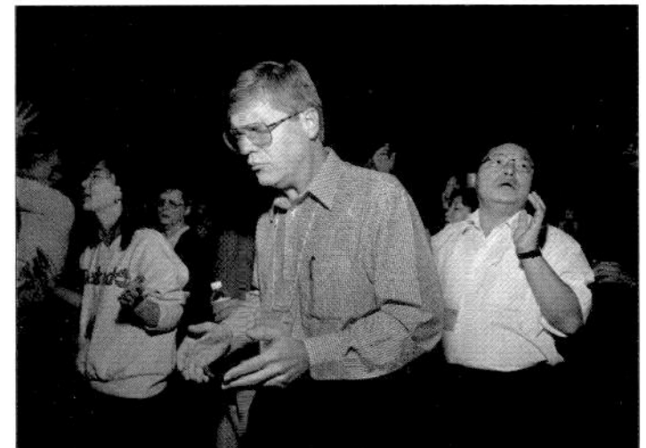

Toronto Airport Christian Fellowship,
Toronto, Canada, 2000

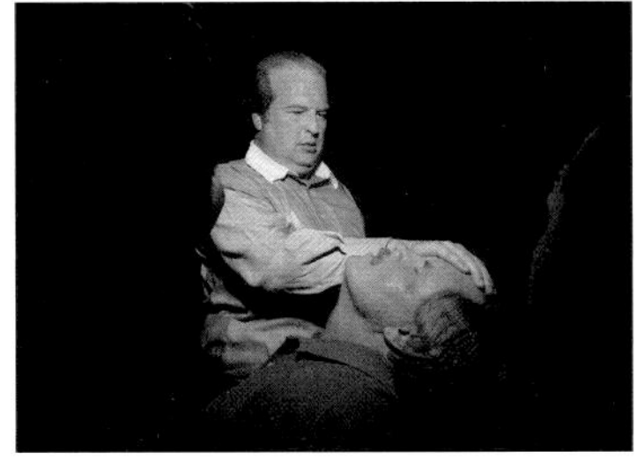

Revival Ministries International, Tampa, FL, 2003

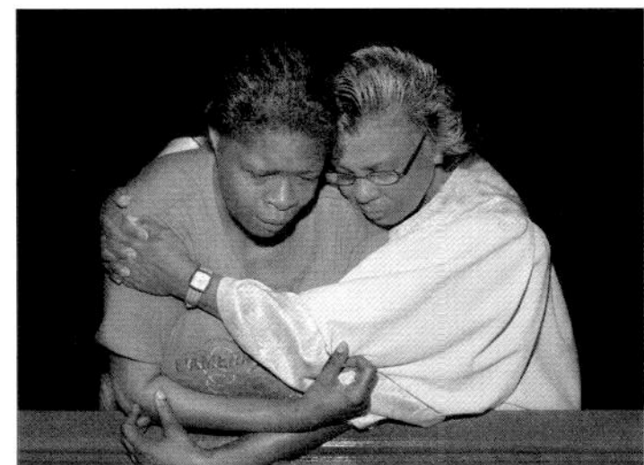

Greater Hurst Chapel AME Church,
Sarasota, FL, 2004

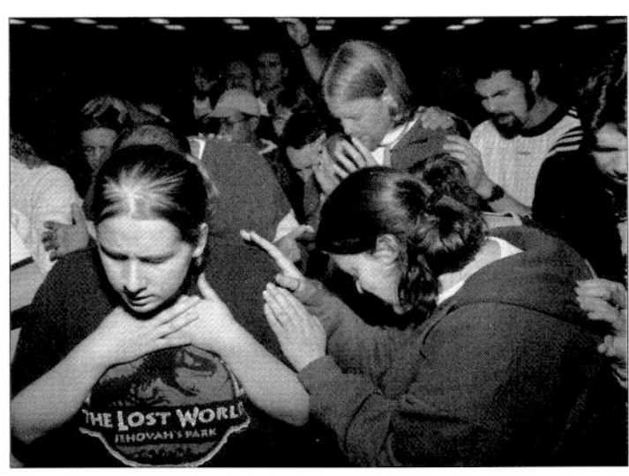

Brownsville Revival School of Ministry,
Pensacola, FL, 1999

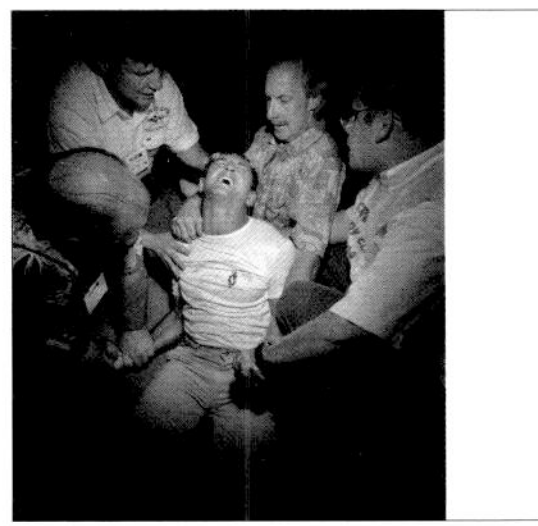

Global Awakening, Belem, Brazil, 2004

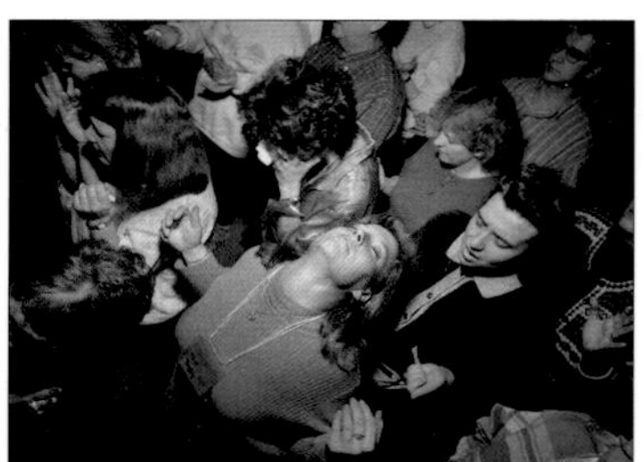
Toronto Airport Christian Fellowship, Toronto, Canada, 1999

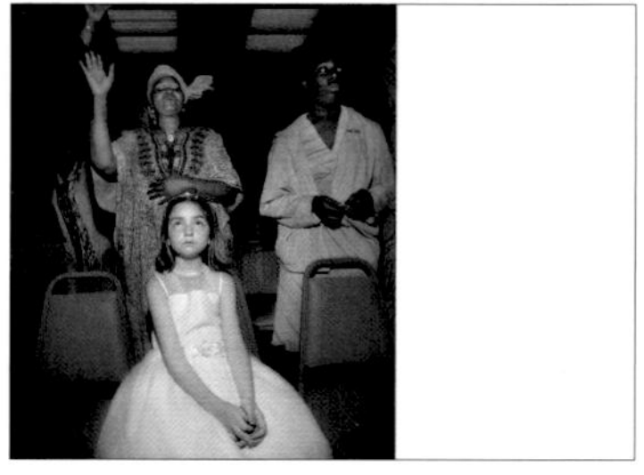
Harvest Tabernacle, Sarasota, FL, 2004

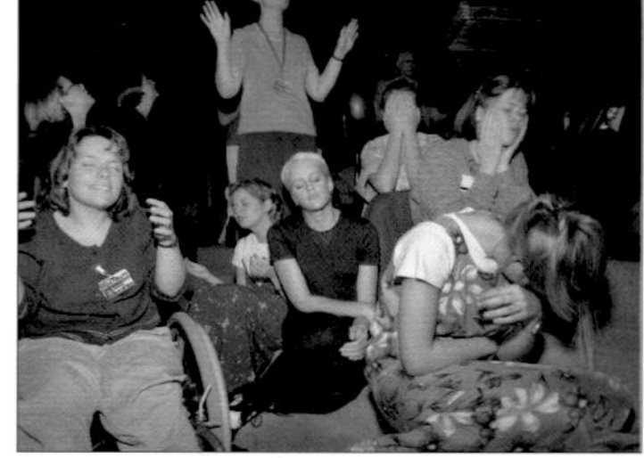
Brownsville Assembly of God, Pensacola, FL, 1999

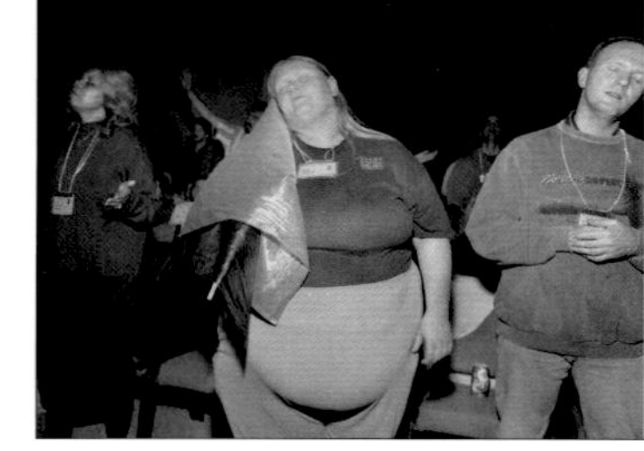
Toronto Airport Christian Fellowship, Toronto, Canada, 1999

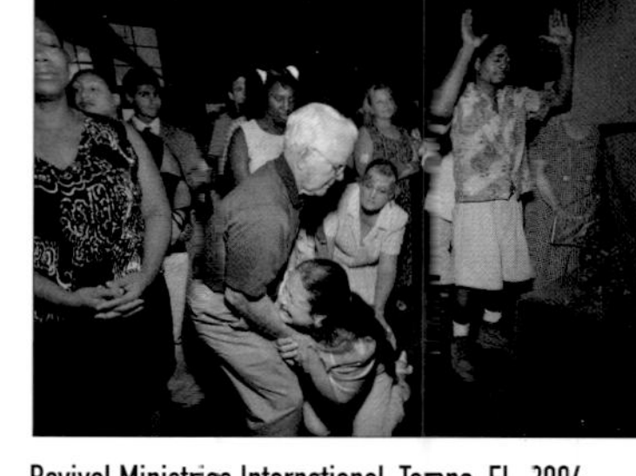
Revival Ministries International, Tampa, FL, 2004

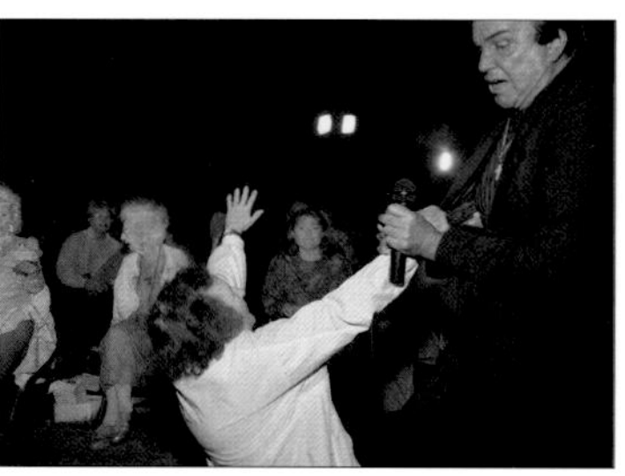
Miracle Tent, Sarasota, FL, 1999

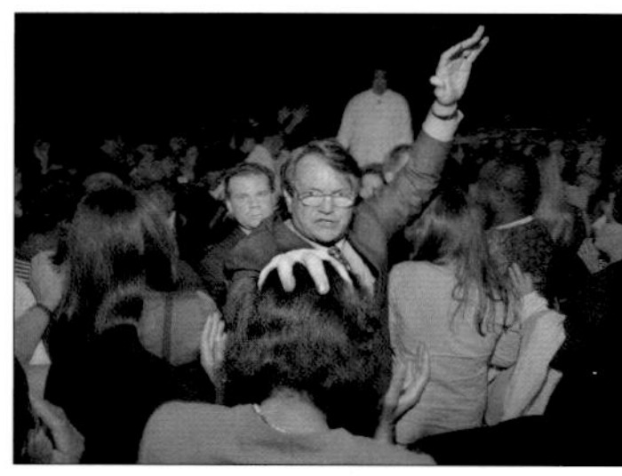
Revival Ministries International, Tampa, FL, 2003

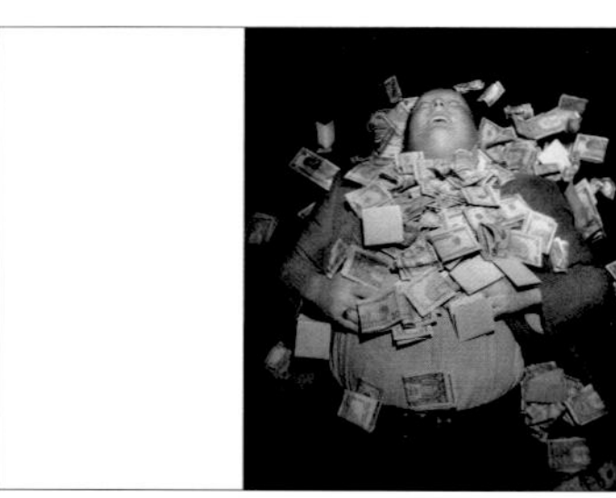
Revival Ministries International, Tampa, FL, 2004

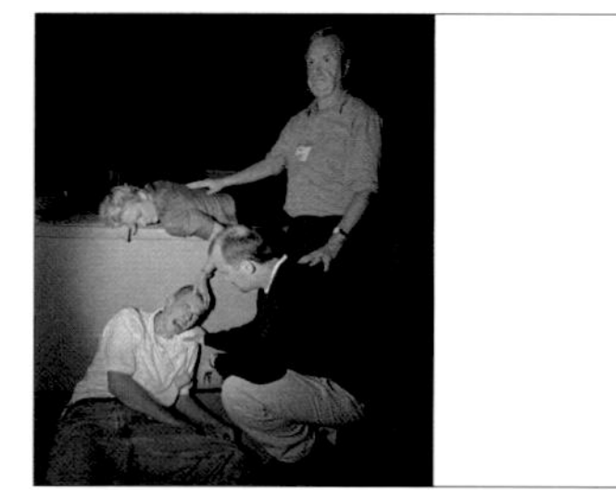
Toronto Airport Christian Fellowship, Toronto, Canada, 2000

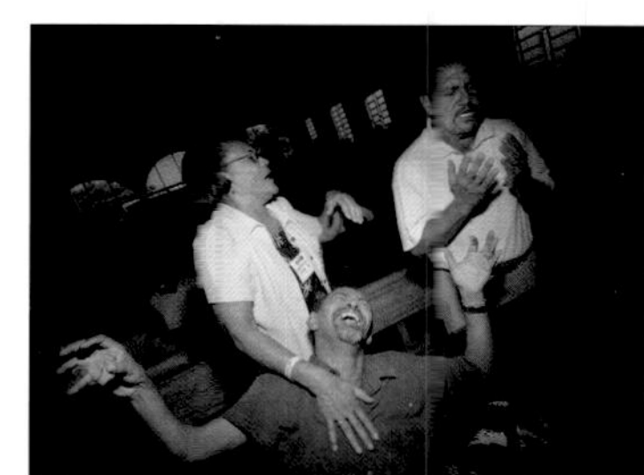
Global Awakening, Belem, Brazil, 2004

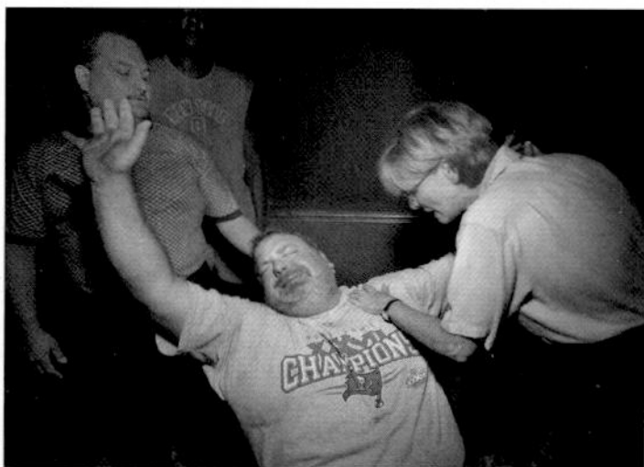

Without Walls International Church, Tampa, FL, 2004

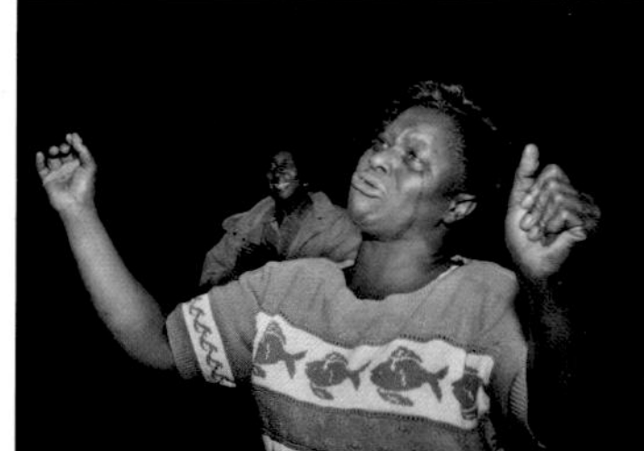
Miracle Tent, Sarasota, FL, 1999

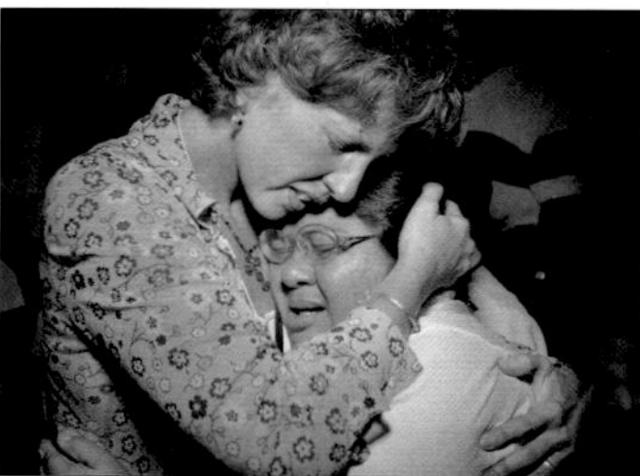
Global Awakening, Fortaleza, Brazil, 2004

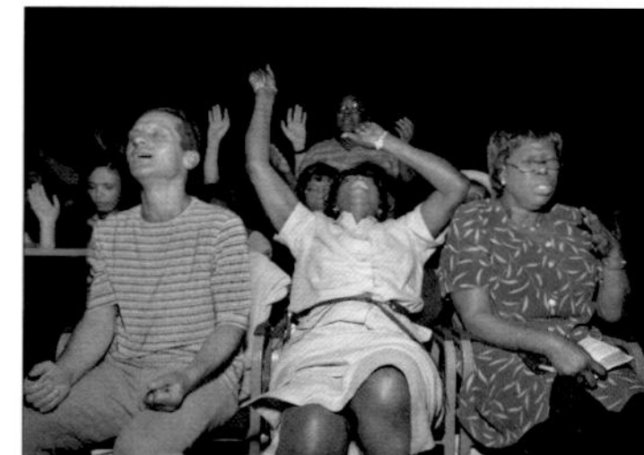
Kensington Temple, London, England, 2003

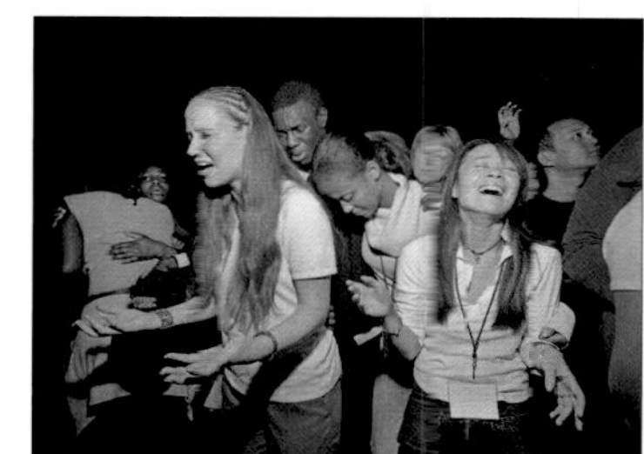
Kensington Temple, London, England, 2003

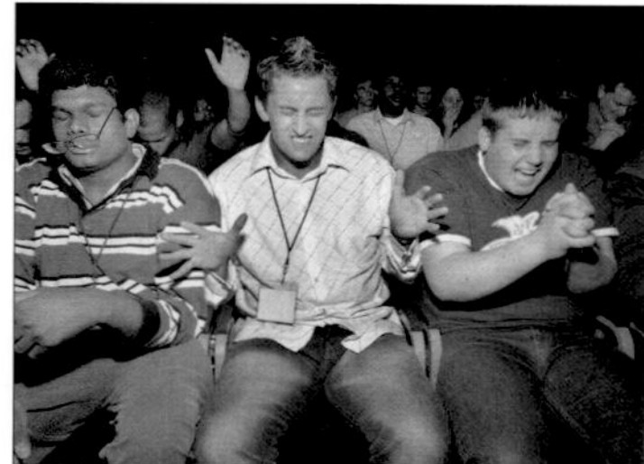
Kensington Temple, London, England, 2003

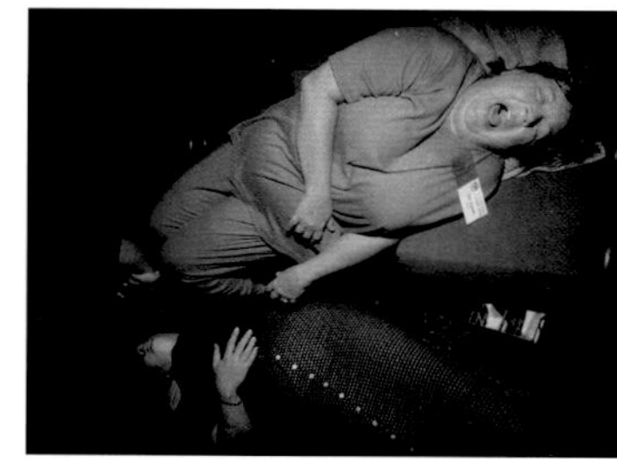
Revival Ministries International, Tampa, FL, 2002

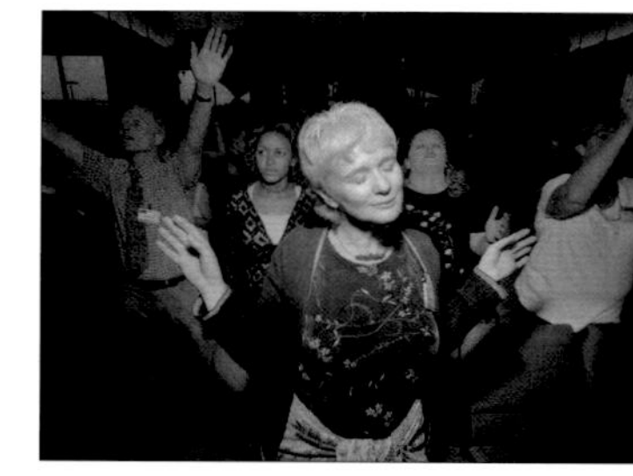
Revival Ministries International, Tampa, FL, 2004

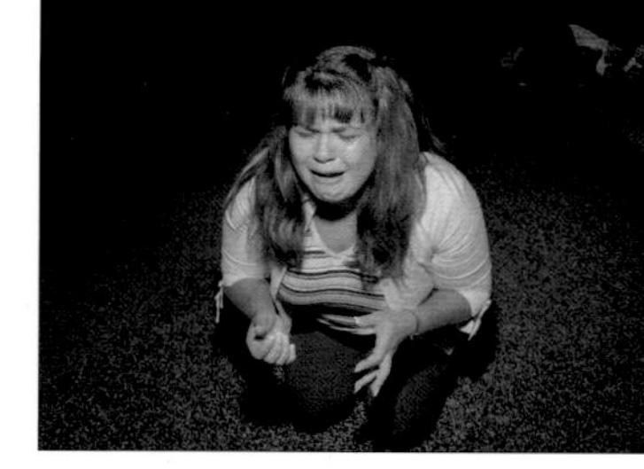
Revival Ministries International, Tampa, FL, 2003

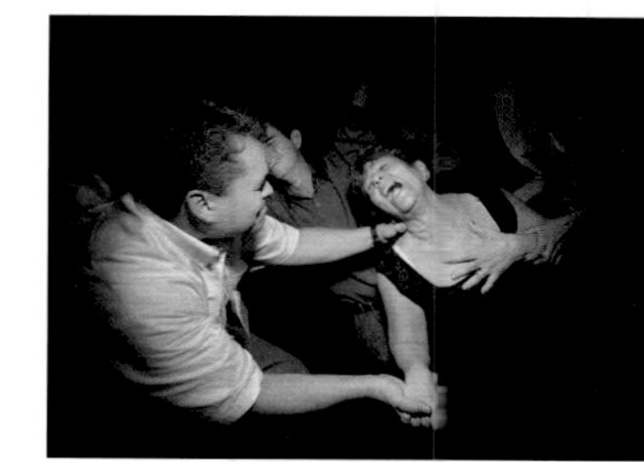
Global Awakening, Belem, Brazil, 2004

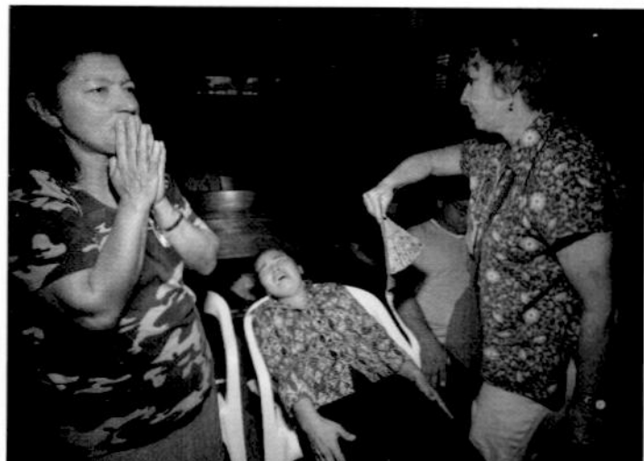
Global Awakening, Belem, Brazil, 2004

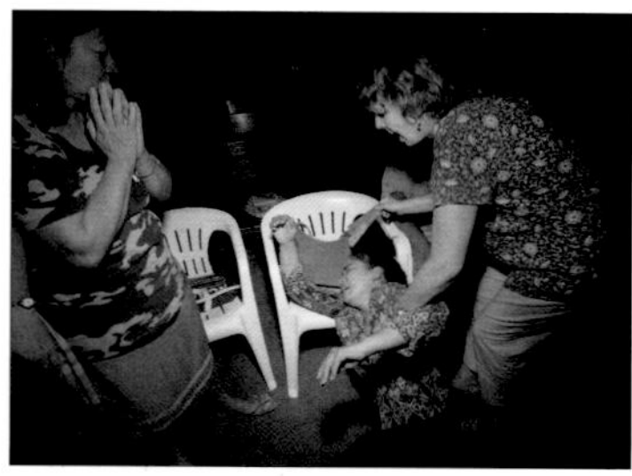
Global Awakening, Belem, Brazil, 2004

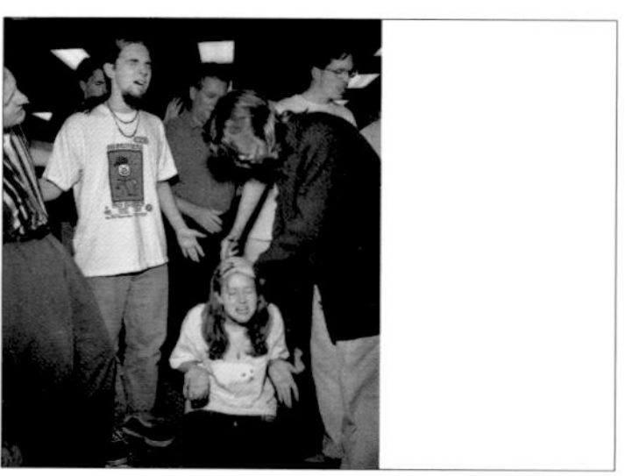
Brownsville Revival School of Ministry, Pensacola, FL, 1999

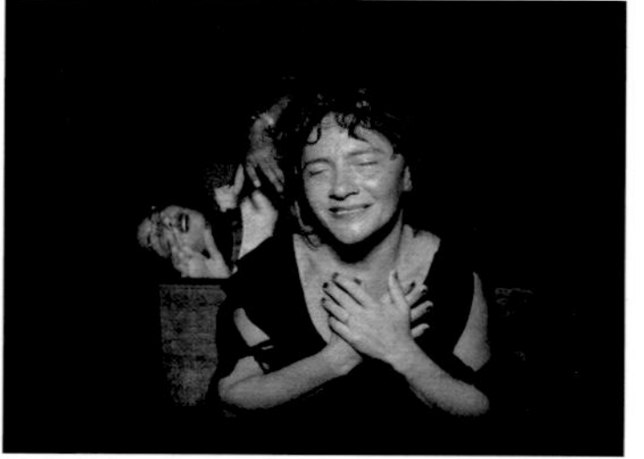
Global Awakening, Fortaleza, Brazil, 2004

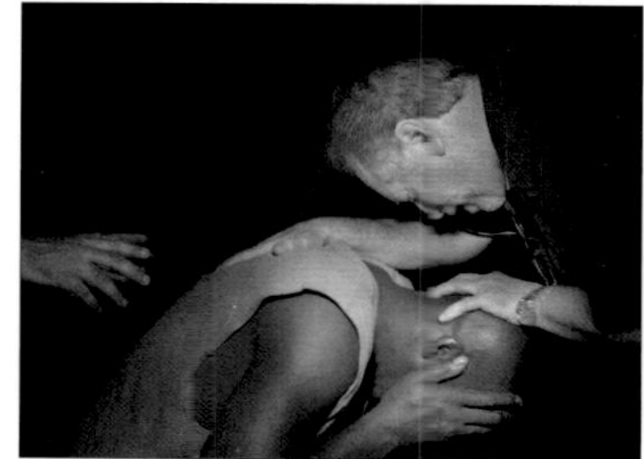
Without Walls International Church, Tampa, FL, 2004

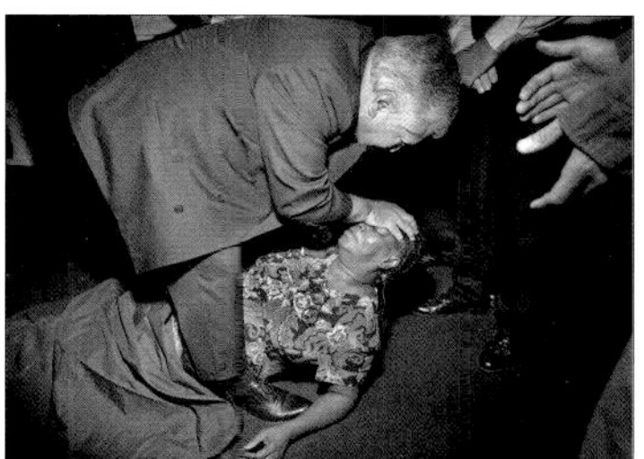

Harvest Tabernacle, Sarasota, FL, 2004

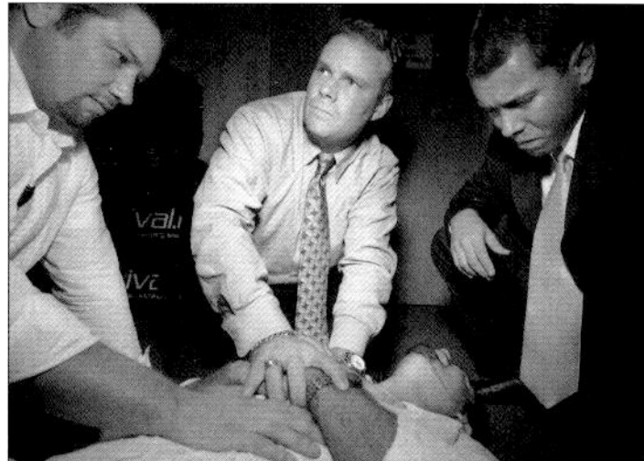

Revival Ministries International, Tampa, FL, 2004

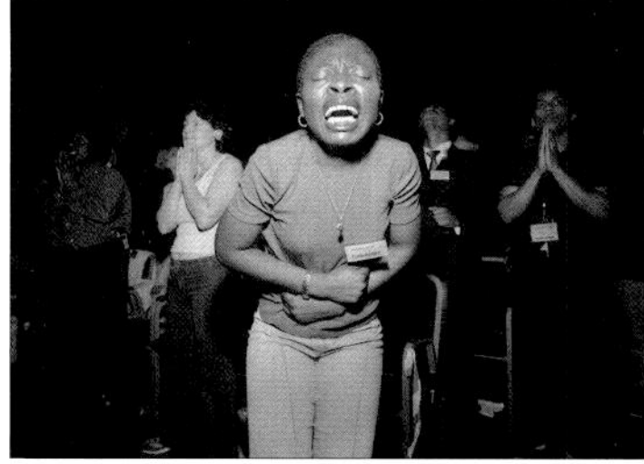

Kensington Temple, London, England, 2003

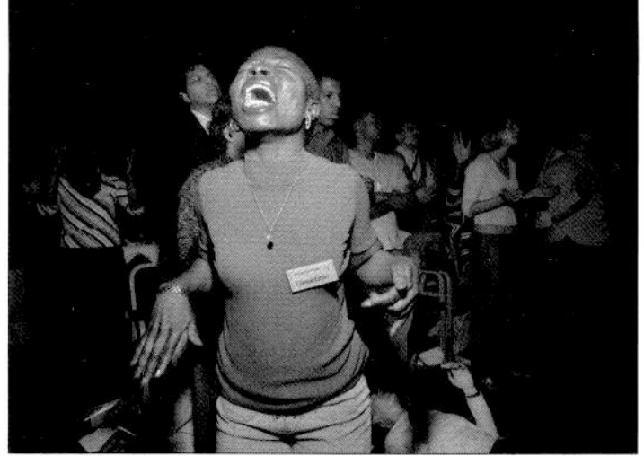

Kensington Temple, London, England, 2003

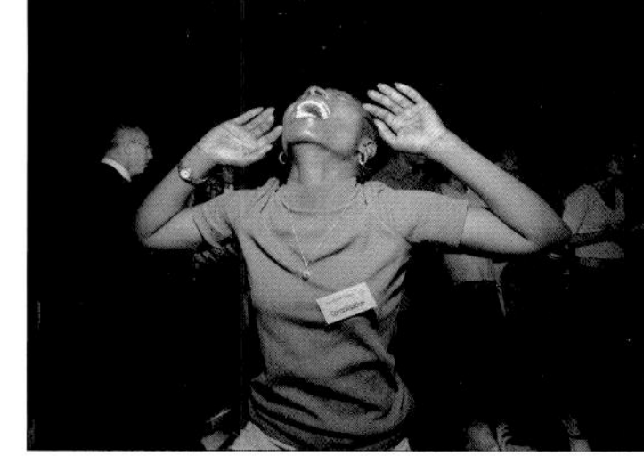

Kensington Temple, London, England, 2003

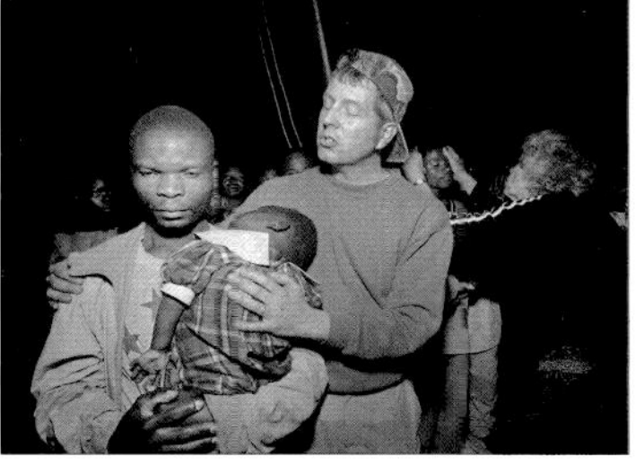

Iris Ministries, Iapala, Mozambique, 2004

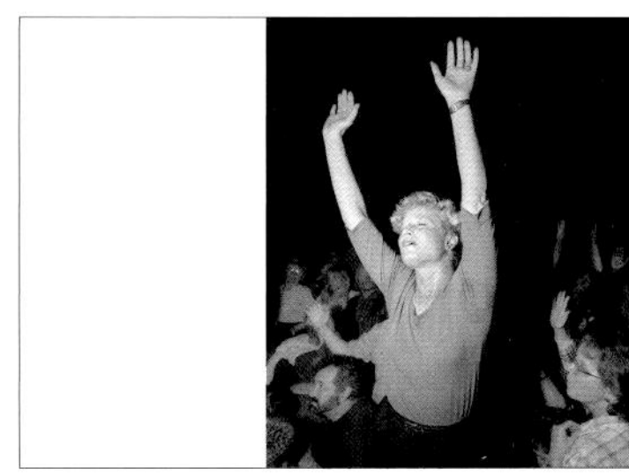

Toronto Christian Airport Fellowship,
Toronto, Canada, 2000

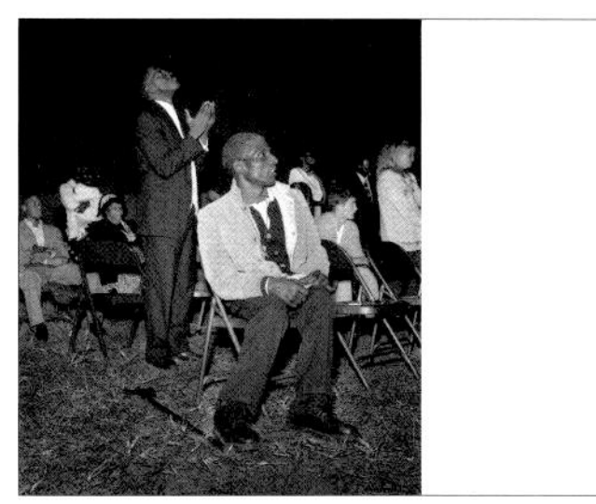

Miracle Tent, Sarasota, FL, 1999

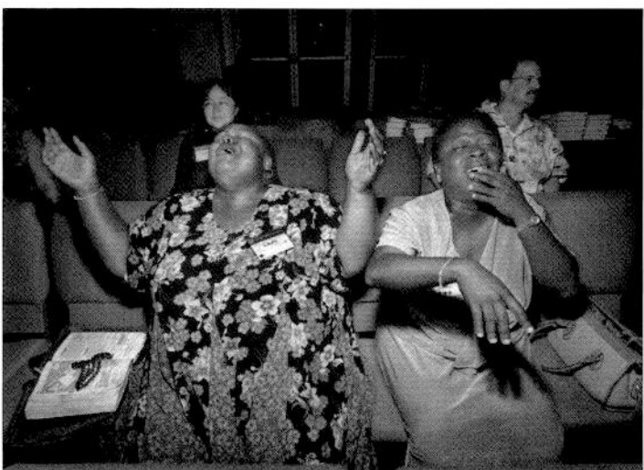

Revival Ministries International, Tampa, FL, 2004

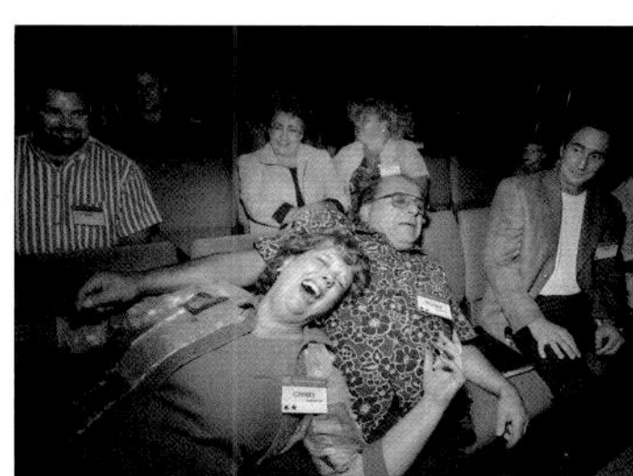

Revival Ministries International, Tampa, FL, 2004

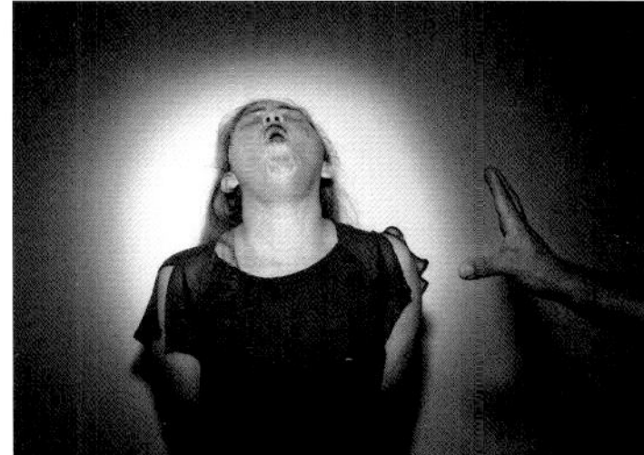

Global Awakening, Fortaleza, Brazil, 2004

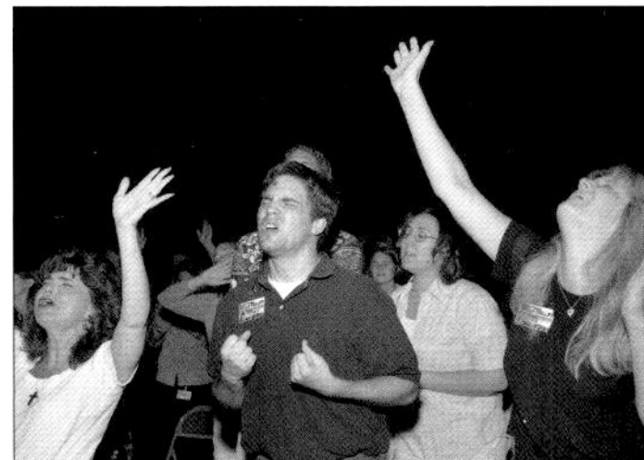

Brownsville Assembly of God, Pensacola, FL, 1999

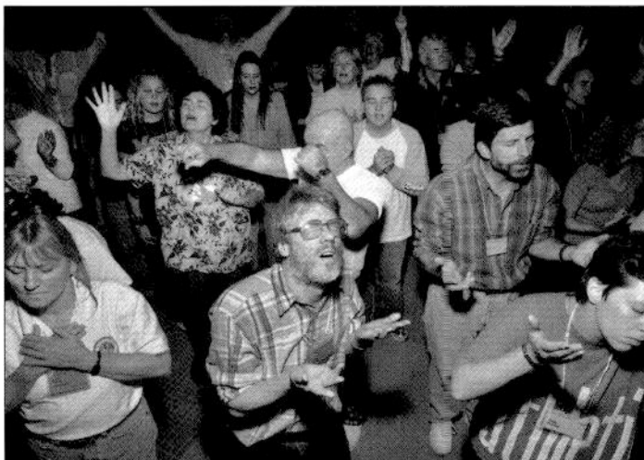

Toronto Airport Christian Fellowship,
Toronto, Canada, 2000

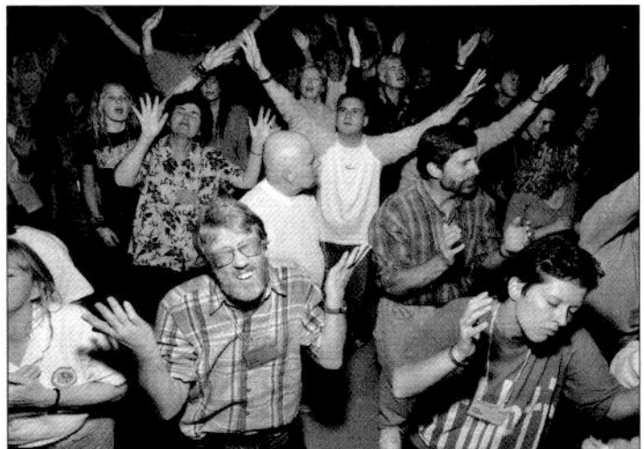

Toronto Airport Christian Fellowship,
Toronto, Canada, 2000

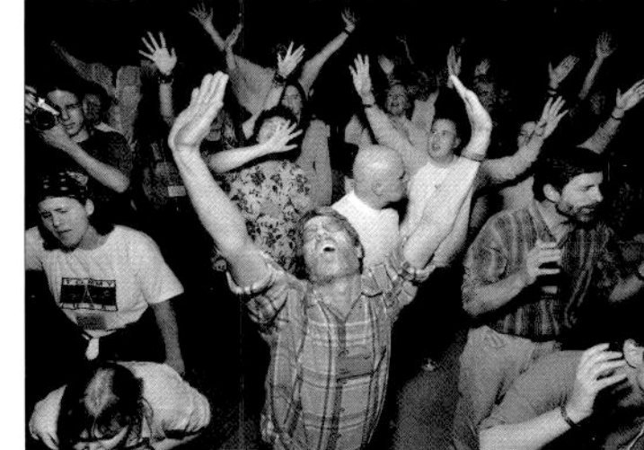

Toronto Airport Christian Fellowship,
Toronto, Canada, 2000

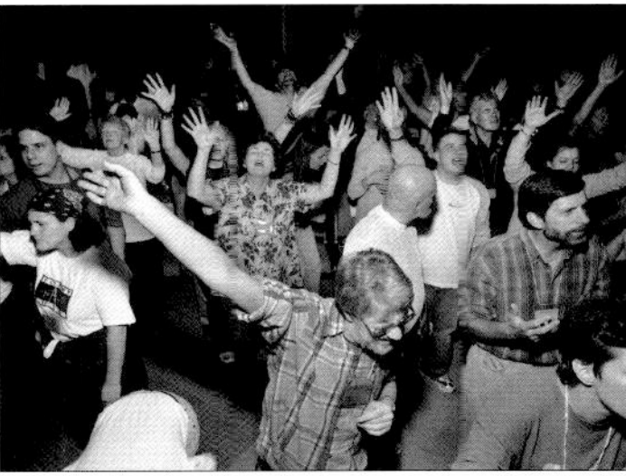

Toronto Airport Christian Fellowship,
Toronto, Canada, 2000

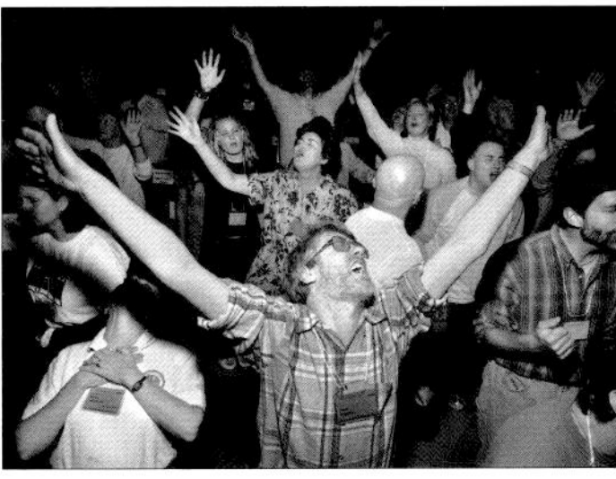

Toronto Airport Christian Fellowship,
Toronto, Canada, 2000

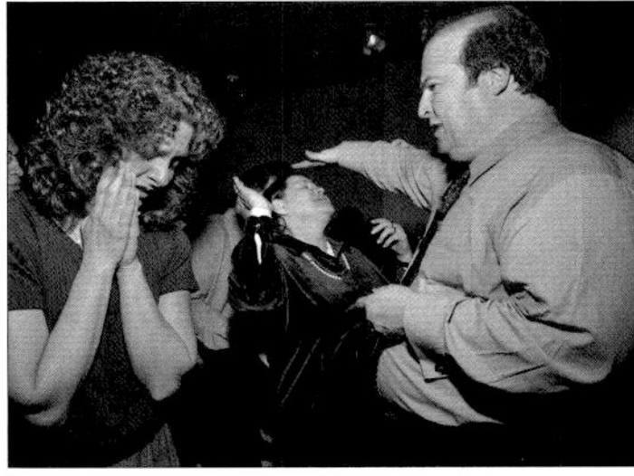

Revival Ministries International, Tampa, FL, 2002

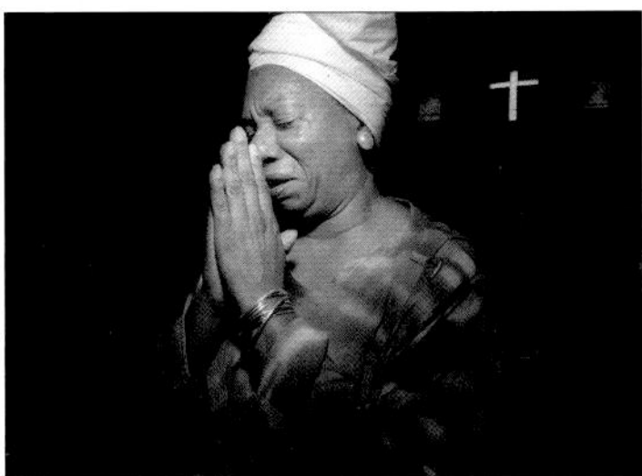

Greater Hurst Chapel AME Church,
Sarasota, FL, 2004

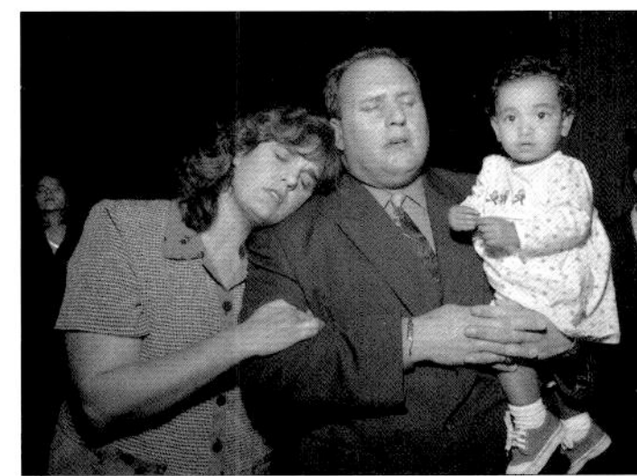

Revival Ministries International, Tampa, FL, 2003

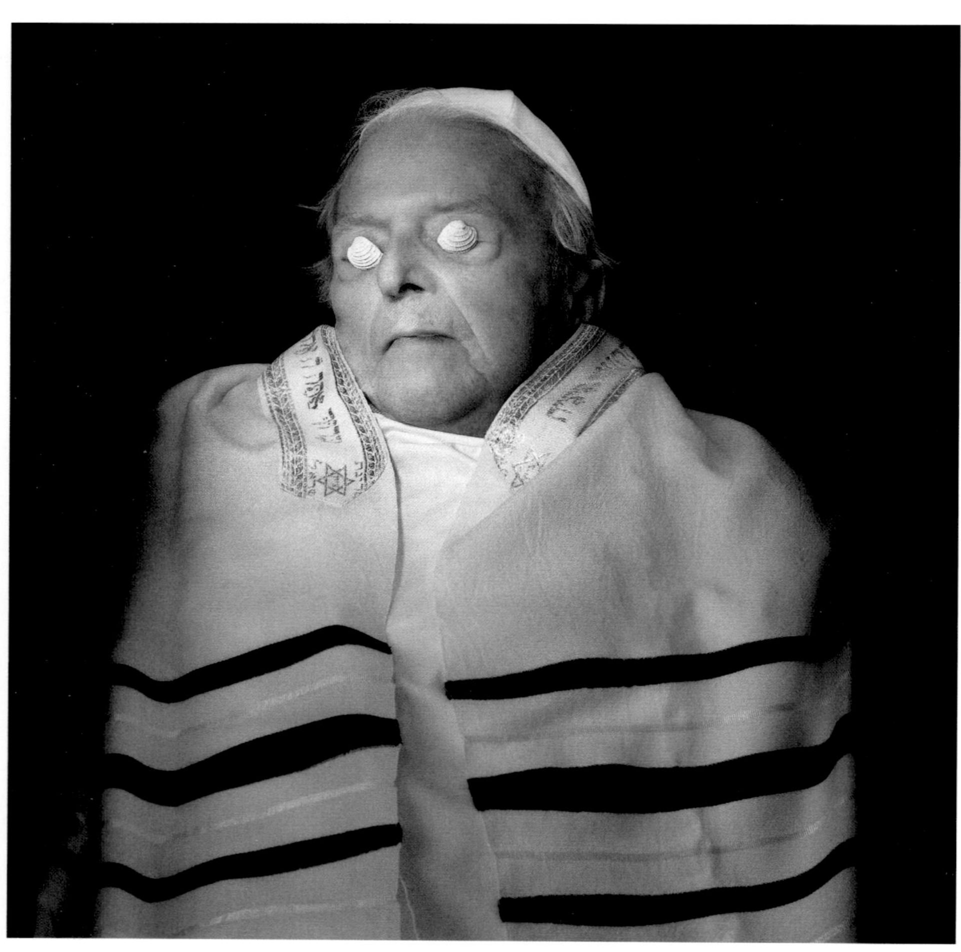

Daniel Katzman
1924–2004

ACKNOWLEDGEMENTS

While I was documenting the Toronto Airport Christian Fellowship, I commented to a group of congregants how I was amazed that my photography had brought me to God. I was quickly corrected, "No Steven, it was God that brought you to photography." I smiled, nodded in agreement, and continued to photograph with this blessing.

The Face of Forgiveness started out as a way to add to my portfolio, and was never intended to be the book you are holding in your hands, nor a life-changing experience. Throughout the course of this project, I have been embraced, encouraged, and blessed. I would like to give special thanks to Adonica and Rodney Howard-Browne, Revival Ministries International; Heidi and Rolland Baker, Iris Ministries; Randy Clark and Tom Ruotolo, Global Awakening; Carol and John Arnott, Toronto Airport Christian Fellowship; John Kilpatrick and Dr. Michael Brown, Brownsville Assembly of God; Mazie Rojas, Greater Hurst Chapel; Colin Dye, Kensington Temple; Jim Minor, Harvest Tabernacle; Leroy Jenkins; and all of the additional people I have met. Although strangers to me, their tears became my tears, their laughter became my laughter, and their celebration became my song. All this they have freely offered me. Now, through my photographs, I want to freely offer you my experience, strength, and hope.

On the technical side of the aisle, I personally scanned and created all of the files with an Imacon Flextight 848 Scanner. I am indebted to the generosity and technical help provided by Chris Cudzilo, John Lane, Dean Lambert, LexJet; Les Brown, Justin Stailey, Bogen Imaging; Lorry Rosen, Quantum Instruments, Inc.; Peter Turo, Photo-Tech; John Pannozzo, Mark Dale, Daniel Barrett, Iryna Moskalenko, Color Byte Software; Mary Tandourjian, Martin Kerver, Hanamühle Fine Art; Janice Wendt, nik multimedia, Inc.; Liz Quinlisk, gmb GretagMacbeth; Bill Lindsay, Wacom; and Lisa McCormack, Extensis. I would also like to thank Skip Cohen, Bill Hurter, *Rangefinder*; Maureen and Brooks Jensen, *LensWork*; and Warren Marcus, New Day Pictures; who have previously recognized the importance of my work.

I am greatly indebted to my parents, Ruth and Daniel—their ideals, values, and social conscience I embrace as my own; the desire to make our world a much better place than when we found it, the need to plant not just one tree, but a forest for future generations.

For my son, Justin, who has constantly tried my patience while we were both growing up, who has made me a better father because our love has endured throughout our personal trials and tribulations, providing a cornerstone for greater love and understanding.

Sharon, your unconditional love has given me strength and courage to walk into darkness, creating an environment that nurtured my creativity. You have added fuel to my fire, giving me the confidence to challenge the unknown, taking nothing for granted except the next photograph.

THE FACE OF FORGIVENESS
Salvation and Redemption

Published in the United States by powerHouse Books,
a division of powerHouse Cultural Entertainment, Inc.
68 Charlton Street, New York, NY 10014-4601
telephone 212 604 9074, fax 212 366 5247
e-mail: forgiveness@powerHouseBooks.com
website: www.powerHouseBooks.com

First edition, 2005

Library of Congress Cataloging-in-Publication Data:

Katzman, Steven, 1950-
The face of forgiveness : salvation and redemption : photographs / by Steven Katzman ;
text by Bill Johnson.-- 1st ed.
p. cm.
ISBN 1-57687-250-5
1. Evangelicalism--Pictorial works. 2. Evangelicalism. I. Title.

BR1640.K38 2005
779'.82--dc22
2004060121

Hardcover ISBN 1-57687-250-5

Separations, printing, and binding by EBS, Verona

Book design by Kiki Bauer

A complete catalog of powerHouse Books and Limited Editions is available upon request; please call, write, or kneel down on our website.

10 9 8 7 6 5 4 3 2 1

Printed and bound in Italy